Dynamic Benefit-Cost Analysis

Dynamic Benefit-Cost Analysis

Evaluation of Public Policy in a Dynamic Urban Model

Joseph A. Maciariello
Union College and University

Lexington Books
D.C. Heath and Company
Lexington, Massachusetts
Toronto London

Library of Congress Cataloging in Publication Data

Maciariello, Joseph A
Dynamic benefit-cost analysis.

Expanded version of the author's Ph.D. dissertation, New York University.
Bibliography: p. 169.
Includes index.
1. Expenditures, Public. 2. Cost effectiveness. I. Title.
HJ7451.M18 350'.722 75-522
ISBN 0-669-98020-x

Published simultaneously in Canada.

Printed in the United States of America

International Standard Book Number: 0-669-98020-x

Library of Congress Catalog Card Number: 75-522

To the memory of my father Lawrence and our son Joe

Contents

List of Figures

List of Tables

Acknowledgments

This book could not have been written without the help, constructive criticism and advice of Professor William J. Baumol who served as my dissertation adviser at New York University. My debt to Professor Baumol is overwhelming.

Professor Hourmousiz G. Georgiadis was a constant source of inspiration to me during my studies at New York University, both inside and outside the classroom. He has my profound thanks and admiration. I also owe a debt of gratitude to Professor Solomon Fabricant of New York University for his help.

Financial support for this book was provided to a large extent by Union College. I have Deans Martin Lichterman and William Weifenbach, and Professor Alfred L. Thimm to thank for that assistance. Professor Donald S. Holmes of Union College and Ms. Arlene Larsen of the Rensselaer Polytechnic Institute Computer Center provided valuable technical assistance on the computer hardware and software requirements. Professors D. W. Griesinger and Thimm of Union College provided continuous intellectual encouragement for this work.

Mr. Stephen Anchukaitas provided early technical assistance on the computer programming requirements of this project, and Mr. Richard Levinson aided in the preparation of the figures. I am grateful to each of these talented young men.

Acknowledgments are due to Professor Paul A. Samuelson and the editors of *The American Economic Review* for permission to reproduce passages from an article by Professor Samuelson; to Mr. William D. Bourne, General Manager of the Sacramento Regional Transit Authority for his permission to reproduce the Sacramento Transit Authority Case which appears in Appendix C of this volume, and to Charles H. Haar and the Eno Foundation for permission to reproduce passages from an article by Mr. Haar which appeared in the *Traffic Quarterly*.

Most of the typing and much of the editing of this volume were performed by Mrs. Elinor Lambert, whose many skills and patience were very important to me over the three-year period during which it was prepared. Finally, I am grateful beyond words to my wife Judy, whose general assistance with the tedious work that appears in the appendixes was to me second in importance only to her constant encouragement and understanding.

Dynamic Benefit-Cost Analysis

1 Introduction to Static Benefit-Cost Analysis

The primary purpose of this volume is to present a new procedure for evaluating a class of public-expenditure decisions which cannot be evaluated properly by existing methods. This new procedure, however, should not be thought of as one that makes existing static methods obsolete, but rather as one that should be used in all cases where the assumptions of static analysis are not met in reality. I will argue at many different points in this volume that these assumptions are violated very frequently in the real world—so frequently, indeed, that we should examine the dynamic properties of each problem area before using static methods of evaluation.

Nevertheless, static methods of benefit-cost analysis are quite useful in many applications, and the dynamic procedure described in this book utilizes many of the compromises with the requirements of pure economic theory found in a typical static benefit-cost study. For both these reasons, I believe it useful to begin with a brief introduction to static benefit-cost methods before addressing ourselves to the dangers of these methods. The plan of this volume, therefore, is as follows: first, review conventional methods of benefit-cost analysis and their assumptions; second, explore the dangers of these methods; third, construct a dynamic procedure for evaluating public projects; fourth, evaluate the implications of the procedure for each element of a benefit-cost study; and finally, distinguish, among all categories of public expenditure, those which lend themselves to evaluation by static methods from those which require dynamic methods, and ask whether it is possible, when the full institutional realities of the budget-making process are considered, to use the latter methods to construct a systematic procedure for making rational public-expenditure decisions.

We now summarize the purpose and methods of benefit-cost analysis as practiced conventionally.[a] This discussion will serve as a point of departure for later chapters.

---

[a]I refer the reader interested in more detail than is contained in this chapter to one or more of the excellent surveys and applications which have made their way into the literature. In particular, see Robert Dorfman (Ed.), *Measuring Benefits of Government Investment* [44], Otto Eckstein, *The Economics of Project Evaluation* [50], Jack Hirschleifer, James C. DeHaven, and Jerome W. Millman, *Water Supply, Economics, Technology and Policy* [76], John V. Krutilla and Otto Eckstein, *Multiple Purpose River Development* [89], Richard A. Musgrave, "Cost-Benefit Analysis and the Theory of Public Finance" [110], A. R. Prest and R. Turvey, "Cost-Benefit Analysis: A Survey" [123], and Ralph Turvey, "On the Development of Cost-Benefit Analysis" [150].

The Purpose of Benefit-Cost Analysis

Benefit-cost analysis is a practical tool that can be used by government to select among alternative expenditures those it should undertake in order to carry out its economic role—a role which includes a requirement that it provide goods and services to remedy what otherwise would be a suboptimal allocation of resources in the economy.

Government is required to provide goods and services because of the presence of so-called *externalities* in the private market. Externalities, or external effects, occur in the economy when the production or consumption of a good provides to individuals benefits or costs other than those normally provided to parties of a market transaction. The benefits or costs thus provided to members of a society *in total* are either smaller or larger than the benefits received or costs incurred by the individual parties to the market transaction.

In other words, an externality is present when there is interdependence among utility or production functions and the absence of either compensation to injured parties (in the case of detrimental externalities) or payment to providers (in the case of beneficial externalities). The term "technological externality" is often used to describe these external effects, since production or utility functions are physically interrelated.

The presence of external effects means that either costs are incurred or benefits are received by parties outside the market transaction. Because costs or benefits "spill over" to parties external to these transactions, outputs of these goods are not produced at levels considered optimum from society's point of view. An optimum allocation of resources for society requires that the production of each good be carried to the point where its marginal social utility (or benefit) is equal to its marginal social cost. But unless marginal social utility is equal to private utility and marginal social cost is equal to marginal private cost, the private market transaction will not produce an optimum allocation of output for a given good. When external effects are present, parties to a market transaction will not themselves equate marginal *social* cost with marginal *social* utility. The presence of external effects, therefore, provides the justification for government to interfere with private transactions in order to bring social costs into equality with social utility, thus remedying an otherwise suboptimum allocation of resources. This interference occurs through the provision of public goods.

Two categories of public goods, differing only in the extent of the presence of externalities, may be defined. Each poses its own problems for a benefit-cost procedure. Musgrave [109] has designated these two categories as social goods and merit goods. We now discuss each type of public good.

Social and Merit Goods and Benefit-Cost Analysis

Certain public expenditures, such as those required to purchase defense, flood control protection, highways, and judiciary services, are made by government because the private market cannot adequately supply them, even though these goods are desired by the public. These social goods are identified by the widespread presence of external effects in their provision.

A social good confers a benefit on almost everyone and, unless payment is received from everyone, the social benefits (i.e., the benefits to all citizens of the nation) will exceed the private benefits to those who make payment for the good. Those who make payment cannot prevent those who don't from enjoying benefits from the provision of the good, nor do those who purchase the good evaluate the benefits to others in determining the level of their purchases. Externalities are present in social goods because those who pay cannot exclude the remaining citizens of the political jurisdiction from enjoying benefits in amounts approximately equal to those enjoyed by parties to the transaction. Furthermore, because of the presence of these pervasive external effects, private transactions simply will not provide an optimum level of output for these goods.

To summarize, while goods of a social nature may conceivably be offered by the private sector, the price mechanism cannot be used to prevent those who don't pay the market price from enjoying the benefits *fully*. The external effects provided by such goods are not merely incidental to the provision of these goods, but are a distinguishing characteristic of these goods.

Merit goods, however, provide external effects which are merely incidental to a private transaction and are more local in their incidence than are the external effects of social goods. These are public goods which are provided in large quantities by the private sector, but at a level less (or greater) than socially optimum, that is, at a level where the marginal social benefits are greater (or less) than marginal private benefits. To remedy this suboptimal allocation of resources, government attempts to expand or contract these merit goods. Examples of merit goods include public expenditures on education, health, and housing, and taxation on the sale of liquor. Each of these goods is provided by the private market but at a level less (in the case of education, health, and housing) or greater (in the case of liquor) than optimum.

Although the presence of external effects creates a need for government intervention, this intervention should take place only if the social utility derived from such action exceeds the social costs, including the social cost of opportunities forgone by such an expenditure. The practical impossibility of measuring social utilities has forced all investigators to approximate true social utilities with a quantitative assessment of benefits. If the requirement that benefits exceed costs is met, we can be fairly certain that the *economic welfare* (i.e., real income) of the nation will be advanced rather than retarded by public expenditures. The requirement that social utilities exceed social costs for public goods provides the justification for subjecting each public expenditure, except those intended solely to alter the existing distribution of income, to the benefit-cost criterion. The procedure does not, however, ensure that total welfare (i.e., happiness) is increased, for we only approximate changes in true social utilities by estimating social benefits.

Benefit-cost analysis, therefore, is a procedure used to attempt to remedy a suboptimal use of resources. We now examine the elements of this procedure. Once we have reviewed all the elements, we will examine some additional complications that may arise, including problems arising from our attempt to use estimates of social benefits as a proxy for social utilities.

Elements of a Benefit-Cost Study

Numerous compromises with the requirements of economic theory are necessary in order to provide a quantitative evaluation of public projects. A parallel may be drawn here between the types of compromise required in a benefit-cost study and the types required to arrive at a correct measure of national income (or business income, for that matter). In national income accounting it is necessary to make many compromises in order to solve the conceptual, statistical, and analytical problems that prevent us from arriving at a true measure of national income, and even after much laborious work we are warned by the national income accountant that estimates of gross national product and national income and their movement should be used only as the roughest indicator of overall welfare. Likewise, the business accountant warns of the limitations of financial accounting statements for determining the true health of a business.

Similarly, the requirements of pure economic theory are simply too demanding for most practical benefit-cost studies, and compromises are required at virtually every step of a typical study. Many ingenious solutions to difficult evaluation problems have been made in past static studies. Many more compromises remain to be worked out. We now examine the elements of a typical static study along with the compromises that are made typically for each element.

1. Evaluation of Social Benefits

In all applications of benefit-cost analysis, economists have used the second-best procedure of estimating benefits in monetary terms as quantitative surrogates for true changes in social utilities, since quantitative estimates of true social utilities are beyond the scope of current estimation procedures. Benefits, however, even in a monetary sense, are not arrived at simply for most public goods. They are more easily measured in the case of merit goods, where the public good has a counterpart in the private market, the price of which may be used as an approximation to the benefits of the merit good. But there can be no precise counterpart, since merit goods involve externalities and these, by definition, do not have market values. We must, therefore, be satisfied with approximations, and market prices provide useful first approximations to social benefits.

Difficult as the benefits of merit goods are to evaluate, the benefits of social goods pose even more difficult problems, for here there are no good market substitutes, since social goods are simply not sold normally. Unless the social good is an intermediate product to a final good which is sold on the private market, or unless one can estimate savings in costs and employ these savings as estimates of social benefits, the benefit side of benefit-cost analysis breaks down and a political procedure must be substituted to solve the basic evaluation problem. Once the overall evaluation is made in the political process, however, project evaluation may often proceed to evaluate incremental adjustments to these social goods through a cost-savings approach to benefit estimation. For example, once the desired level of judicial services is provided, new configurations may be evaluated using the estimated cost savings of the old as an estimate of benefits of the new.

2. Estimation of Social Costs

When economists speak of estimating the social costs of a public project, they mean social "opportunity costs." The measure of a public project's true social cost is what society forgoes in real wealth in order to undertake that project. The upshot of this requirement to measure opportunity costs is that if resources contemplated for use on public projects are otherwise unemployed, the social opportunity cost for employing them is zero during the time period in which they otherwise would be unemployed. If resources contemplated for use on public projects displace other productive effort, the market prices of these resources should be used as the social opportunity cost of these resources.

The opportunity-cost principle provides the economic justification for government to provide employment during periods of large-scale unemployment, for during these periods the opportunity cost to society of employing unemployed labor resources is zero. Projects that are marginal during periods of full employment become profitable during periods of widespread unemployment.

3. Static Framework of Analysis

The standard method of analysis in benefit-cost studies involves a principle that may be called "with and without" analysis. The idea is simple enough: the path of the existing system is compared to the modified path of the economic system with the project. All the nonpecuniary incremental economic effects of the new project over time are counted as benefits and costs of the proposed project.[b] The assumption, however, is always that the existing system is stable and in equilibrium at the time the project is introduced, and that the internal dynamics of the existing system do not materially affect the size of the benefits and costs of the new project. Benefits and costs are estimated over the life of the project under the assumption that present conditions will continue over the life of the project unless altered by the project itself.

The assumption of a static structure avoids the necessity of uncovering the underlying social production functions upon which new projects operate. Much more will be said in Chapter 2 about this static procedure and the problems encountered with its assumptions.

4. The Social Discount Rate and the Present-Value Criterion

Because social costs of public expenditures should reflect true opportunity costs of utilizing otherwise employable or potentially employable resources of the private sector, we are required to charge to public projects the opportunity cost of capital diverted from the private sector to the public sector. That is, we should require that public investments yield *at least* the social return over time which would otherwise be earned by these funds in the private sector from which they must be withdrawn. This requirement is met in benefit-cost analysis by selecting an opportunity-cost rate of return for the purpose of discounting social costs and benefits associated with the public project.

The social discount rate is used for calculating the present value of net benefits for a social project. It serves as our decision criterion for determining the acceptability of projects. Formally, the criterion requires that we accept projects which produce a positive net present value (NPV), defined as follows:

$$NPV = -S_0 + \frac{S_1}{(1+r)^1} + \frac{S_2}{(1+r)^2} + \frac{S_3}{(1+r)^3} + \ldots \frac{S_n}{(1+r)^n}$$

[b]A pecuniary external effect of a project is defined as a change in the market price of products or factors of production which results from a project. These external effects, as distinct from technological external effects, are excluded from estimates of benefits and cost under conventional procedures. According to Prest and Turvey [123, p. 160], "we are concerned [in cost-benefit analysis] with the value of the increment of output arising from a given investment and not with the increment in value of existing assets."

where $S_0, S_1, \ldots, S_n$ represent net benefits for each of the time periods in the life of the project and r represents the social discount rate.

The most operational procedure for estimating the social discount rate is to compute a weighted average social rate of return representing production and consumption forgone in the private sector. The rates of return forgone in production and consumption are weighted according to estimates of the portion of funds which will be taken from each sector for the purpose of making the investment. The rates of return forgone should be computed on a pretax basis, since taxes are paid to society and are part of what society forgoes when it removes funds from the private sector. Furthermore, because we attempt to estimate the net social return forgone, we must attempt to increase the pretax private return if beneficial externalities are forgone by undertaking the project, and to decrease it if detrimental externalities are forgone. Finally, if detrimental externalities are a side effect of a public project, they should be deducted from the social benefits.

5. *Provision for Uncertainty*

There are a number of standard techniques for making provision for the uncertainty associated with our estimates of benefits, costs, project life, and the social discount rate. They include:

1. Adding an arbitrary uncertainty factor to the social discount rate. This produces a more conservative assessment of net benefits by raising the rate at which they are discounted.
2. Establishing an expected value for benefits, costs, project life, and the discount rate by estimating a subjective probability distribution for each element whose value is uncertain. The expected value of each distribution is then taken as a certainty equivalent for the parameter for the purpose of computing the present value of net benefits.
3. Arbitrarily reducing estimates of distant benefits, truncating the procedure at a short project life, or making the discount rate a positive function of time. Each of these methods has the effect of decreasing the weight accorded distant benefits and costs in the calculation.
4. Subjecting the net present value to worst-case values of uncertain parameters to determine whether these extreme values alter the acceptability of the project. If the project passes the sensitivity tests, we can then be more certain of its acceptability regardless of the uncertainty in our estimates of parameter values.

Procedure No. 4 seems the least arbitrary one and it has the additional advantage of being quite operational, especially when carried out by computer. These advantages tend to make it the preferred procedure for making provision for uncertainty in public projects.

To summarize, each of the five major elements of a typical benefit-cost study requires us to make compromises with the requirements of pure economic theory in order to arrive at a quantitative economic evaluation of a public project. Even after this difficult task has been completed, however, we still must take certain additional precautions to ensure that a project which passes the benefit-cost criterion actually improves both economic efficiency and welfare. One of the most obvious sources of difficulty is the need to conduct interpersonal comparisons of utility for those who gain versus those who lose from a project in order to satisfy the requirement that welfare actually be advanced by the public expenditure in question. Another difficulty concerns the likely suboptimization of social returns in the private sector, whose various parts earn unequal social rates of return. Each of these difficulties creates the possibility that individual projects which pass the benefit-cost criterion may not actually improve welfare. We now examine these problems.

Interpersonal Utility Comparison Problems

The benefit-cost criterion leads us to choose projects which improve the allocation of resources and therefore the level of real national income, regardless of the distribution of income which results. Welfare, however, is advanced by projects which raise the level of happiness or utility in society. Since utility is very difficult to measure in even the roughest sense, we utilize benefits to approximate it. This procedure has its dangers, since it uses a change in monetary benefits as a proxy for a change in utility (and therefore welfare). Trouble arises if those who gain from a project evaluate their gains lower in terms of *utility* than those who lose. If this happens, welfare is actually retarded by the project. Welfare economists have tried to develop rules of thumb to aid policy makers in the difficult but necessary task of making judgments regarding changes in utility which result from a project. We now discuss these various welfare criteria which may be used qualitatively to supplement the results of our benefit-cost studies.

The Pareto welfare criterion is by far the best known among welfare criteria. It permits us to consider a change beneficial if someone is helped by the project and no one is harmed. However, very few policy measures lead to such results. Moreover, the Pareto criterion leaves us with an infinite number of possibilities among which it cannot choose, since each possible distribution of income can produce a Pareto optimum. The criterion is silent regarding the "proper" distribution of income. Even in those instances where economic efficiency is improved by a project to no one's detriment, externalities in consumption mean that we cannot be absolutely sure that total welfare has been enhanced. Since interpersonal utility comparisons and judgments regarding the proper distribution of income must be made in policy decisions, the Pareto criterion is of little help. Unfortunately, these difficulties plague all welfare criteria.

The Kaldor-Hicks criterion was designed to evaluate changes which harm some and help others. The criterion stipulates that a change is beneficial if those who gain assign a higher monetary value to the gains than the losers assign to the losses they incur from the project. However, the criterion also runs into utility comparison problems. First of all, compensation is not actually required under the Kaldor-Hicks criterion; if it were required, the Pareto criterion would be met—the change actually would benefit some and harm no one. Second, the utility attached to the monetary value by the gainer may not be higher than the utility attached to the monetary value by the loser, even though the gains are evaluated at a higher monetary value than are the losses. Therefore, we are in no position to assume that there has been a net increase in total welfare. Third, as Scitovsky pointed out [141], if the Kaldor-Hicks criterion is actually met but compensation is not paid, the resultant changes from the project may alter the distribution of income to such an extent that the losers may actually find it profitable to compensate the gainers for a new move back to the status quo. Scitovsky consequently proposed a double criterion requiring that gainers evaluate their gains at a monetary value higher than the losers evaluate their losses and that losers do not find it profitable, with the resultant distribution of income, to bribe the gainers to revert to the status quo ante.

Although the Scitovsky double criterion does avoid the embarrassing possibility of contradictory Kaldor evaluations of a pair of alternatives, it still does not provide the interpersonal utility comparisons required to judge whether the gains accruing to the winner have a higher utility to him than the losses accruing to the loser. It also ignores the desirability of the redistribution of income which the project involves.

Little [93] has extended the Scitovsky criterion to incorporate explicit value judgments concerning the "goodness" of the resultant income distribution. Under Little's criterion, a change is an improvement if the Scitovsky double criterion is satisfied and policy makers judge the resultant income distribution to be an improvement. Little, however, provides no criteria for judging income distributions, nor does his criterion overcome the interpersonal utility comparison problem. However, avoiding a value judgment regarding the distribution of income is itself a value judgment placing high normative value on the existing distribution of income.

In summary, none of the preceding welfare criteria provides a firm footing for allocation decisions based on the use of benefit-cost analysis alone. Benefit-cost analysts are compelled to agree with Baumol [8, p. 400] that any search for an overall welfare criterion must necessarily be sterile and rest upon utility comparisons. Certainly, the use of benefit-cost analysis as a policy tool cannot be justified on the basis of welfare economics alone. In practice, it must be supplemented with the judgment of policy makers concerning the equity and desirability of the resultant changes in the distribution of income brought about by the project. On this question, we should expect policy makers to disagree.

Even without the ability to make interpersonal comparisons of utility, if everything else were well, the Little criterion would seem to provide a reasonable basis for policy decisions, with value judgments regarding interpersonal utility changes and income distribution being made by policy makers. Benefit-cost analysis could then be carried out subject to distributional constraints. Other things, however, are not all well.

Second-Best Problems

The requirements for a Pareto-optimum solution are met under the purely competitive market structure in the absence of externalities. Since prices under this kind of a regime are everywhere equated to marginal social utilities and marginal social costs, marginal social benefits equal marginal social costs for all outputs. If prices in only one sector of the economy exceed marginal social costs, a government policy which brings prices into equality with marginal social costs will improve aggregate economic welfare. This is the case so long as government projects in that policy sector have social benefits which are greater than (or equal at the margin to) social opportunity costs.

However, if prices *generally* deviate from marginal social costs, as is more likely the case in our economy, economic welfare is not necessarily increased by government projects which by themselves produce social benefits greater than social costs. That is, an application of the optimality rule in only one sector of the economy is likely to produce relatively more output in that sector than is socially optimum. This means that higher social returns might be made available to society by the expansion of outputs in the relatively profitable sectors of the private economy. Under these conditions, government intervention via benefit-cost analysis may actually move us away from rather than toward a welfare optimum. These results follow directly from the theorem of second-best, which has been generalized by Lipsey and Lancaster [92].

The reason for these results is that a Pareto-optimum solution implies that just the right social amount of each good is produced in the economy. If prices deviate from marginal social costs, however, some goods will be produced at too low a level of output from the point of view of society. In addition, if we assume reasonably full employment, other goods will be produced at too high a level of output, since these latter industries will utilize some resources which under an optimum arrangement would be employed elsewhere.

However, this technical problem of second-best is not likely to be very serious for benefit-cost analysis if we insist on removing capital from those sectors with relatively low marginal social returns (i.e., those with relatively high output) and put these funds to use in projects which have relatively high marginal social returns (i.e., those which are otherwise produced at relatively low volume).

To summarize, a mechanistic application of benefit-cost analysis to public-sector income and expenditure decision making is an error. The unmodified benefit-cost analysis rule would be valid in a world where the above assumptions of a Pareto optimum held and where the existing income distribution was somehow considered ideal by society. In reality, we are required to supplement this criterion with judgments regarding the desirability of the allocation of output and the distribution of income which results from the project.

The Case for Benefit-Cost Analysis

After discussing the many compromises necessary in order to perform a benefit-cost study and the difficult conceptual problems posed by the need to make interpersonal comparisons of utility and by matters of second-best, one might wonder just what the overwhelming justification is for benefit-cost analysis. One must only look at alternative procedures available for expenditure decisions in order to understand the desperate need for a systematic procedure.

Alternative procedures leave expenditure decisions almost *solely* to the political process, where power and political relations rule in decision making. No assurances can be given that decisions arrived at without analysis in the political process will yield even a fraction of the social return that may be earned by equivalent resources left to the private sector of the economy. We have many examples of public projects which were ill-conceived and actually made matters worse. We will review some of these examples in the next chapter.

While the assumptions required for a Pareto optimum are most certainly not met in our economy, there is a significant amount of competition in virtually every nonregulated sector of the economy. Benefit-cost analysis attempts to bring a similar standard of efficiency to the public sector, to which huge amounts of resources are currently being transferred. The only procedure almost certainly worse than benefit-cost analysis is one which ignores an explicit comparison of benefits and costs for each public expenditure. The strongest support for the benefit-cost procedure, therefore, is the need to ensure that public projects yield social returns at least as high as those private projects which they displace. A liberal dose of common sense should also accompany its use in the political process.

2 The Dangers of Static Methods in Benefit-Cost Analysis

Current social problems have characteristics that make them difficult to analyze fully. They are complex, which means that causes and effects are manifold and separated in time. Potential solutions that attack symptoms of these problems are likely to fail or result in only small benefits. These problems often cut across agency lines, making thorough analysis difficult to carry out. Data sufficient to provide solutions to such problems are often sparse or totally unavailable.

Even when the intricate cause-and-effect relationships of a problem area are identified, a tool for evaluating the economic consequences of proposed solutions is required. This means that good estimates must be made of the dynamic time path of benefits and costs of proposed programs. Often, however, even this is insufficient for purposes of policy, since questions of "who benefits" and "who bears the costs" are often dominant in the minds of policy makers.

Standard static methods of benefit-cost analysis cannot (by definition) capture the underlying time-varying behavior of a social system. It is often necessary to understand this behavior in order to make good estimates of the dynamic time path of benefits and costs of proposed programs. Therefore, if static methods are applied to evaluate programs affecting complex social systems, they are likely to lead to choices that are essentially incorrect, or choices that may even make matters worse.

The preceding chapter provided a brief description of the purpose and methods of benefit-cost analysis. We turn in this chapter to examine some actual applications of static methods. We will illustrate how they can lead to incorrect choices when applied to problem areas that are themselves inherently unstable. Then we will examine the properties of these complex systems that make dynamic analysis essential for a proper evaluation of programs affecting these systems. Finally, at the end of this chapter, we present an outline of the remainder of the volume.

The Dangers of Static Estimates of Benefits and Costs: Three Illustrative Examples

1. Introduction

In addition to immediate benefits and immediate costs, public projects often produce secondary or induced dynamic effects upon other economic variables. These induced effects, which include nonpecuniary external effects, must be incorporated into estimates of benefits and costs. The customary method of incorporating these side effects is to estimate, in a rough and ready manner, the difference in net benefits *with* and *without* the proposed project over the life of the project. This difference constitutes the measure of net benefits that is used to evaluate the desirability of the proposed project.

Although it is no trivial matter to measure immediate benefits and costs, induced dynamic effects pose an even more difficult problem. In order to measure them accurately, we must evaluate the influence a proposed project has on the dynamic time path of the system being considered. As we shall see presently, by reviewing three examples, economists have not in most cases considered the time path of the system under investigation.

2. *An Example from Urban Renewal*

Rothenberg, in a well-known study [126, pp. 196-7], uses the following model to summarize his economic evaluation of five *completed* residential redevelopment projects in a blighted area of Chicago:

Let: GPC = gross project cost

AC = cost of acquired real estate in site (acquisition cost)

L_O = market value of land acquired in site

I_O = market value of improvements acquired in site

R = resource expenditures in project other than acquisition cost

TC = total resource costs of project

Then; $GPC = \text{AC} + \text{R}$

$AC = L_O + I_O$

$TC = I_O + R$

(since I_O, but not L_O, is lost to society through the project)

So: $TC = (AC - L_O) + R = GPC - L_O$

and total benefits (TB) are given by

$TB = (L_1 - L_0)$ + (spillover effects) + (changes in social costs of slums)

In his detailed model, Rothenberg [126, pp. 177-183] attempts to isolate the portion of increased land values resulting from redevelopment projects, as opposed to those *induced* by income and population changes. The projects *themselves* are not assumed to affect population and income. The differences between estimated preproject and postproject land values constitute his measure of benefits: $L_1 - L_0$ in the total benefits (TB) equation.

Rothenberg's model is an example of a static and ex-post benefit-cost evaluation of urban renewal projects. Although he points out many problems with his analysis, and warns against taking it seriously, his method is not, in my view, appropriate for the economic evaluation problem that is posed by urban redevelopment projects. Rothenberg makes no attempt to measure the effect of these projects on the time-varying stream of benefits and costs of the unmodified urban system.

Increased land values clearly represent only one possible effect of urban redevelopment. Redevelopment projects may (and often do) influence movements of population and industry; increase municipal costs; reduce municipal revenues; and affect property tax levies, thus affecting cumulative revival or deterioration processes existing in the urban area *without* the projects. These processes and the influence of redevelopment on them are missed totally by Rothenberg's model.

Spillover effects (pecuniary and nonpecuniary), not measured by Rothenberg's procedure, might well have been detrimental on balance. For example, the projects may have stimulated an exodus of some affluent members of the community (as a result of higher property taxes induced by the redevelopment projects?), thus raising the costs of municipal services for those property owners who remained behind. These interrelated dynamic components in an urban system influence the time path of benefits and costs set off by redevelopment projects. There is no reason to believe that Rothenberg's static and one-year estimates of benefits and costs represent even remotely the true time-varying benefits and cost of the redevelopment projects. Nor is there any reason to believe that the method employed evaluated directly the true effect of these projects on the time-varying stream of benefits and costs of the current unmodified arrangement for even the period of time that was considered.

Moreover, I would simply echo the criticism levied on this procedure by Prest and Turvey [123, p. 191] when they described Rothenberg's illustrative example as "an ex-post one" that "introduces problems which are irrelevant to the ex-ante calculations" required by decision makers if the analysis is to be of any use for public policy. That is, if public policy analysis is to be useful, it must focus on the likely future effects of proposed projects, a task which requires insight into causal relationships in the problem area.

In order to evaluate an urban redevelopment project properly, Rothenberg requires a model of the urban area affected by redevelopment. Such a model is needed to trace the incremental effect of the project through time on the time-varying behavior of net benefits enjoyed by the citizens of the urban area without the project. It is essential, although by no means a trivial task, to determine the effects of the redevelopment project on population, income, housing, and property taxes.

The static analysis did result in a favorable economic evaluation of the redevelopment projects studied by Rothenberg. However, without a knowledge of the time-varying stream of net benefits produced by the existing urban system, one has no assurance that the projects are truly desirable. If the projects did stimulate an exodus of affluent population from the municipality, there is a good chance that they actually produced more costs than benefits. We cannot be sure that the static tool employed in this case will lead us to correct choices.

The typical real-life urban area is rarely in a state of equilibrium. Any procedure that evaluates an urban project as though the system were stable, as Rothenberg's does, must fail to capture the dynamic effects of a proposed project.[a]

3. An Example from Urban Mass Transportation

Baum and Gutowsky [6] have completed an extensive economic evaluation of the Sacramento Transit Authority to determine its economic effects upon the citizens of Sacramento and the surrounding metropolitan area.[b] The analysis is based on data compiled from a survey of transit passengers taken during May 1968, plus additional research on the value of travel time and on the level of pollutants produced by automobiles. In a nutshell, benefits of the transit system are calculated by estimating the incremental social costs that would result if the transit system were eliminated—social costs that include increased air pollution as most of the previous riders of the mass transit system switch to automobiles.

In addition, the following social costs (social benefits of the transit system) are taken to result from the closing of the transit system:

1. Incremental congestion costs to auto users, computed at four alternative hourly dollar values for waiting time.

[a]The recent description of an econometric urban simulation research project being carried out by Engle *et al.* [53] leads me to believe that these omissions are now being corrected. The econometric model consists of three submodels of the Boston metropolitan area [53, p. 87]: "A macroeconomic nonspatial model of output, employment, and income distribution; a model of long-term adjustments of population and capital stocks; and a model of spatial allocation." Although the authors claim that the primary purpose of the econometric model is "to evaluate the costs and benefits of a hypothetical set of alternative development patterns for Boston," they have not provided a set of equations to measure net benefits.

[b]A major portion of this study is included in this volume as Appendix C.

2. Incremental welfare costs and lost wages for citizens unable to work as a result of reduced public transit.
3. Lost revenue from operations.

The costs of retaining the transit system were calculated by estimating:

1. Weekday and weekend operating costs, including charter costs.
2. Opportunity costs of the capital employed in the transit system.

In addition to favorable benefit-cost ratios, ranging from 2.12 to 2.79 depending upon the value assigned to travel and waiting time, the transit system was estimated to reduce pollutants by more than 1,283 tons annually. Although Baum and Gutowsky decided not to estimate the social value of the reduced level of pollution (i.e., the social value of the reduction in the level of this externality), this is certainly a benefit of the transit system which would make its benefit-cost ratio even more favorable.

Without denigrating the truly important contribution of this study to the benefit-cost literature, we must recognize its limited usefulness for purposes of policy. First, the economic evaluation was carried out for one year only. Second, it is another example of an ex-post analysis. Third, although the authors mention the dynamics of automobile and mass transportation, they ignore them totally in their benefit-cost model and estimation procedure. For example, they point out [6, p. 12] that:

> Since World War II the national trend has been for riders to desert public transit in favor of automobiles which adds to street congestion and slows transit service. This diversion reduces transit revenues, increases congestion and transit system costs which in turn triggers a reduction in schedules motivating more transit patrons to substitute private autos; thus completing a vicious cycle with our cities suffering from the resultant smog, congestion and devotion of more and more land to the private automobile.

Had the authors attempted a thorough dynamic analysis of these relationships, they might have found reasons for the public's preference for automobiles other than the unavailability of mass-transit service.

Mass transit creates changes in patterns of living that may produce large costs or benefits for residents of a municipality. For example, Muth [111, p. 308] points out that improved transportation is a major cause of urban decentralization and suburbanization. Improved rapid mass transit may speed the exodus of middle- and upper-income citizens from the city to the suburbs, thus decreasing municipal revenues and increasing the costs to those remaining in the central city.[c] Costs and benefits of such changes are

[c]The data used by Baum and Gutowsky show that citizens using mass transit in Sacramento in 1968 were members of families with median incomes approximately $1,800 lower than those citizens using automobiles, indicating that mass transit is an inferior good. The data imply that as the relative income rises, the demand for mass transit tends to diminish. Therefore, while improvements in mass transit should expedite the movement of middle-income families away

not constant over time; they certainly cannot be captured by a static and incomplete benefit-cost evaluation procedure.

The preceding quotation provides a good starting point for determining the components of a dynamic model for the Sacramento Transit Authority. In addition, a dynamic model of the problem would have to incorporate the influence of mass transportation projects on migration, per capita net income, assessed valuations, municipal revenue, and housing patterns.

In summary, Baum and Gutowsky have accumulated many valuable data indicative of the relative benefits of mass transit as against the automobile, but have used a tool that is not adequate for selection among public investments of projects in the transportation field. Their analysis is far too static and omits too many important feedback relationships, and may lead us to public investment choices that actually deteriorate welfare.

4. Examples from the Economic Evaluation of Investments in Human Capital

This section examines the status of the applications of benefit-cost analysis to investments in human capital. Unlike the two previous examples, each of which related specifically to a single study, this section reviews the current controversy concerning the efficacy of the many attempts to measure the economic returns resulting from investments in human capital.

Much recent evidence indicates that estimates of the rate of return on investments in human capital, particularly investments in education, have erred on the upward side. In this section, we sample some of that evidence, and attempt to explain how such errors have come about.

In reviewing the voluminous literature on investment in human capital, one certainly does not find any consensus about expected returns to education; nor about the likely success of efforts of economic research to find answers to such rate-of-return questions. However, in a sampling of prominent articles in this field, e.g., the collection in Blaug [18], one is struck by the relatively high estimates of rates of return, both social and private, to primary, secondary, and college education in the United States.

The basic procedure employed in estimating returns to education is to compare lifetime earnings of a group having a specified level of education with earnings of a group having the nearest lower level of education. Using

---

from central cities, the effects on upper-income city residents may be more indirect. Improvements in mass transit tend to attract additional passengers of middle income, thus reducing traffic congestion and waiting time, which tends to reduce the cost of waiting incurred by automobile travelers. Since the opportunity cost of waiting should be higher for the relatively affluent passengers, their costs tend to be reduced most by the reduced level of congestion that results from improved mass transit. Therefore, improvements in mass transit may expedite the decentralization of both middle- and upper-income families of central cities.

this procedure, Hansen [18, p. 146], for example, estimates that social rates of return for males in the United States are about 15.0%, 11.4%, and 10.2% for primary, secondary, and college education respectively. Since Hansen does not try to separate the effects of education from other factors influencing income, such as sex, race, intelligence, socioeconomic status, home background, and pure chance, his estimates must be considered highly inaccurate at best.

Becker [17] and Morgan *et al.* [108], in well-known studies, have attempted to refine earlier studies and, through the use of multivariate analysis, to isolate the independent influence of education on income. They independently concluded that education was the major factor influencing incomes in the groups studied.[d]

A number of economists and policy makers have criticized this work sharply. Their criticisms go right to the heart of the procedures employed in these rates-of-return analyses. They all believe that, since we are *unable* to specify a production function relating inputs of the education process to improvements in the productivity of labor, we are unable to identify accurately the independent effects of education on income. For example, Bowles states[20, p. 12]:

> Without an estimate of the technology of education (the production function) the relationship between the opportunity cost and expected benefits of particular policies must be little more than guesswork.

The debate among economists on the value of rate-of-return calculations of investment in education, as summarized by Blaug [18, pp. 222-231], involves an evaluation of the issues raised by Bowles. The use of multivariate analysis to determine the effect of education upon earnings is beset both by identification problems and by the high correlation among the values of many of the independent variables influencing income. While we may be fairly certain, as most calculations show, that education is a factor influencing income, we cannot overlook the hazards besetting the attribution to education of a definite portion of observed income differences among workers *without* some knowledge of the manner in which all the factors influencing earnings *interrelate* to cause earning differences.

With these problems in mind, Samuelson [134, p. 172] has also joined the debate on the side of those who believe that estimates of returns "are biased on the high side." He states:

> . . . it is very hard to separate the certifying and selecting function of education from what it adds . . . The statistics simply will not enable us to know whether identification bias is 10 percent, 50 percent, or 90 percent. This original suspicion has been heightened by the findings of the Coleman Report that the relationship between money spent on schooling and performance is a complex one.

[d]The estimates of rates of return to education computed by Morgan *et al.* (4-6%), however, were well below those computed by Becker.

While the Coleman study [32] does not imply directly that education is unrelated to income, it does conclude that the amount spent by government on education does not improve the learning process. However, if additional expenditures effect little improvement in cognitive skills, how can we be sure that such expenditures improve the quality of labor, as some estimates of economic returns indicate?

Two recent major studies lend further support to arguments that rate-of-return calculations have been on the high side. The New York State Commission on the Quality, Cost, and Financing of Elementary and Secondary Education [117] has found a strong correlation between test scores (or cognitive skills) and socioeconomic status. Students whose parents have high incomes and are highly educated tend to do well in all the standard measures of cognitive skills, and those who are on the bottom of the socioeconomic ladder do the worst. Thirty-nine socioeconomic characteristics of the students, and *not* expenditures per student, were found to explain (p. 133) "approximately 65% of the variation among schools" of New York State in the percentage of students whose performances were considered below the minimum competence level in arithmetic and reading. These data generally support the findings of the Coleman study and imply that increased expenditures on primary and secondary education do not necessarily improve the learning process, a process which seems to be influenced to a far greater degree by the socioeconomic status of students.

The link between cognitive skills and income was not investigated thoroughly by the commission. Jencks and his associates [80, p. 215] have recently taken up this question. They estimate that only 24-29% of the differences in income between sons of upper-middle and lower-class families can be attributed to extra schooling. When men of similar background, cognitive skill, educational level, and occupational status were compared [80, p. 226], "only 12 to 15% less inequality" was found among them than was found among individuals picked at random. Jencks *et al*. find that socioeconomic background, race, cognitive skills, occupation, education, and test scores do have some influence on income; but, they suggest, luck, personality, and skills other than normal cognitive skills probably have just as much influence.

We can only conclude from this summary of investigations into investment in human capital that past evaluations have not produced a consensus on the make-up of the education-income-education relationship. Recent evidence reviewed previously indicates that the relationships are far more complex than some economists have thought. Until we have an education production function, including an accepted theory of learning, we can say little with confidence regarding the effect of new educational programs upon income. A systematic evaluation of the influence of education inputs (among many others) on productive capacity, through time, seems to be required in order to measure the returns to education accurately.

Education provides still another example of a complex social system in which dynamic feedback components pervade many of the relationships between it and income. Although these dynamic relationships have not been included thus far in benefit-cost studies, some economists have identified them. Burkhead [29, p. 89], for example, has identified the vicious cycle among the poor: low income-low aspirations-poor education-low income *ad infinitum*. This cycle is a reinforcing dynamic feedback loop in the complex income-education-income relationship that cannot be captured accurately by static benefit-cost models.[e]

In summary, we have examined in this section some evidence on benefit-cost evaluations. We have discussed several problems besetting static methods now used to estimate benefits and costs of a certain category of public expenditures. For each example reviewed, we found that dynamic relationships seemed to be important for a proper evaluation of public programs. These relationships were simply not captured by the methods used.

Limitations of the Least-Squares Criterion for Benefit-Cost Models

A serious problem besets the use, for purposes of policy, of a least-squares criterion or any related criterion of "goodness of fit" in a linear model, even if the model is a dynamic one. To illustrate, assume that the actual dynamic behavior of the key variable of a social system can be represented by the solid oscillating curve in Figure 2-1.[f]

The least-squares line in Figure 2-1 provides a better fit (i.e., a lower value of the squared error term) than the dynamic model represented by the broken oscillating curve. Although the least-squares line is likely to provide a better prediction of the state of the social system at any specific date in the

[e]The fact that we possess limited knowledge of education and health production functions has not escaped policy makers. At a recent symposium [114] sponsored by the National Academy of Engineering, policy makers gave overwhelming testimony indicating that recent education and health programs had offered small or even negative returns. The programs that backfired all looked promising at the outset. Comments by Francis Keppel, formerly U.S. Commissioner of Education, on the "Present Limits of Education Change" called attention to the absence of data concerning educational production functions, and to the absence of reliable data relating an increase in expenditures on education to improvements in education at the primary and secondary levels.

Our knowledge concerning investment in health care programs appears equally imperfect. Wholey [81, Vol. 1, p. 461] finds: "The interrelationships among the effects of environment, education, and medical care make it very difficult to predict the improvements in health which would result from improvements in the delivery of health care. The results of health programs are usually not ascertainable for some years." Wholey implies that dynamic elements are also important for health systems.

[f]This figure is similar in intent, although somewhat different in construction, to a diagram contained in Forrester's *Industrial Dynamics* [62, p. 126].

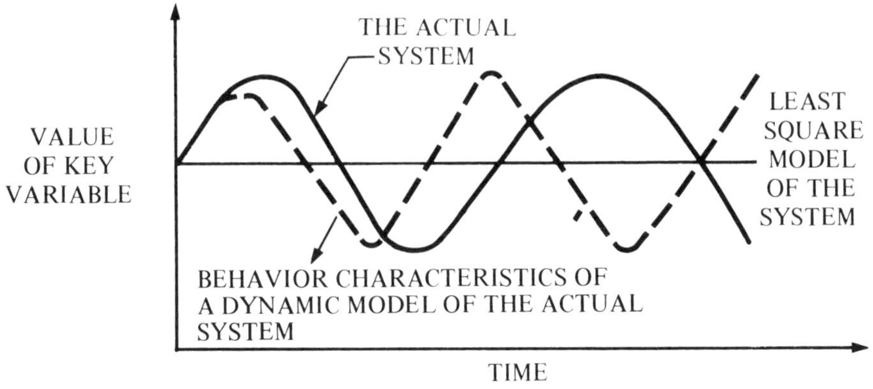

Figure 2-1. Least-Squares vs. Dynamic Model

future, it does not display any of the oscillatory behavior characteristics of the actual system.

The dynamic nonlinear model, on the other hand, does have behavior characteristics (e.g., period and amplitude characteristics) similar to those of the actual system. If we are also confident that the structure and parameters of the model are those that actually produce the observed dynamic behavior, the model can be more useful for the evaluation of potential policy changes than is the least-squares model, even though its predictions of specific states of the system are less accurate than those of the least-squares model. This problem can arise in all linear regression models.

To build a realistic *nonlinear* regression model to represent the system as it is affected by urban redevelopment, mass transportation, and education programs, we require many observations for each important variable influencing the system in reality. For these and many other social systems, the data requirements for estimation of such nonlinear models simply cannot be met, at least not at this time.

Regression models and related goodness-of-fit criteria have been used extensively in benefit-cost studies (e.g., by Morgan et al. [108] and by Taubman and Wales [145]). In some instances (e.g., Taubman and Wales), allowances have been made in such models for nonlinear effects. Almost without exception, however, the data are derived from cross-section analysis (i.e., cross-section data on incomes for one or, at best, two years only). Moreover, the analyses without exception (at least to my knowledge) have been carried out on an ex-post basis.

If benefit-cost analysis is to be effective in helping us choose among projects, it must permit us to evaluate *specific* projects in an ex-ante manner. This means that valid dynamic models of underlying systems are prerequisites to successful estimates of benefits and costs of such projects, even though the data requirements of such models may be stringent.

Outline of Chapters 3 through 8

In the next four chapters, a comparative-dynamic procedure for benefit-cost analysis is described, a procedure that attempts to resolve *some* of the problems that have been reviewed in the preceding section. All the difficulties are not resolved perfectly; compromises are necessary at every step of the way. The objective is to design a procedure that allows us to proceed safely with benefit-cost analysis as a tool for project selection.

An urban model is used to illustrate the procedure because it is characterized by pervasive dynamic effects. Since dynamic effects characterize all public goods, in varying degrees, a valid procedure for benefit-cost analysis must be capable of evaluating their consequences properly. In addition, many domestic programs affect citizens of either urban or suburban areas. An urban model is essential for benefit-cost evaluations of such programs.

Any procedure we can hope to utilize must be a second-best, perhaps even a third-best, one (i.e., one for which second-best properties have not been proved formally), since the *best theoretical* procedure would require us to perform precise interpersonal utility comparisons; to have perfect foresight in the estimation of social benefits, costs, and the discount rate; and to assume that marginal social costs and benefits are everywhere equal except in the policy sector under evaluation.

Yet these exacting requirements of welfare economics must serve as a guide for the design of second- or third-best policy tools in order to ensure that these tools will offer a high probability of increasing welfare. The objective of the procedure, therefore, is to provide the *best practical* policy tool for the evaluation of projects imbedded in complex systems, even though such a procedure cannot satisfy the exacting requirements of pure welfare theory. Because these exacting requirements cannot be met in reality, this procedure must suffer from some of the deficiencies of conventional benefit-cost analysis.

The proposed procedure deals primarily with a class of problems that affect complex systems, a class that is likely to include many current social problems.

I shall proceed by constructing an explicit dynamic urban simulation model that predicts the course of events, over a 25-year period of time, both with and without each of four independent proposed public projects. The model will be described in Chapters 3 and 4. I will subject the model to an extensive sensitivity analysis in Chapter 5 to locate those parameters to which the key variables of the model are most sensitive. Then, in Chapter 6, the proposed projects will be evaluated by finding the discounted present value of the stream of benefit and cost differences between the basic system and the modified system. This will constitute our measure of net benefits, and will serve as the criterion for project acceptability. Each benefit-cost evaluation of Chapter 6 will be subjected to many plausible values of the most crucial parameters in order to determine how sensitive each original evaluation is to possible errors in estimation of the most sensitive parameters. This second sensitivity analysis will tell us how much uncertainty, in a qualitative sense, exists as to the validity of our recommendations.

Then, in Chapter 7, we will see that the procedure permits us to examine directly the role of the following issues, fundamental for benefit-cost analysis:

1. The provision for uncertainty.
2. The selection of an appropriate social discount rate.
3. The treatment of dynamic effects.
4. The evaluation of the effects of proposed projects on the intertemporal distribution of income.
5. The establishment of boundary conditions necessary to partition the public systems that are affected by individual projects to allow effective benefit-cost evaluation of proposed projects.
6. The validation of benefit-cost models.

Finally, Chapter 8 contains an analysis of the role static and dynamic methods of benefit-cost analysis should play in actual public-expenditure decisions in a democracy, taking full account of the institutional realities of the budget-making process and of the characteristics a rational decision should exhibit within this process.

3 A Comparative-Dynamic Partial Urban Model

In this and the next chapter, a comparative-dynamic partial urban model is described. The model is used in Chapters 5 and 6 to illustrate a comparative-dynamic procedure for benefit-cost analysis.

The partial urban model is a simulation model of medium size. Difference equations are used to represent a typical urban municipality—a municipality that has many features of a large northern central city of the United States.

A version of Baumol's [11] model of unbalanced productivity growth is linked both with a spatial model and a model of urban services and expenditures. Net-benefit equations for typical groups of citizens residing in the municipality are built into the model's structure explicitly.

The model differs significantly from other explicit dynamic urban models of the Forrester variety [61], in that it emphasizes unbalanced productivity growth as a major source of municipal fiscal pressure, and provides an explicit criterion of choice among projects.

For us, the primary purpose of the urban model is to illustrate the comparative-dynamic procedure for benefit-cost analysis. The model's structure and most of its parameter values have some empirical support, but the model represents only part of the complex set of forces at work continuously in a typical urban environment. Nevertheless, I do believe the model to be useful, in a very limited way, for purposes of public policy.

The model allows us to represent some of the policy choices of a typical central city—a task that is not at all trivial, since surrogate quantitative criteria for many policy choices are difficult to find.

The model represents *some* of the complex forces at work in a typical large central city of the United States. It does not purport to contain *all* important relationships, but rather attempts to capture a few important relationships that are likely to provide us with some help in understanding (and improving) reality. In this respect it is not unlike most mathematical models of complex phenomena.

The functional forms of some crucial equations lack empirical support totally. We hypothesize quantitatively in these instances, using economic theory as a guide, and hope that the results of the simulations themselves can provide a clue to plausible forms for these equations. Many of the data necessary for completion of the specification of these equations are simply not available, and in many cases where some evidence does exist, there are only a few observations of poor quality.

The partial model differs from econometric urban simulation models in that it concentrates almost exclusively on identifying valid structural relationships. The specification of functional forms and the determination of parameter values for most equations are given secondary and tertiary priority respectively. This strategy is followed for two reasons:

1. Our data for structural relationships are likely to be far better (although by no means complete) than our data for equation forms and parameter values.
2. Valid structural relationships *may be* far more important for an understanding of the complexities of reality; i.e., the values for key variables of a model representing a complex economic system may be relatively insensitive to changes in most equation forms and parameter values—at least this is Forrester's assertion [62, pp. 117-118], which I will test in Chapters 5 and 6.

In order to describe and evaluate the model in a manageable way, I have segmented it into five interrelated sections and subdivided its presentation into two chapters. Section I is described fully in this chapter and Sections II through V are described in detail in Chapter 4.

Section I deals with some of the dominant forces that produce fiscal pressures in a typical municipality. Fiscal pressures arise predominantly from wage increases granted to municipal employees who perform municipal tasks characterized by relatively low productivity growth in output per man-hour—wage increases that are equal, as a percentage of labor costs, to those granted to nonmunicipal employees who perform tasks characterized by relatively high productivity growth in output per man-hour. This section is, accordingly, labeled "Unbalanced Productivity Growth." For reasons that will become clear in Chapters 5 and 6, the variables contained in Section I of this model are those that are most crucial for the success of any effort to model a typical urban area. The omission of unbalanced-productivity-growth considerations from *all* previous urban simulation models constitutes the single greatest deficiency of these explicit urban models.

In Section II, increases in costs that arise from increases in municipal employee wages are summed with the previous year's costs to arrive at current municipal costs. Annual benefits are also distributed to each typical family. The results of this "Municipal Costs and Benefits" section are utilized in Section IV to determine tax assessments.

The municipality is assumed to be composed of two typical groups of citizens: the affluent and the poor. Since the members of each group are widely perceived in the political process to posses common interests, the economic consequences of urban programs are evaluated as they influence these two groups. This evaluation is carried out in Section III, the "Net Family Benefits" portion of the model.

The affluent are assumed to base location decisions upon two factors: annual municipal costs for each affluent family, and opportunity loss vis-à-vis services provided to similar affluent families in an adjacent suburb. The poor are assumed to make location decisions on the basis of net benefits enjoyed by poor families in other areas within a feasible zone of migration.

Net benefits of proposed projects are measured by computing changes to the net costs for the affluent and net benefits for the poor. Calculations of net benefits to various citizens are necessary if we are to determine the desirability of proposed projects. Previous econometric and feedback urban models have excluded such calculations.

Section IV of the partial urban model is the "Municipal Population and Housing" section. The population levels and mix determine the quantity and quality of the housing stock in the municipality. The housing stock is assumed to consist of two homogeneous classes: affluent housing and poor housing. Population arrival and departure decisions based on the net benefits determined in Section III influence the population and housing levels of Section IV.

Property-tax rates and assessed valuations are determined in Section V, "Municipal Taxation and Revenue." Municipal revenue is assumed to be collected in an amount sufficient to produce a balanced municipal budget. This is accomplished by adjusting tax rates to assessed valuations in a manner which produces just enough revenue to cover municipal costs. Total assessed valuations in the municipality are adjusted to reflect changes that occur over time in the quantity and quality of the housing stock in the municipality.

This brief summary illustrates the three characteristics of the model that differentiate it from both the Lowry [94] and Forrester [61] urban models. First, it includes unbalanced productivity growth as a crucial factor creating urban fiscal pressures. Second, it contains an explicit choice criterion in Section III that attempts to incorporate dynamic effects. Finally, the model tends to be more comprehensive than the Lowry model and, unlike the Forrester model, an attempt is made to test the model's structure and its parameter values empirically.

Before describing the details of the model, we examine the simulation methodology employed to construct the model. Then we describe Section I of the model. Finally, we examine the empirical evidence supporting Section I.

Summary of the Simulation Methodology

I have elected to use the simulation technique and the DYNAMO compiler program developed by Forrester and his group at the Massachusetts Institute of Technology.[a] DYNAMO (from DYNAmic MOdels) is a compiler program which assumes that the model to be simulated can be described by a set of differential equations. Since DYNAMO is a digital computer program, however, the equations of the model must consist of a corresponding set of first-order difference equations.

Although any programming language could have been used, DYNAMO possesses many salient features not found in other simulation programs. The two major advantages are its adaptability to cumulative feedback processes and its computing efficiency. Other advantages include a flexible user-oriented, rather than computer-oriented, input format and built-in delay, noise, and plotting subroutines. All these other advantages, and especially the first, are helpful for modeling at the policy level.[b] I will provide a brief summary of this modeling technique to facilitate our discussion of the model. Its advantages will become apparent shortly.

The stock variables of the model are represented by level (L) equations which are first-order difference equations. The stock variables, calculated at point *K*, are assumed to depend upon the level of that variable at point *J* plus the flows that cause the stocks to change during the elapsed time interval that separates point *J* and point *K*. The flow variables of the model are represented by rate (R) equations. They indicate the manner in which the flows within the system are controlled. The time period between calculations of level equations is the solution interval; it is represented in all level equations by *DT*.

Level equations have the following form:

$$\text{Value}.K = \text{Value}.J + DT * \text{Rate of change}.JK \qquad \text{(L)}$$

The *current* value of a level (i.e., at point *K*) is computed by adding to or subtracting from the previous value the change that has occurred since the level was calculated last. The solution interval *DT* specifies the period of time during which the flow variable is assumed to be constant. The algebraic expression on the right-hand side of the level equation is the derivative of the value, assumed constant, over the time interval *J* to *K*. The level equation, therefore, carries out the process of integration. The accuracy of

---

[a]This technique is not fully described in any one source, but can be distilled from Forrester's *Industrial Dynamics* [62]. *Urban Dynamics* [61], and *Principles of Systems* [60]. The compiler program instructions are contained in *DYNAMO II User's Manual* [124] by Alexander L. Pugh III.

[b]Although I have chosen to use the DYNAMO compiler program, I do not accept fully the Forrester philosophy of dynamic modeling or the results he achieves. It is my view that Forrester oversimplifies, to an unacceptable degree, empirical data collection and validation problems and therefore takes his results far too seriously. However, because the *results* have been oversold, his entire modeling structure, including the compiler program, is in danger of falling into disrepute. In my view, this would be unfortunate, since the principles of feedback systems which underlie his entire structure. and which are built into the compiler program, are of great use in benefit-cost analysis, as I intend to show. I will also show that empirical problems may be reduced significantly, for policy purposes, by this approach.

the integration can be controlled by the choice of the value for *DT*, with smaller time periods yielding finer calculations.

Rate equations are calculated at point *K* for the time interval *KL*, using information from levels computed at point *K*. They are taken to be functions of levels and constants (C) only, and are assumed to remain constant during interval *KL*.

Rate equations are often subdivided to provide clarity and improve exposition. Algegraic subdivisions of rate equations are called auxiliary (A) equations. Auxiliary equations are evaluated after level equations, upon which they (as do rates) depend, but prior to rate equations. Unlike rate and level equations, auxiliary equations can depend upon one another in a chain.

To begin a simulation, level values are equated to specified initial conditions (N). Rates are then computed for time period *KL* ($t + 1$ in time notation) utilizing initial-level values. Levels are then calculated for time *K* (t) utilizing rates of the immediately preceding time period *JK* ($t - 1$). The process continues in an iterative manner. When auxiliary variables are employed, the complete order of calculation is as follows: auxiliaries, rates, and levels. Initial conditions and constants must be specified prior to a simulation.

The rate and auxiliary equations permit us to incorporate nonlinearities into the model. Rate equations may contain the product or ratio of two or more variables. Rate or auxiliary equations may contain various types of relations including those given by tables; logarithmic, delay, and exponential functions; and random-number generators. These capabilities allow us to evaluate complex nonlinear systems of first-order difference equations, which is nearly impossible using analytical methods. Although we lose the ability to evaluate the system directly at a specified point in time, we gain the ability to evaluate complex nonlinear systems such as the social systems that benefit-cost analysis is called upon to evaluate. The partial urban model is such a complex system of 12 level equations. It is not feasible to evaluate it by analytical methods.

With this background we turn to Section I of the partial urban model.

Section I: Unbalanced Productivity Growth[c]

In the unbalanced-growth section of the model, I have adopted Baumol's premise [9, p. 426]:

[c]Each level, rate and auxiliary equation of the model is identified by the symbol L, R, or A placed to the right of it within parentheses. Initial conditions for level equations and values for constant parameters are identified without equation numbers. Many equations necessary for proper computer execution of the system, but not essential for an understanding of the system, are omitted from this chapter. They are, however, included in Appendix A, where all the equations of the computer model are listed and numbered.

> . . . that economic activities can, not entirely arbitrarily, be grouped into two types: technologically progressive activities in which innovations, capital accumulation, and economies of large scale all make for a cumulative rise in output per man hour and activities which, by their very nature permit only sporadic increases in productivity.

The technologically progressive activities are likely to be those where labor is only one input in the ultimate product. The technologically nonprogressive activities are likely to be those where labor is virtually the only input and where labor services are, therefore, the only output.

Labor costs in the progressive sector for time K are given by

$$LCPS.K = LCPS.J + DT * (MWIPS.JK - MPIPS.JK) \quad (1,L)$$

where $LCPS.J$ = the level of labor costs in the progressive sector at time J

DT = the solution interval

$MWIPS.JK$ = the increase in money wages in the progressive sector during the time period JK

$MPIPS.JK$ = the monetary value of increases in productivity during the time period JK

The solution interval DT is set equal to one year in all level equations of the urban model. Labor costs in the progressive sector are therefore computed annually. Annual wage increases that exceed (money) productivity increases raise money labor costs in the progressive sector. Level equation (1,L), therefore, simply reflects the positive effect of wage increases and the negative effect (i.e., the offset) of productivity increases on total labor costs in the progressive sector.

The initial condition for equation (1,L) is represented by $LCPS$, and it is the value that $LCPS.J$ takes in the first period. In order to estimate its numerical value, we must now adopt some simplifying assumptions about the municipality and its economy. We assume that the municipality consists of 10,000 families,[d] 6,000 affluent and 4,000 poor. Each family is supported by one wage earner. The *affluent* wage earners are assumed to be employed in the nonprogressive sector. Each wage earner *residing* in this municipality earns his entire income in activities taking place within the boundaries of the city, and *initially* there is full employment in the municipality.

A typical affluent wage earner is, initially, assumed to earn $10,000 annually. A typical poor wage earner is, initially, assumed to earn $3,000

---

[d]It is necessary to restrict the size of the population to a relatively small number in order to prevent calculations of the model from becoming unmanageably large. All other characteristics of the model represent those of a relatively large central city. The size of the population used should do little damage to the results.

per year. Since all 4,000 poor employees are assumed to be employed in the progressive sector at an annual wage of \$3,000, total labor costs in the progressive sector are \$12,000,000. The initial-condition *LCPS* for equation (1,L) is, accordingly, \$12,000,000.

Increases in money wages in the progressive sector are described by

$$MWIPS.KL = NPPI * (LCPS.K * PPI.K) * E\emptyset P \qquad (2,R)$$

where *NPPI* = the normal annual rate of growth in productivity in the progressive sector

LCPS.K = labor costs in the progressive sector

PPI.K = the percentage of residents employed in progressive activities at time *J* that are residents of the municipality at time *K*

EØP = a factor that relates an increase in wages to normal annual growth in productivity

Equation (2,R) asserts that labor achieves annual wage increases that are a function of average improvements in output per man-hour in the progressive sector. The parameter *NPPI* is set equal to 3.1%.

LCPS was defined by equation (1,L). The constant parameter *EØP* is a factor that represents the ability (or inability) of labor to negotiate wage increases equal to or in excess of percentage gains in productivity. A factor of 1.0 implies that wages in the progressive sector increase at the rate of productivity increases. If labor is capable of extracting inflationary wage increases, *EØP* will be greater than 1.0. We assume *EØP* equals 2.0. This implies that wages in the prrgressive sector increase at twice the rate of growth in productivity. Inflation is thereby introduced into the model at an average annual rate of 3.1%.

After the initial period, the division of the work force between progressive and nonprogressive activities depends upon location decisions of firms. These decisions are affected by the available labor supply existing in a municipality, and themselves affect migration of labor to the municipality. The composition of the work force and the total product of the municipality over time, therefore, depend upon many variables *not included* within the model at present. Simplifying assumptions are introduced into equations (2,R) and (6,R) by way of the auxiliary variables *PPI.K* [equation (3,A)] and *PNPI.K* [equation (7,A)] to deal with these complexities of reality.

The variable *PPI.K* serves to raise or lower total labor costs of the progressive sector [i.e., *LCPS.K* of equation (2,R)] above or below their level calculated by equation (1,L). The result is a change in the normal increase in money wages [equation (2,R)], and therefore in labor costs to the progressive sector [equation (1,L)], that reflects the results of the migration patterns of the previous period *JK*. The variable *PPI.K* is one that alters the structure of activities performed in the municipality, slowly and arbitrarily, in accordance with migration patterns to and from the municipality. If *no* in-migration should occur during period *JK*, no adjustment is made to *LCPS.K* in order to calculate increases in money wages for period *KL*—increases in money wages are simply a function of productivity gains (*NPPI*) and the inflation factor (*EØP*). If there is migration of the poor into or out of the municiplaity during period *JK*, labor costs for time *K* will be increased or decrease respectively, in proportion to the migration, for purposes of computing increases in money wages for the period *KL*. The variable is computed as follows:[e]

$$PPI.K = PLP.K/PLP.J \qquad (3,A)$$

where $PLP.K$ = the number of poor families in the municipality at time K, defined by equation (23,L)

$PLP.J$ = the number of poor families in the municipality at time J

The monetary value of productivity increases, which paritially offsets the impact of wage increases on costs in the progressive sector, is given by

$$MPIPS.KL = NPPI * (LCPS.K * PPI.K) \qquad (4,R)$$

where *NPPI*, defined above for equation (2,R), is the normal increase in productivity in the progressive sector, and *LCPS* represents the labor costs of the progressive sector, defined in equation (1,R). This simply states that annual productivity gains, which are subtracted from labor costs in equation (1,L), are of a monetary value equal to the normal percentage increase in productivity multiplied by the level of labor costs at the beginning of the period *KL*. The variable *PPI.K* was defined by equation (3,A); it increases or reduces labor costs to reflect migration patterns for purposes of computing the productivity offset to rising money wages.

Labor costs in the nonprogressive sector are given by

$$LCNPS.K = LCNPS.J + DT * (MWINPS.JK - MPINPS.JK) \qquad (5,L)$$

where $LCNPS.J$ = the level of labor costs in the nonprogressive sector at time J

---

[e]We could replace *PPI.K* with an alternative assumption that provides automatic employment for all poor migrants at the wage rate prevalent for a typical poor wage earner in the municipality at the time of migration. I believe that assumption would be more damaging to reality than the assumption contained in *PPI.K*, because as soon as we preclude unemployment for any potential poor migrant, we eliminate one of the key variables that historically has discouraged migration (see Kuznets in Eldridge and Thomas [52, pp. xxiii-xxxv]). The model can be moved closer to reality by introducing a business sector and a labor market explicitly. I am currently extending the model in this latter direction.

$MWINPS.JK =$ the increase in money wages in the nonprogressive sector during period JK

$MPINPS.JK =$ the monetary value of the productivity increases of time period JK

The initial condition $LCNPS$ for equation (5,L) is \$60,000,000. This value is arrived at by multiplying the number of employees in the nonprogressive sector by their annual wage. Each of the 6,000 affluent employees is assumed to be employed in the nonprogressive sector at an annual wage of \$10,000. Increases in money wages in the nonprogressive sector are assumed to be equal to the rate of growth of productivity in the *progressive* sector, multiplied by earnings over productivity ($E\emptyset P$) in the *progressive* sector and labor costs in the *nonprogressive* sector. The annual rate of increase in money wages in the nonprogressive sector (as a percentage of labor costs) is therefore assumed to equal the rate of the progressive sector. The equation describing this is

$$MWINPS.KL = NPPI * (LCNPS.K * PNPI.K) * E\emptyset P. \qquad (6,R)$$

Labor costs in the nonprogressive sector $LCNPS.K$ have been defined by equation (5,L): $NPPI$, also defined previously, has been set equal to 3.1%, and $E\emptyset P$ is assumed to equal 2.0.

The auxiliary variable $PNPI.K$ gives the proportion of workers employed in the nonprogressive sector of the municipal economy at time K as a percentage of those employed at time J. It is defined formally by

$$PNPI.K = PLA.K/PLA.J \qquad (7,A)$$

where $PLA.K =$ the number of affluent families in the municipality at time K, defined by equation (24,L)

$PLA.J =$ the number of affluent families in the municipality at time J

Equation (6,R) implies that employees of the nonprogressive sector bargain for wage increases that are equal, as a percentage of labor costs, to those attained in the progressive sector. Since labor costs in the progressive sector do not increase at as rapid a rate as those of the nonprogressive sector (as a result of the productivity offset in the progressive sector), the actual rate of increase in money wages in the progressive sector, as a percentage of employee wages, soon becomes smaller than the rate of increase in money wages of employees in the nonprogressive sector.

By equations (3,A) and (7,A) we have incorporated one additional assumption. The two sectors are assumed to be sealed off from one another; labor mobility from one sector to the other is therefore precluded in this model.

The monetary value of annual growth in productivity in the nonprogressive sector is given by

$$MPINPS.KL = NPINPS * (LCNPS.K * PNPI.K) \qquad (8,R)$$

where $NPINPS$ = a constant representing the normal annual increase in productivity in the nonprogressive sector

$LCNPS.K$ = the previously defined [equation (4,L)] level of labor costs in the nonprogressive sector

$PNPI.K$ = the percentage of residents employed in nonprogressive activities at time J that are residents of the municipality at time K [defined by equation (7,A)].

I have set $NPINPS$ equal to zero, which implies that productivity is constant in the nonprogressive sector. The annual level of income produced in the municipality is given by

$$WSLM.K = NAS.K + NPS.K \qquad (9,A)$$

where $NAS.K$ = the normal level of wages and salaries earned in nonprogressive activities by affluent employees

$NPS.K$ = the normal level of wages and salaries earned in progressive activities by poor employees

The level of wages and salaries of affluent families that earn their income in the municipality is defined by

$$NAS.K = NAS.J + DT * (MWINPS.JK) \qquad (10,L)$$

where $MWINPS.JK$ is the money-wage increase in the nonprogressive sector, defined by equation (6,R). The initial value NAS is set equal to \$60,000,000, which represents the product of the initial level of annual salaries for an affluent family (i.e., \$10,000) and the initial level of population of affluent families (i.e., 6,000).

The level of wages and salaries of poor families that earn their income in the municipality is calculated similarly from

$$NPS.K = NPS.J + DT * (MWIPS.JK) \qquad (11,L)$$

where $MWIPS.JK$ is the increase in money wages in the progressive sector, defined by equation (2,R). The initial value for NPS is set equal to \$12,000,000, which is the product of the level of wages for a poor family (i.e., \$3,000 a year) and the initial level of population of poor families (i.e., 4,000).

Some Empirical Evidence on the Assumptions of Section I

We now examine the empirical evidence (or lack of it) supporting the structure, equation forms, and parameter values of Section I. The assumptions, and therefore the empirical evidence, fall conveniently into four categories: (1) the solution interval, (2) the technological characteristics of activities, (3) the assumptions regarding wages and income, and (4) the dynamic composition of municipal activities.

1. The Solution Interval

A solution interval (i.e., *DT*) of one year was chosen for all the level equations of the model. The interval of one year corresponds to the time period over which many of the flow rates represented in the model are, in reality, constant. For example, wages and salaries are commonly adjusted on an annual basis. Rates of growth of productivity and property taxes are commonly computed on an annual basis. In addition, a common period for discounting benefits and costs in reality is one year. For these reasons, I believe that an annual period is a reasonable unit for most of the flow rates of the model. In only a very few cases do the flow rates represented in the model change more frequently than at yearly intervals. No great violence is done to reality, therefore, by the assumption of an annual solution period.

2. The Technological Characteristics of Activities

Although activities in this simplified economy have been classified as either progressive or nonprogresive, a look at the empirical evidence presented by Fuchs [63, p. 51] indicates that there is in fact great variation in the rate of change in output per man within and among industry groups. The average rate of change in output per man from 1956 to 1965 varied from −1% in the contract construction industry to 5.8% in the communications and public utilities industry.

However, the data do illustrate a significant difference in the average rate of growth in output per man in the three major industry groups that comprise the economy of the United States. Average output per man during the 1956-1965 period grew at an annual rate of 4.7% in agriculture, 3.1% in the industrial sector, and 1.8% in the service sector. Within the service sector, wholesale and retail trade output per man grew at 2.9%, while the rate of productivity growth in financial institutions was only 1.6%; general government had a zero rate of growth in average output per man during this period.

The significant difference in growth rates of output per man among the three sectors does suggest that it is legitimate to classify activities into two groups: those that have relatively high rates of growth in productivity and those that have relatively low rates of growth in productivity. Any attempt to divide the economy into many small sectors by average productivity-growth rates would soon become unmanageable. We therefore accept the helpful classification of activities into these two broad categories, even though it is an oversimplification.

The justification for the productivity estimates used in equations (4,R) and (8,R) for progressive and nonprogressive activities is found in the data provided by Fuchs. The 3.1% estimate of normal growth in productivity assumed for progressive-sector activities is Fuch's [63, p. 51] estimate of the average growth in output per man in the industrial sector during the 1956-1965 period. Although this estimate is plausible, it is assumed by equation (4,R) of the model to be constant. Productivity-growth rates, in reality, tend to be cyclical, thus making any single-rate figure somewhat questionable unless we restrict ourselves to a one-year estimate only.

Although Fuchs estimates a productivity-growth rate of 1.8% for the service sector, he includes many progressive activities within that sector—activities in which labor is only one of many inputs. Therefore, 1.8% clearly overstates the sporadic increases in productivity that we expect for nonprogressive activities. Fuchs does estimate, however, a zero growth rate for activities of general government in the period 1956-1965. Since we are interested in the effect of unbalanced productivity growth on municipal costs, I believe the use of a zero rate in equation (8,R) for nonprogressive activities is justified for any simple model such as ours.

By equations (3,A) and (7,A) respectively, all the poor were assumed to be employed in activities characterized by high rates of growth in productivity and all the affluent were assumed to be employed in activities characterized by relatively low rates of growth in productivity. We now examine this premise.

Fuchs [63, p. 21] has shown that service-sector employment as a percentage of total employment in the United States has risen steadily, and in 1965 reached 55%. In addition, the service sector is characterized by relatively low growth in productivity, 1.8% during the 1956-1965 period. Although there are some relatively progressive activities in the service sector, most have low or sporadic increases in productivity. We also know that approximately 40% of all service workers are engaged in managerial or professional activities. These activities tend to yield relatively high wages, but relatively low rates of growth in productivity. In addition, more than 30% of the employment in the industrial and agricultural sectors consists of supervision and highly skilled (craft) activities. The latter activities yield relatively high salaries, and are characterized by low or sporadic growth in productivity.

The preceding estimates suggest that a large percentage of the affluent are employed in activities characterized by relatively low rates of growth in productivity. Therefore, our assumption that all the affluent are employed in the nonprogressive sector, while simplistic, is not completely arbitrary.

The poor, on the other hand, are likely to be low in skill. Low-skill activities are prime candidates for technological innovations and are likely, in the main, to be characterized by relatively high rates of growth in productivity.

3. Wage and Income Assumptions

By equations (2,R) and (6,R) we assumed that the rate of increase in money wages would be slightly higher for employees of the nonprogressive sector than for employees of the progressive sector, although wage increases as a percentage of labor costs would be equal in both sectors. Historical data do not support such a *pattern* of money wages, but more recent experience does.

Fuchs [63, p. 143] shows that most service-sector earnings (i.e., earnings of the relatively nonprogressive sector) lagged *behind* the industrial sector during the 1929-1965 period for employees of comparable age, education, sex, and color. Interindustry differences were explained largely by two factors: unionization and demographic differences. Fuchs's regression results attribute 82% of the interindustry differences to these factors, with unionization explaining most of the wage differentials.

The intensive unionization that has occurred more recently within the service sector, particularly the unionization of municipal employees, makes it entirely plausible that nonprogressive employees will negotiate wage-rate increases at least as high as those received by comparable employees of the progressive sector, and possibly higher. For example, recent data published by the Bureau of the Census [152, p. 119; 153, p. 123] show that average annual salaries of all elementary and secondary school teachers in public schools have increased from $5,995 in 1964 to $8,560 in 1970—an average annual rate of approximately 6.0%. More current data (through 1972), cited by Schultze et al. [138, p. 323], indicate that teachers have fared even better. These investigators find that "since 1966, average teacher salaries have increased at an annual rate of almost 8 percent—about one third faster than wages in general."

These data seem to suggest that we have passed the time when wage increases of the service sector lag behind those of the industrial sector. In certain areas of the service sector, and especially among municipal employees, wage-rate increases appear to be higher than in the relatively progressive sector.

Of course, we cannot assume this relationship to be stable. However, the monopolistic power of municipal employee unions (i.e., citizens cannot purchase many municipal services from another supplier) may ensure wage-rate increases at least as great as those achieved in the progressive sector. Therefore, the wage-rate assumptions underlying (2,R) and (6,R) appear plausible and in line with recent experiences, but certainly imperfect, as are most estimates of the outcomes of collective bargaining (a process whose outcome is usually considered indeterminate). In any event, it is *not* essential to the model that we adopt the wage relationships that appear in equations (2,R) and (6,R). All we require is that the relationship between wage increases of the two sectors be specified. An alternative, but equally plausible, assumption is that the rate of wage increase, as a percentage of employee wages, is equal for employees of each sector.

The separation of the population into two income classes and the wage assumptions for each class are drastic simplifications of reality. Certainly a broad middle class does exist. Here again, a full and accurate representation of reality would require more detail and would soon become unmanageable. Nevertheless, the literature of urban economics is filled with evidence that in-migration patterns of the poor and out-migration patterns of the affluent influence the dynamics of central cities profoundly. Therefore, the poor-affluent family dichotomy used in the model is a manageable, though highly simplified, view of the income characteristics of urban residents.

Our assumption of a 150% initial ratio of affluent ($10,000 annual income) to poor ($3,000 annual income) families requires comment. Campbell and Sacks [30, p. 22] provide data, as of 1959, regarding the percentages of families with annual incomes under $3,000 and over $10,000 by size of standard metropolitan areas. In central cities of metropolitan areas in 1959, 17.6% of all families earned less than $3,000, and 16.5% earned more than $10,000. The ratio of families that earned more than $10,000 to families that earned less than $3,000 in 1959 was therefore 93.9%. Although this figure holds for the nation as a whole, it is clear from the same data that this ratio varies by region and by the size of central cities. Our assumption in Section I of a 150% initial ratio (i.e., 6,000 affluent to 4,000 poor), therefore, assumes a central city that has relatively more affluence than the 1959 norm. The assumption, however, is entirely plausible.[f]

One additional wage and income assumption requires comment. By equations (3,A) and (7,A) we have made the assumption that the two sectors are sealed off from one another. When power relationships enter into wage-rate determination, as they do in collective bargaining, the rate of increase in money wages in each sector is *not* dependent on mobility

---

[f]A search of the data on metropolitan disparities compiled by the Advisory Commission on Intergovernmental Relations (1, p. 11) leads one to their conclusion "that very few meaningful generalizations about economic, social, and racial disparities can be applied to all metropolitan areas."

between sectors. Therefore, the assumption that the two sectors are sealed off from one another, while unrealistic, may not distort the values of key variables of the model significantly. The assumption, to be sure, is absolutely necessary in order to construct a manageable simulation model.

4. The Dynamic Composition of Municipal Activities

After the initial period, the division of the work force between progressive and nonprogressive activities in the municipality depends upon location decisions of firms and households. Location decisions are affected by the available labor supply in a municipality, and the decisions themselves affect migration of labor to the municipality. Although location decisions of households are included in Section IV of the model, location decisions of firms are omitted completely from this model. Quite *arbitrary*, but fairly *harmless*, assumptions are made about the behavior of the labor market as surrogates for the *actual* operations of the labor market. These assumptions are introduced into the model by the auxiliary variables *PPI.K* [equation (3,A)] and *PNPI.K* [equation (7,A)]. These variables change the technological composition of activities in the municipality through their effects on the growth of wages and labor costs in the economy.

The variables *PPI.K* and *PNPI.K* raise or lower labor costs of the progressive and nonprogressive sectors above or below their calculated levels to reflect the effects of migration patterns of the previous period on the structure of activities within the municipality. If no migration occurs during the period *JK*, no adjustment is made to labor costs (i.e., *LCPS.K* and *LCNPS.K*) in equations (2,R) and (6,R) for the purpose of calculating increases in money wages for the period *KL*—increases in money wages are simply a function of productivity gains (*NPPI*) and the inflation factor (*EØP*). If, on the other hand, there is migration of poor and affluent families during the period *JK*, labor costs in the relevant sector for time *K* will be increased (in the event of in-migration) or decreased (in the event of out-migration) in proportion to the migration, for purposes of computing wage increases. Similarly, as labor costs for each sector are altered, the value of productivity gains for each sector is altered accordingly by equations (4,R) and (8,R). Therefore, *PPI.K* and *PNPI.K* are the variables that slowly alter the structure of activities of the municipality in accordance with migration patterns to and from the municipality.

We could replace the variables *PPI.K* and *PNPI.K* with alternative assumptions that (a) provide continuous full employment for all migrants to the municipality at the prevailing wage, and (b) consider all families that leave the central city for an adjacent suburb to be employed in that suburb and not in the central city. I believe these assumptions would be more damaging to reality than the assumption represented by the variables

PPI.K and *PNPI.K*, for two reasons: (1) If we preclude unemployment in the central city for poor migrants, we omit one of the key variables that has discouraged migration historically, according to Kuznets (in Eldridge and Thomas [52], pp. xxiii-xxxv]). (2) If we assume that the affluent who depart to the adjacent suburb also leave their jobs behind, we ignore reality; for in reality such moves do not normally involve a job change, but rather involve a decision to live in the suburb and commute to a job in the central city.

The variables *PPI.K* and *PNPI.K* can be replaced profitably, and Section I can be moved closer to reality, by a more explicit treatment of the business sector of the municipality. However, until a more explicit treatment of the business sector is incorporated into the model, we must use rather crude surrogates such as those employed in Section I of this model. One redeeming quality of such a crude approach is that in a simulation model the forms of such equations can be altered easily to test the sensitivity of key variables of the model to alternative assumptions. This process will be illustrated in Chapter 5.

Summary

This completes our discussion of Section I of the model. The assumptions of this section appear plausible, although they simplify reality significantly. The assumptions of unbalanced productivity growth and inflation result in an annual increase in municipal costs of approximately 6%, since almost all municipal employees, as we shall find in Chapter 4, are engaged in non-progressive activities. These cost pressures and their impact on household location decisions are described in the next chapter.

4 A Comparative-Dynamic Partial Urban Model (Continued)

In this chapter we continue our description of the partial urban model. Municipal fiscal pressures can easily be shown to increase cumulatively with the aid of the assumptions of unbalanced productivity and wages of Section I, given the large proportion of municipal employees that are engaged in nonprogressive activities. These pressures and their effects on population, income, and housing are described in this chapter by Sections II, III, and IV of the partial urban model.

Municipal costs are accumulated in Section II, and assumptions are made there about the distribution of municipal benefits. Family benefits and costs are combined in Section III in order to arrive at a measure of annual net benefits. These net benefits serve as the basis for household location decisions, which are described in Section IV of the model. Location decisions influence the quantity and quality of housing and the technological structure of municipal activities. The effects of location decisions on housing are described in Section IV of the model, while the technological structure of activities in this simple economy is governed by equations (3,A) and (7,A) of Section I.

Assessed values of housing and property-tax rates are determined in Section V. Assessed values and tax rates are set, in every instance, to produce municipal revenue just sufficient to meet the municipal costs computed in Section II. These tax data are also used in Section III to compute municipal costs per family.

We turn presently to a detailed description of each of the four remaining sections of the model. After each section, we examine the empirical evidence supporting the assumptions. Finally, we review the entire model and the methodology, and suggest areas where the model can be improved.

Section II: Municipal Costs and Benefits

In our model, annual municipal costs are assumed to rise, predominantly as a result of increased wages for municipal employees. For simplicity, therefore, we ignore all other increases in municipal expenditure except those associated with municipal labor costs, and assume a price elasticity of demand for municipal services of zero. The equation for municipal costs is

$$MC.K = MC.J + DT * MECI.JK \qquad (12,L)$$

where $MC.J$ = the level of municipal costs in the preceding year

$MECI.JK$ = annual wage increases for municipal employees

The initial value for equation (12,L) is set equal to zero, since we assume that all municipal costs begin at year 1.

Increases in municipal employees costs are given by

$$MECI.KL = PNPEM * (LCNPS.K - LCNPS.J) + PPEM * (LCPS.K - LCPS.J) \quad (13,R)$$

where $PNPEM$ = the proportion of employees in the nonprogressive sector that are employed by this municipality

$(LCNPS.K - LCNPS.J)$ = the annual change in total labor costs of the nonprogressive sector of this economy

$PPEM$ = the proportion of employees in the progressive sector that are employed by the municipality

$(LCPS.K - LCPS.J)$ = the annual change in total labor costs of the progressive sector of this economy

Because we have created a simplified economy in which all activities are classified as either progressive or nonprogressive, we must make further assumptions regarding the composition of the municipal work force in order to illustrate the fiscal pressures that result from unbalanced growth of productivity. These assumptions, introduced by equation (13,R), are discussed presently.

The parameter *PNPEM* in equation (13,R) is set equal to 5.37%, and the parameter *PPEM* is set equal to .056%. This means that 5.37% of all employees in the nonprogressive sector, and .056% of all employees in the progressive sector of this municipal economy are assumed to be employed by this municipality. Over 90% of municipal employees are, therefore, assumed to be employed in the nonprogressive sector. This produces cumulative cost increases in the model, since municipal employees are assumed to bargain for wage increases equal (as a percentage of labor costs) to those granted in the progressive sector, where wage increases are offset partially by productivity increases. Cumulative increases in municipal costs may occur without causing a shift of employees from municipal activities to nonmunicipal activities if the demand for municipal services is relatively price-inelastic and income-elastic.

While we have assumed this municipality to bear a constant share of the labor costs of the economy, a change in the size and composition of the population will alter the size and composition of the labor force and, therefore, the annual rate of municipal cost increases. Municipal costs increase continuously because of wage increases granted to municipal employees that are in excess of productivity increases. If, however, poor families migrate into the municipality and affluent families migrate out, the relative composition of activities within the economy also changes becoming relatively more progressive. This is accomplished by the assumptions underlying equation (2,R) of Section I. The migration of additional poor families into the municipality serves to offset partially the effect of municipal employee wage increases on *total* municipal costs, although municipal costs for a typical affluent family still increase, as we shall see later.

If affluent families migrate into the municipality and poor families migrate out, the relative share of activities falling into the nonprogressive category does increase, thus increasing the normal increment in municipal employee costs and total municipal costs (although municipal costs for a typical affluent family may actually decline). This is accomplished by the assumptions underlying equation (6,R) of Section I.

To summarize, equation (12,L) states that municipal costs rise as the result of increases in municipal employee costs, which are shown by equation (13,R) to consist of annual increases in wages that exceed productivity increases significantly, and to a lesser extent as a result of the changing income composition of the population in the municipality.

We now come to the evaluation of annual benefits by citizens of the municipality. It would be quite simple to equate the value of benefits to citizens with municipal costs, and distribute them equally to all families of the municipality in order to arrive at a measure of net benefits. This would be incorrect for two reasons. First, each family evaluates municipal services differently and subjectively; and second, there is an element of opportunity cost for each family representing the level of services forgone as a result of locating in this municipality rather than in the best alternative location.

I have made the assumption that each affluent family residing in the central city incurs an opportunity loss relative to the benefits offered in the best alternative location. In addition, the opportunity loss is considered to be the result of disparities between the central city and its suburbs in expenditures for public education. A typical affluent family residing in the municipality perceives its opportunity from living in the central city (measured here as a negative benefit) as follows:

$$RSSIA.KL = -NSDA * (NAS.K * NPME)/PLA.K \qquad (14,R)$$

where $NSDA$ = the annual rate of services forgone by affluent citizens of the municipality

$NAS.K$ = the total annual level of wages and salaries earned by affluent employees

$NPME$ = the normal percentage of income that the affluent spend on public education

$PLA.K$ = the total number of affluent families residing in the municipality

The above equation approximates the true opportunity loss experienced by the affluent residents of a central city. It does so by recognizing that expenditures for education are the most important expenditures of local governments so far as affluent families are concerned, and that the quality of primary and secondary public education, as approximated by expenditures per student, is deteriorating in central cities relative to outside suburban areas.

The constant $NSDA$ gives the annual rate of deterioration of central city schools relative to suburban schools as a percentage of annual income spent by the affluent of central cities on education. It is assumed to be equal to 6.0%. The constant $NPME$ gives the percentage of affluent income spent on public education in central cities. We have set it equal to 2.3%.

The two remaining terms in equation (14,R) are defined elsewhere: $NAS.K$ by equation (10,L) and $PLA.K$ by equation (24,L).

The annual benefits that potential poor migrants *perceive* in a central city are not only those associated with municipal services, but also those associated with employment opportunities. The annual benefits that a poor family perceives for itself in this municipality as against those it perceives elsewhere are assumed to be approximated by the following equation:

$$RSSIP.KP = NPISP^* \{(WSLM.K - WSLM.J)TPL.K\} \qquad (15,R)$$

where $NPISP$ = a factor representing the relative attractiveness of this municipality, in dollar terms, for poor in-migration as a function of per capita income produced in the municipality

$(WSLM.K - WSLM.J)$ = the annual change in income produced in activities within the boundaries of the municipality

$TPL.K$ = the total number of families residing in the municipality

This equation, in words, states that a typical poor family perceives its annual improvement in economic welfare in this central city, as against that attainable elsewhere in the logical zone of migration, as a function of the change in per capita income produced in the central city. Municipal income per family represents both a proxy for employment opportunities and a source of funds for municipal services. We begin by assigning a value of 10% to *NPISP*. The other variables in equation (15,R) are defined elsewhere: *WSLM.K* by equation (9,A) and *TPL.K* by equation (22,L).

Some Empirical Evidence on the Assumptions of Section II

We now examine the empirical evidence supporting the structure, forms, and parameter values of the municipal cost and benefit equations.

1. Municipal Costs

In equation (12,L) we made the simplifying assumption that municipal costs increase only as the result of increases in municipal employee costs. It is clear that municipalities do incur both capital costs and increases to capital costs. Labor costs, however, as Schultze reports [138, pp. 294-296] represent more than half of local government costs, and comprise the segment of municipal costs that has risen spectacularly in the 1957-1970 period, creating the current fiscal problems of central cities. In addition to increases in labor and capital costs, municipal expenditures, and especially expenditures on education, tend to increase as income increases.

Fuchs [63, p. 43] has estimated an income elasticity of demand of 1.07 for state and local expenditures over the 1942-1957 period. Fabricant [54, p. 125] has estimated an income elasticity of .90 for state and local expenditures in 1942. Income has been shown by Campbell and Sacks [30, p. 173] to be "more highly correlated with expenditures than with taxes, indicating that income operates more strongly on the demand side than on the supply side. The greater the income difference, the greater the difference in services demanded. This influence of income is greater for education than for non-education services."

Rising capital costs *may* create a fiscal problem as serious as rising municipal employee wages, but in reality they should not, for two reasons:

1. Capital expenditures, unlike expenditures for mandatory municipal services, may be postponed.
2. Capital goods are produced in the relatively progressive sector of the economy where wage increases are offset at least partially by increases in productivity, so that prices for these goods should rise less rapidly than prices for mandatory services.

Increases in municipal expenditures that arise directly from increases in municipal income should result in the provision of more or better municipal services. These increased expenditures are likely to be met with far less resistance than are increased expenditures that are not accompanied by more or better services.

Three additional comments must be made with regard to equation (12,L). First, there seems to be little evidence that the migration of the poor to a central city results immediately in any extraordinary demand on public service. Evidence found by Campbell and Sacks [30, p. 118] and by Tilly [146, p. 166] indicates that only a slight increase in local costs (in the short run at least) is attributable to migration of the poor alone.[a] Since short- and intermediate-run effects have the greatest effect on net-present-value calculations, any long-run cost increases resulting from the migration of the poor can perhaps be ignored fairly safely. Second, the data available in Campbell and Sacks [30, p. 119] seem to indicate that diseconomies of scale characterize certain traditional municipal functions—diseconomies that raise per capita unit costs of supplying police, fire, and sanitation services for large cities. The magnitudes of these diseconomies are, however, unknown. Third, equation (12,L) contains the assumption that municipal expenditures are completely price-inelastic (i.e., they have a price elasticity of zero). This assumption, although simplifying, is not arbitrary. The mandatory nature of most local expenditures certainly makes the demand for all local expenditures relatively price-inelastic.

To summarize, equation (12,L) takes into account only the major source of fiscal pressure—increases in municipal expenditures as a result of rising employee wages. Other variables are indeed important for a complete explanation of municipal expenditures. An alternative form of equation (12,L) might incorporate a unitary income elasticity of municipal expenditures in addition to increases in wages. Although we shall experiment with this alternative form of equation (12,L) in the next chapter, we must recognize that all estimates of the income elasticity of municipal expenditures are subject to the difficulty of separating price and income effects. This difficulty is one of identifying expenditure increases that result from price increases caused by unbalanced productivity growth as opposed to those that result from changes in the incomes of municipal inhabitants.

We now examine the plausibility of the assumptions of equation (13,R) regarding the composition of the municipal work force. Fuchs estimates [63, p. 51] a rate of growth in output per man of 2.2% during the 1956-1965 period for those activities of government which provide services that are marketed by government. He labels this group of activities "government enterprises" and differentiates them from the activities of government which provide services that are not sold, but rather are provided to citizens

[a]A major reason for this finding is that most local welfare programs are financed predominantly by federal and state funds.

without any incremental charge. These latter activities of government he classifies as "general government." He estimates constant productivity, or a zero rate of growth in productivity, for activities of general government during the same 1956-1965 period.

The above data indicate that activities of government enterprises are relatively progressive, whereas those of general government are relatively nonprogressive. We find from these same data that 91% of government employees were engaged in activities of general government, whereas only 9% were engaged in government enterprises during the 1956-1965 period. This implies that 91% of the total government work force in the United States was engaged in relatively nonprogressive activities and 9% in relatively progressive activities during this period.

We begin our justification of equation (13,R), then, by assuming that municipal activities follow the national characteristics, and can be classified as 91% nonprogressive and 9% progressive. This estimate of the proportion of total workers employed in the nonprogressive sector makes economic sense. The dominant expenditure of municipalities is for education, accounting (as we shall soon see) for about 50% of all nonaided local expenditures. Other major categories of expenditure include fire, pllice, health, and social services. All these activities employ labor as an input almost exclusively. Productivity in all these activities tends to be constant from one year to the next, except for sporadic increases.

We need one more piece of information to justify our assumptions on the size and composition of the municipal work force. We must estimate the share of income earned by employees of the municipality in order to estimate the share of the total municipal work force employed by the municipality itself. Obviously, only the roughest sort of estimate is possible unless we consider a specific city. We shall, therefore, strive to find plausible values only, recognizing that the actual values of these parameters vary significantly from city to city, as illustrated by recent U.S. Department of Commerce data [151].

We find from Campbell and Sacks [30, p. 7] that roughly 9% of GNP was purchased by state and local government from 1962 to 1965. In addition, we assume that approximately 60% of these state and local government purchases were made by local government. This figure of 60% represents an approximation from additional data presented by Campbell and Sacks [30, p. 6]. They show that the state portion of state and local expenditures has been expanding from 19% in 1922 to 35% in 1963-1964. The 60% assumed for the local portion of state and local expenditures is a crude extrapolation of this trend to provide us with a plausible value *only*.

Using the very rough estimates above, we find that approximately 5.4% of GNP (i.e., 60% of 9.0) was purchased by local government in the 1962-1965 period. From our previous assumptions about the technological structure of municipal activities, we know that approximately 91% of municipal activities may be considered nonprogressive, whereas approximately 9% are progressive. In addition, we know from equations (1,L) and (5,L) of section I that the total product in our model in the initial period is $72,000,000. Of this total product, 5.4% is to be produced by the municipal government itself in the initial period. Since municipal activities are 91% nonprogressive and 9% progressive, some 5.37% of nonprogressive activities must be municipal services, whereas .56% of the economy's progressive activities must be activities of the municipal government. It is in this way that we justify the values of 5.37% and .56% assigned respectively to *PNPEM* and *PPEM* in equation (13,R). These estimates, although crude, will allow us to proceed with the model while recognizing that, if key variables of the model are sensitive to small percentage movements in these parameters, then the parameters (and the assumption that they are constant) will require closer examination.

Two additonal comments are necessary on equation (13,R). A slight income effect on municipal wages is introduced as the labor costs of each sector change to reflect migration patterns to and from the municipality. As evidence presented earlier indicated, the precise nature of the income effect on municipal expenditures is much more complicated than that represented by equation (13,R). However, a changing income composition of the municipality will probably influence expenditures on education most significantly. Campbell and Sacks [30, p. 150], using 1957 data, show that local expenditures on education are strongly related to income levels. They estimate that the income elasticity of demand for education in central cities is unitary, and that the income elasticity for outside areas is 1.2. Education activities tend to be nonprogressive in character. Therefore, a wealthier community is likely to have a higher ratio of nonprogressive to progressive workers than a poorer one, since education expenditures are the dominant category of expenditures for local governments, accounting for 43.5% of locally financed expenditures in 1965, according to Sacks [128, p. 148]. This is implied, although very crudely, by equation (13,R).

2. *Municipal Benefits*

We have established that expenditures on education are the largest locally financed expenditures made by municipalities, and that these expenditures are income related.

The quality of education in central cities appears to be deteriorating relative to outside areas. Sacks points out [128, p. 159] that locally financed per capita education expenses grew at the rate of 2% per year from 1957 to 1962 in the central cities in a sample made up of 36 standard metropolitan areas, and at the rate of 8% outside central cities. On all other measures of the quality of education, the areas outside central cities have been shown by Sacks to be forging ahead of central cities.

The strong income-education relationship, on the demand side, leads us to believe that the deterioration of central city schools, relative to schools of outside areas, should make a typical affluent family relatively worse off in a central city than in one of its higher-income suburbs, since its public education demands are likely to be frustrated (assuming everything else to be reasonably equal). In addition, Campbell and Sacks [30, p. 123] indicate that in 1962 per capita taxes were higher by $24 in central cities, with approximately half the amount derived from property taxes. The higher property-tax levies per capita in central cities, and the lower expenditures on education per capita in central cities, reflect the relatively greater importance (or higher per capita unit costs) of other traditional functions in central cities.

The preceding data suggest that the affluent are relatively better off in outside areas than in central cities. Property taxes are no lower in central cities than in the suburbs, but education services are apparently much better, and improving, in areas outside central cities. In equation (14,R) we set *NSDA*, the money value of the services forgone by a typical affluent family when it chooses to remain in or enter the central city, at 6.0%. This rate is the difference in the annual growth rate of expenditures on education between areas outside central cities and central cities, calculated from the Sacks study. It may understate the true deterioration in the economic welfare of the affluent in central cities relative to the affluent in the suburbs.[b] In addition, there is no reason to assume that in reality *NSDA* is constant.

We now must comment on the value assigned in equation (14,R) to the normal annual percentage of income that a typical affluent family spends on education (*NPME*), i.e., locally financed education expenditures as a percentage of annual income. The median annual income in a sample of central cities of 36 metropolitan areas, taken in 1957 by Campbell and Sacks [30, p. 118], was approximately $6,000. Per capita nonaided education expenditures in central cities in 1957 were $42.24, or 22% (roughly) of total per capita expenditures.

Since family income was computed on the basis of three persons per family, unaided education expenditures per family amounted to $136.72, or approximately 2.3% of median family income. I have, therefore, set the normal proportion of affluent income spent on education *NPME* equal to a constant 2.3%.

---

[b]The esthetic properties of the suburbs are no doubt a very important factor influencing migration, especially if coupled with housing subsidies and improved means of transportation to central cities.

We must recognize the estimate of *NPME* to be a very rough guess about the value of what may be a very important parameter. There is no reason to expect that this will remain stable over time, and there is every reason to expect great variability in this ratio among central cities, as all the data, such as those of Schultze [138, p. 328], show. If we find the key variables of the model to be sensitive to this parameter, we will carry out our benefit-cost analyses using several alternative but plausible values of *NPME*.

One additional assumption of equation (14,R) requires comment. As affluent families depart from the municipality, the income earned in the nonprogressive sector of the economy will be received in part at least by families residing in the adjacent suburb. The variable *NAS.K* then begins to overstate the income of affluent family residents and equation (14,R) begins to produce opportunity loss figures that are greater than 6% of *normal* affluent expenditures on education. This form implies that, as affluent families depart from the municipality, the opportunity loss for those that remain increases. The poorer a central city becomes, the more abnormal (i.e., the greater) the opportunity loss is assumed to be for those affluent families who remain. This form is appealing intuitively, since it implies that the more affluent central cities will have better school systems relative to their affluent suburbs than will the poorer central cities relative to the *same* suburbs.

We now examine the assumptions underlying equation (15,R). There we assumed that potential poor migrants perceive benefits of migration to the central city as a function of the change in municipal income per capita produced within the boundaries of the central city. Equation (15,R) is very speculative, but per capita income as a proxy for employment opportunities is, from all indications, the dominant variable influencing migration to a central city. This, of course, implies that poor families *perceive* their benefits from a central city to be a function of employment opportunities. We approximate these opportunities as some unknown function (i.e., *NPISP*) of the annual change in per capita family income produced in the municipality. Quite arbitrarily we assigned a value of 10% to *NPISP*. This is necessary since the "constant" is obviously important, but quite qualitative in nature. Once we observe the extent of the effect of this parameter on key variables in the model, we may be able to gauge its magnitude better by choosing a value that, when all other model variables are considered, leads to *observed* migration patterns.

The empirical evidence that does exist on migration indicates that municipal services do not play a *dominant* role in attracting poor migrants. Tilly [146, p. 151] finds employment, and the prospects for employment, far more important than municipal services in influencing poor migration to central cities. In his words [146, p. 167], "the quality of public services does not seem to make much difference to the flow of migrants and the migrants who do come place no exceptional demand on services."

The Advisory Commission on Intergovernmental Relations [1, p. 128] finds that:

> Indigents tend to migrate to urban centers in search of employment, to join relatives, and, perhaps, because they know a city has a welfare program which will assure them a minimum of assistance.

Employment opportunities, from every indication, seem to be the key variable influencing migration of the poor to central cities and must, along with municipal services, be perceived by the poor as benefits. These opportunities are, I believe, a function of municipal income as the form of equation (15,R) specifies.

Before we leave the subject of migration, we should observe that past patterns of migration may not continue indefinitely into the future. In addition, data on migration do not indicate any general pattern that has persisted through time. All we can say is that the waves of migration that have occurred throughout the history of the United States appear to have been motivated primarily by economic opportunities, as Kuznets (in Eldridge and Thomas [52, pp. xxiii-xxxv]) has indicated.

This completes our description of Section II of the model and the empirical evidence supporting it. The structure and equation forms appear fairly realistic and most values of parameters have at least some empirical support.

The municipal costs accumulated in equation (12,L), and the benefits computed by equations (14,R) and (15,R), are distributed to residents of the municipality in the next section. Family costs for typical affluent and poor citizens are combined there with benefits to produce a measure of net benefits. These net benefits cause population movements and alterations in the housing stock which are described in Section IV.

Section III: Net Family Benefits

Section III of the model reports net benefits for each of the poor families and net costs for each of the affluent families of the municipality. Both net benefits and net costs are reported over time.

The model begins at zero costs for a typical affluent family. Net benefits (i.e., benefits minus costs) for a typical poor family, however, are initially (i.e., at time zero) set equal to $3,000. This reflects the immediate relative attractiveness of this municipality for poor inhabitants; for potential unemployed poor migrants, it represents the annual wage expected upon migration.

Incremental benefits, computed in Section II, result from each group's perception of the benefits or opportunity loss in this municipality relative to the benefits that are perceived in the next logical place of residence (i.e., the suburbs for the affluent and, say, the relevant zone of migration for the poor). The incremental costs computed in this section result, it is assumed, from increases in property-tax levies for each family of a typical group.

Annual net costs, including opportunities forgone for a typical affluent family, are given by

$$NCLA.K = NCLA.J + DT * (RSSIA.JK - RCIA.JK) \qquad (16,L)$$

where $NCLA.J$ = the net costs for a typical affluent family at time J

$RSSIA.JK$ = the perceived annual change in services for the affluent relative to the change experienced by the affluent in a relevant adjacent suburb (normally a negative number)

$RCIA.JK$ = the annual cost increase, in dollars, for the affluent of this municipality

The initial condition for equation (16,L) is zero, as stated above.

The annual rate of increase in costs for a typical affluent family in this municipality is given as follows:

$$RCIA.KL = MCA.K - MCA.J \qquad (17,R)$$

where $MCA.K$ = the level of municipal costs at time K for an affluent family

$MCA.J$ = the annual level of municipal costs for an affluent family at time J

RSSIA was given by equation (14,R) of Section II.

It might appear that we have attached a peculiar meaning to equation (16,L). We have avoided the difficult (or impossible) job of estimating the *value* attached to urban services, over time, by the affluent. In its place we have substituted a measure of opportunities forgone (*RSSIA*) for a typical affluent family. Therefore, equation (16,L) really represents the addition of two items of cost: the annual increase in costs and the benefits forgone by a typical affluent family.

The annual level of municipal costs for a typical affluent family is given by

$$MCA.K = (MTR.K * AVAH.K)/AH.K \qquad (18,A)$$

where $MTR.K$ = the municipal tax rate (dollars per thousand) at time K

$AVAH.K$ = the total assessed valuation of affluent housing

$AH.K$ = the total number of affluent housing units in the urban area

The variables $MTR.K$, $AVAH.K$ and $AH.K$ are described below in Section IV, "Municipal Population and Housing."

The annual net-benefit level for a typical poor family is given by

$$NBLP.K = NBLP.J + DT * (RSSIP.JK - RCIP.JK) \quad (19,L)$$

where $NBLP.J$ = net benefits for a typical poor family at time J

$RSSIP.JK$ = the perceived annual change in services for a poor family of this municipality relative to those perceived in the relevant zone of migration

$RCIP.JK$ = the actual rate of cost increase for the poor

The initial condition for *NBLP* is \$3,000 for the reasons cited at the beginning of this section.

Equations for the annual rate of increase in costs for a typical poor family (*RCIP*), and for total municipal costs for each poor family (*MCP*), are as follows:

$$RCIP.KL = (MCP.K - MCP.J) \quad (20,R)$$

and

$$MCP.K = (MTR.K * AVPH.K)/PH.K \quad (21,A)$$

where the variables have meanings for the poor corresponding to those of equations (17,R) and (18,A). In addition, we make the simplifying assumption that municipal costs for the poor (*RCIP*) are *equal* to those experienced elsewhere.

In summary, Section III contains many technical, as opposed to behavioral, relationships, many of which are *not* controversial. Unfortunately, Section IV is just the opposite, requiring many behavioral assumptions.

Section IV: Municipal Population and Housing

We assume in Section IV that the municipality contains a housing stock of 10,000 family units, consisting of 6,000 affluent and 4,000 poor units. The housing stock and mix are assumed to change as a function of population arrivals and departures. The total family population is given by

$$TPL.K = TPL.J = DT * (PMP.JK + PMA.JK) \qquad (22,L)$$

where $TPL.J$ = the number of families in the municipality at time J

$PMP.JK$ = the number of poor families arriving *or* departing during the period JK

$PMA.JK$ = the number of affluent families arriving or departing during the period JK

The initial condition TPL for equation (22,L) is set equal to 10,000 families, which simply represents the initial total family population level of the municipality.

The population levels of poor and affluent families are computed separately. The population level of the poor is given by

$$PLP.K = PLP.J + DT * (PMP.JK) \qquad (23,L)$$

and the population level of the affluent is given by

$$PLA.K = PLA.J + DT * (PMA.JK). \qquad (24,L)$$

The initial condition for equation (23,L) is 4,000 families; for equation (24,L) the initial condition is 6,000 families.

Population *movement* of affluent families is assumed to occur one-half year after the decision to leave or enter the municipality. It is shown by

$$PMA.KL = DELAY1(PADA.JK, AMD) \qquad (24,R)$$

where $DELAY1$ = a DYNAMO function that calls an exponential delay subroutine

$PADA.JK$ = the rate of affluent population movement *decisions*

AMD = the average delay between the decision to move and the actual move

$DELAY1$ in equation (22,R) is a function that allows us to show a gradual adjustment of affluent moves to decisions-to-move with an average delay of six months separating the moves from the decisions.

Population arrival and departure decisions of the affluent are assumed to be based on net costs. We begin to approximate the function by the following equation:

$$PADA.KL = TABHL\ (PADAT,\ NCLA.K,\ -\$10{,}000,\ \$10{,}000,\ \$5{,}000) \qquad (26,R)$$

where $TABHL$ indicates that the function is found in a table of values called $PADAT$ that relates population movement (i.e., the dependent variable) to changes in *NCLA.K,* the net-cost (including opportunity loss) level for a typical affluent family at time *K*. The three numbers on the right-hand side of equation (26,R) relate directly to a table which is again arbitrarily given by

$$PADAT = -300/-150/0/150/300. \qquad (26,T)$$

The dependent variable of equation (26,R) takes the values of the table that are given in equation (27,T) as follows:

1. When net costs for a typical affluent family reach −$10,000 [i.e., the initial number in equation (26,R)], 300 affluent families are assumed to leave annually [i.e., the initial number in equation (27,T)] therefore, *PADA.KL* assumes a value of −300.
2. When net benefits reach +$10,000, we assume that 300 affluent families enter the municipality annually; i.e., the last value in the table is the value assumed by equation (26,R).
3. When net costs for a typical affluent family are zero, no movement occurs; the middle value of the table is zero.
4. When net costs reach −$5,000, 150 affluent families leave the municipality annually; therefore, the second value of the table function is −150.
5. When the net costs reach $5,000, 150 affluent families enter the municipality annually.
6. When any other intermediate net-benefit value occurs, the function performs a linear interpolation between points in the table to arrive at the value of the dependent variable *PADA.KL*

If, in any case, net benefits exceed $10,000 or are lower than −$10,000, the extreme values of +300 and −300 respectively will continued to be used annually.

The quality of housing in the municipality is assumed to be dependent upon the income level of the inhabitants. When movement decisions are made, the housing structures of previous users remain; they are either occupied by newcomers or left vacant. We assume that the housing stock and quality change only by a process of conversion. If new homes are constructed, they are assumed to be constructed over a time period identical with the time period required for conversion.

The quantity of the affluent housing stock is given by

$$AH.K = AH.J + DT * (PMA.JK/DAHF) \qquad (28,L)$$

where *AH.J* = the quantity of affluent housing in the municipality at time *J*

PMA.J = the movement of the affluent population during *JK*

DAHF = the delay, after population movement, required for housing to filter *up* or *down*

In equation (28,L) we assume that affluent housing increases or decreases as affluent families enter or leave the municipality. Rather than enumerate all the variables influencing the supply and demand for housing, I have attempted to approximate the housing-market adjustment mechanism by the use of a well-known process called "filtering." Lowry [95, p. 363] defines filtering as "a change in the real value of an existing dwelling unit within the distribution of housing rents and prices in the community as a whole." I have set the parameter *DAHF* equal to 11 years.

Equations (22,L) through (28,L) were concerned with affluent population and housing. We turn now to a group of equations, almost identical in form, that describe characteristics of the housing of the poor population.

The population movement of poor families is given by

$$PMP.KL = DELAY1(PADP.JK,PMD) \quad (29,R)$$

where all terms have meanings identical to those of equation (24,R) except that they refer to the poor and that the value assigned to *PMD* is one year rather than the six months assumed for the affluent. This difference is an attempt to represent the greater relative mobility of the affluent.

Population arrival and departure decisions of the poor are given as follows:

$$PADP.KL = TABHL\ (PADPT,\ NBLP.K,0,\$10{,}000,\$5{,}000) \quad (30,R)$$

and

$$PADPT = 100/150/200 \quad (31,T)$$

where all terms are as described for (26,R) and (27,T) except that they pertain to the poor. The functional relationship itself, however, is not identical to that stipulated for the affluent. In the preceding equations we see that if annual *net benefits* should reach $10,000 for a typical poor family, 200 poor families per year will enter the municipality, doubling the poor population to 8,000 families in 20 years. If net benefits fall to zero, 100 poor families will leave annually. In any case, if net benefits exceed $10,000 or are less than zero, the extreme values of +200 and −100 respectively will continue to be used as the annual value for equation (30,R).

The equation of housing of the poor is given by

$$PH.K = PH.J + DT * (PMP.JK/PHFD) \quad (32,L)$$

where *PHFD* is the delay required, after a movement in population, for housing to "filter" up or down; it too is assumed to be 11 years. All other terms have meanings similar to those of equation (28,L), except that they apply to the poor. The initial value of *PH* used for this equation is 4,000 housing units, one unit for each poor family.

Some Comments on the Assumptions of Section IV

Section IV is by far the weakest part of the model. While the structural relationships seem plausible, the equation forms and parameter values have very little empirical support.

The assumptions of Section IV of the model fall conveniently into two categories: population assumptions and housing assumptions. We discuss each category in turn.

1. Population Assumptions

Although there is no evidence on the true shape of the functions relating the movement of poor and affluent families to net benefits, the functions specified in Section IV have some intuitive appeal. It is well known, for example, that the cumulative deterioration process taking place in many major American cities is a major effect of recent migration patterns —patterns that include a relatively heavy migration of poor families into certain central cities, and a relatively heavy migration of affluent families from central cities to adjacent suburbs. The poor find central cities relatively attractive (i.e., benefits exceed costs), and the affluent find central cities relatively unattractive (i.e., costs, including opportunities forgone, are greater than benefits). Therefore, although we do not know just how unattractive central cities are to the affluent, or precisely how attractive they are to the poor, we do know that in certain central cities the affluent face a stacked deck and the poor perceive opportunities.

Our knowledge of the functions that relate arrival and departure decisions of the poor and affluent to our measure of net benefits is totally inadequate; nor is there any reason for us to believe that the true function is stable over time. The model does not contain the relationships necessary to relate arrival and departure decisions of the affluent to net costs (including opportunity loss); for it does not contain an explicit description of the relevant suburb, i.e., of the opportunities that the affluent forgo, over time, as a result of residing in the central city rather than in the suburb. Without a model of the relevant suburb, we can only guess at the nature of the functions for affluent arrival and departure. Similarly, the model does not contain the relationships necessary to relate decisions on arrivals and departures of the poor to net benefits; for it does not contain an explicit description of the relevant zone of migration from which the poor emigrate.

If we insert reasonable functions for these relationships, we can at least test the sensitivity of key variables to the parameters of such functions. This will tell us just how pressing it is to obtain accurate estimates of such functions. It certainly is no substitute, however, for a model of the relevant adjacent suburb and zone of migration.

The values of the parameters in the arbitrary functions of equations (26,R) and (27,T) (i.e., the migration equations for the affluent) could have been estimated by regression methods for any one municipality if we possessed a combination of systematic property-tax data for various socioeconomic groups, together with migration patterns for identical socioeconomic groups. The lack of systematic property-tax data is the most serious obstacle to their estimation.

Even if systematic property-tax data were available, regression estimates of this relationship would conceal elements of dynamic interaction between a central city and its suburbs. They would also conceal other more subjective, but equally important, reasons for migration (e.g., esthetic factors). For this reason, I am currently attempting to identify causal dynamic interrelationships between a typical large central city and its suburbs.

As was true of equations (26,R) and (27,T), there is no empirical evidence underlying equations (30,R) and (31,T), i.e., the relationships governing migration of the poor. To my knowledge, there has been no extensive empirical work relating urban migration to the net benefits enjoyed by various groups within the urban area. However, we shall return to this issue in Chapter 5.

To summarize, the relationships relating migration to net benefits may be critical in producing much of the dynamic behavior observed in urban areas. We have represented these relationships in Section IV, although little empirical evidence exists to support (or for that matter, to deny) the relationships established. We will explore alternative shapes of these relationships in the next chapter, and hope the model will provide us with some qualitative insights into the properties of the functions.

2. *Housing Assumptions*

In equations (28,L) and (32,L) we assumed that the quality of housing is dependent upon the income level of the residents. This assumption is supported by Muth's [111, p. 330] empirical investigation of housing in Chicago. He found the most significant determinant of housing quality to be the income level of residents of the municipality. Slum housing and urban decay are the result, predominantly, of poverty. The assumptions on the conversion of housing from one classification of quality to another were simplifying assumptions necessary to avoid the complexities arising from the incorporation of an explicit housing market in the model. These assumptions, including the assumptions that the filtering process takes 11 years, while simplifying, are not arbitrary.

Grebler [66, pp. 17, 55-63], in his study of the housing market of New York's Lower East Side, found that parcels of land changed hands approximately every 11 years during the 1900-1940 time period, a period during which average rents in that area declined from 88% to 62% of the average Manhattan rents. A "filtering-down" process apparently took place over that period of time. Each time a parcel of land was sold, average prices presumably decreased, and the housing stock entered a new and lower relative quality class. The value of 11 years assigned to *DAHF* and *PHFD* in equations (28,L) and (32,L) is a crude estimate, taken from Grebler's study, of the time period required for property to descend (or ascend) from one classification of quality to another in a declining (or rising) area.

In summary, Section IV of the model is certainly incomplete. Two parameters, *DAHF* and *PHFD*, are used as proxies for the workings of the housing market. In addition, only plausible ranges are provided for the values of most of the other parameters. The nature of the functional forms that equations (26,R), (27,T) (30,R) and (31,T) should take is not known. Happily, Section V contains very few problems of this type. Relationships in this section are mainly technical, and few additional assumptions and simplifications are required.

Section V: Municipal Taxation and Revenue

In Section V of the model, the municipal tax rate and municipal revenue relationships are described. Municipal revenue is obtained simply by multiplying the tax rate by the total assessed valuation of housing. Municipal revenue is thus given by

$$MR.K = (AVP.K) * (MTR.K) \qquad (31,A)$$

where $AVP.K$ = the total assessed valuation of municipal property

$MTR.K$ = the municipal tax rate (dollars per thousand of assessed valuation).

The total assessed valuation is given by

$$AVP.K = AVAH.K + AVPH.K \qquad (32,A)$$

where $AVAH.K$ = the total assessed value of affluent housing

$AVPH.K$ = the total assessed value of poor housing

The total assessed valuation of affluent housing is determined by

$$AVAH.K = AH.K * NMAAVH * MAVR.K \qquad (33,A)$$

where $AH.K$ = the total number of affluent housing units

$NMAAVH$ = the normal assessed value for an affluent housing unit

$MAVR.K$ = the municipal assessed-value-ratio factor.

I have assumed the assessed-value ratio of affluent to poor homes to be 1,000/30. This means that *NMAAVH* equals $1,000. Only the ratio is important, since the affluent and poor are assumed to bear all the property taxes.

The municipal assessed-value-ratio factor (*MAVR*) is a device that attempts to approximate, in a crude manner, the political power of the affluent. It is approximated by their relative numbers in this central city in comparison with other central cities. It is calculated as follows:

$$MAVR.K = NPPA/(PLA.K/TLP.K) \qquad (34,A)$$

where $NPPA$ = the normal percentage of affluent families living in central cities, where the 1,000/30 assessed-valuation ratio is assumed to prevail

$PLA.K/TPL.K$ = the percentage of total families of this municipality that are affluent

As the poor become more numerous relative to the affluent, the ratio begins to exceed 1, and the assessed value of the homes of the affluent becomes relatively higher than it is normally.

The assessed value of poor housing is given by

$$AVPH.K = PH.K * NAVPH \qquad (35,A)$$

where $PH.K$ = the number of poor housing units

$NAVPH$ = the normal assessed value of a poor housing unit

NAVPH is, as indicated previously, equal to $30.

Only the assumptions of equations (33,A) (34,A), and (35,A) seem to require justification. The assessed-value ratio of $1,000 to $30 used for equations (33,A) and (35,A) is the ratio that Grebler [66, p. 85] found to hold for the affluent parts of Manhattan as against the Lower East Side in 1950. We shall experiment with alternative values for this in Chapter 5 to observe their influence upon key variables of the model. The political power assumptions underlying equation (34,A) are simplistic. All I claim is that they are plausible and that the political power enjoyed by any one typical group is indeed related to the relative population of that group in the central city.

Conclusion

This completes the description of our partial urban model.[c] There is considerable direct and indirect evidence supporting the structure of the model, but it is still very incomplete. It would be profitable to expand the structure of the model to include (1) a detailed model of migration of the poor from a natural zone of migration to the central city; (2) a model of a relevant suburb adjacent to the central city, representing a feasible alternative of living location for the affluent families of the municipality; (3) a life-cycle analysis of the industries located in, and likely to be attracted to, the central city and the adjacent suburb; and (4) a model of the demographic factors of both the central city and the adjacent suburb.

I am now expanding the structure of the model to include at least four more sections (or modules) that represent these four features.

The specification of some of the equation forms of the present model (e.g., municipal expenditures) must be improved. In addition, although the values assigned to some parameters have considerable empirical support, others can at best be shown to fall within ranges of plausible values, as we have seen.

Although the partial urban model leaves much to be desired for use in benefit-cost analysis, it does offer us an instrument to deal more systematically than is customary with complex urban phenomena. Decisions must and will be made; the task of the analyst is to bring the best available information of all kinds to bear upon issues of public policy. This is a continuous and iterative process. Although the model certainly is imperfect, the only thing worse is to have no model at all for the evaluation of public projects as has been the case in too many of the benefit-cost evaluations carried out in the past.

For the purpose of illustrating a third- or fourth-best procedure for benefit-cost analysis, this model is not only adequate but is well suited to the task. It will allow us to develop a comparative-dynamic procedure that is likely to have wide application in areas of complex social problems. It will provide a framework within which we can examine many of the fundamental issues of benefit-cost analysis. Perhaps most important, it will allow us to resolve some of the present controversy surrounding these issues.

Our procedure for evaluating such complex social programs will be described in the next two chapters. The empirical problems posed by such a procedure will be discussed throughout the remainder of the book, predominantly by evaluating Forrester's assertion [62, p. 172] that key variables in such models should be relatively *insensitive* to wide estimating errors in all but a few parameter values, and to a lesser extent, to the specification of equation forms.

[c] A glossary of notation for the entire model appears at the end of this volume.

Some final notes are necessary on the choice of the DYNAMO Compiler. The partial urban model could have been programmed in another language (e.g., FORTRAN). The language chosen has no influence on the dynamic behavior of the model. However, the language chosen has a considerable influence on programming and computing efficiency. The DYNAMO Compiler accepts the model equations directly, without an intermediate computer-programming step. It includes subroutines for many special functions, including those required for output layouts, scaling, and plotting.

Since successful simulation requires much trial and error, the computing efficiency of a compiler is critical to the success of a simulation model. We should expect the usefulness of a simulation procedure for benefit-cost analysis to be inversely related to its average cost per simulation run. In this respect, DYNAMO is truly remarkable; the average cost per run of a 100 statement model, computed over a 40-year period, is approximately \$1.30. At this average cost, the procedure certainly is economically feasible.

5 Sensitivity Analysis in the Partial Urban Model

Many of the parameters of the model have been assigned values that could be considered plausible only. True values for many of these parameters are simply not known, nor are there always sufficient data available to estimate them empirically.

The absence of data of good quality for the construction of models of social systems is quite normal. We are, therefore, forced to establish good model relationships with limited data. However, if we can show that key variables of a model are insensitive to many parameter values, then plausible values should suffice for all but the most crucial parameters. The primary purpose of this chapter is to test for these crucial parameters.

Sensitivity analysis is the method employed to investigate the relative importance of each parameter. We will vary, systematically, the values assigned to parameters in Chapters 3 and 4 to determine the effect that an erroneous estimate of any one will have on the values of key variables. If we find that values of key variables are insensitive to wide shifts in values of certain parameters, we may conclude that a more precise estimate of these parameters may not be highly important, for it will improve the performance of our model very little. If, on the other hand, we find a parameter to which the model is very sensitive, we must be certain of its true value, for a small error in the estimate of such a parameter will cause relatively large errors in the values of key variables.

Sensitivity analysis also provides us with a technique that helps us to understand the dynamic characteristics of the model. By varying the values of all parameters and comparing new results with those of the basic model, we can determine which parameters are most responsible for the dynamic behavior exhibited by the model. If we conclude that the basic model represents reality accurately, these crucial parameters become logical points for policy actions.

In this chapter, each of the constant parameters, including the values of the two table functions of the basic urban model, will be assigned a range of values. We will be concerned with the relative change in the value of key variables that results from a relative change in a parameter value. We will, therefore, employ the elasticity concept to estimate the sensitivity of key variables to changes in each of the constant parameters. In this manner, the most sensitive parameters will be identified for further analysis.

There are four variables that we shall consider key variables, because changes in these four can initiate a process either of urban revival or of urban decay. They are the net costs and population of affluent families (i.e., *NCLA* and *PLA*) and the net benefits and population of poor families (i.e., *NBLP* and *PLP*). Deterioration or improvement in housing quality occurs, it is assumed, because of migration patterns into and out of the municipality. Migration occurs because of changes in net costs for the affluent and net benefits for the poor, relative to net costs in the adjoining suburbs (for the affluent) and net benefits in other relevant urban and suburban areas (for the poor).

We must now examine the detailed operations of the basic model as a prelude to the sensitivity analysis.

Dynamic Behavior of the Partial Urban Model

The behavior of the model was simulated for a period of 20 years to determine the nature of its time path in the absence of institutional changes. *Partial* results for the basic model (i.e., the values of some of its key variables) are reproduced in Table 5-1.

The key variables shown in each column of Table 5-1 are: (1) time, (2) net costs for a typical affluent family (*NCLA*), (3) net benefits for a typical poor family (*NBLP*), (4) total net costs for all affluent families (*TNCLA*), (5) total net benefits for all poor families (*TNBLP*), (6) total number of affluent families (*PLA*), and (7) total number of poor families (*PLP*). The total net cost and benefit columns are the product of population and net benefits for each typical group. Column 5 results are in millions, while column 6 results are in thousands.

Table 5-1 reports the values for key variables only. Figure 5-1 illustrates the dynamic behavior of four of these key variables. The values for eight additional, secondary variables required for a thorough analysis of model behavior are given in Table 5-2. The values of these secondary variables determine the values of key variables. The values for 10 additional, tertiary variables appear in Appendix II.

As is apparent from column 2 of Table 5-1, net costs rise continuously for a typical affluent family: from $13.80 in year 1 to $2,125 in year 20. This results from a combination of increasing costs and decreasing relative benefits.

The two variables that determine *NCLA* are *RSSIA* and *RCIA* (columns 2 and 4 of Table 5-2). *RSSIA* is the annual opportunity loss for a typical affluent family, and *RCIA* is the annual increase in property taxes paid by a typical affluent family. Year-1 values for these variables are the total initial costs. For example, property taxes (*RCIA*) are $537 for a typical affluent family in year 1. Property taxes increase annually by an increasing dollar amount, $33 in year 2 to $99 (approximately) in year 20. The opportunity loss *RSSIA* rises from $13 in year 1 to $51 (approximately) in year 20.

Table 5-1
Key Variables of the Basic Model

(1) Time E+00	(2) NCLA E+00	(3) NBLP E+00	(4) TNCLA E+06	(5) TNBLP E+06	(6) PLA E+00	(7) PLP E+00
.0	.0	3000.0	.000	12.000	6000.0	4000.0
1.	−13.8	3720.0	−.083	15.066	6000.0	4050.0
2.	−565.9	3748.4	−3.396	15.368	6000.0	4100.0
3.	−614.5	3794.3	−3.687	15.883	5999.2	4186.0
4.	−666.2	3842.4	−3.974	16.420	5966.0	4273.4
5.	−721.4	3893.2	−4.601	16.986	5962.3	4363.1
6.	−779.3	3946.1	−4.621	17.581	5926.1	4455.2
7.	−842.1	4002.0	−4.985	18.209	5519.0	4549.9
8.	−908.2	4060.3	−5.339	18.869	5879.3	4647.2
9.	−978.6	4122.0	−5.743	19.568	5868.5	4747.3
10.	−1053.3	4186.3	−6.135	20.305	5824.8	4850.3
11.	−1133.0	4254.2	−6.583	21.086	5809.7	4956.4
12.	−1217.6	4325.1	−7.015	21.910	5761.6	5065.7
13.	−1307.9	4400.0	−7.509	22.785	5741.8	5178.4
14.	−1403.6	4478.2	−7.985	23.711	5688.5	5294.7
15.	−1505.9	4560.8	−8.529	24.695	5663.3	5414.7
16.	−1614.5	4647.0	−9.048	25.738	5604.3	5538.6
17.	−1730.5	4738.1	−9.644	26.849	5572.9	5666.6
18.	−1853.7	4833.2	−10.209	28.027	5507.4	5799.0
19.	−1985.4	4933.7	−10.858	29.286	5469.1	5935.9
20.	−2125.3	5038.5	−11.469	30.622	5396.2	6077.5

The stock variable *MCA* (column 6 of Table 5-2) accumulates the increases in property-tax levies; affluent property taxes, which exclude the opportunity loss, rise from $537 in year 1 to $1,684 in year 20.

Net benefits for a typical poor family (column 3 of Table 5-1) rise from $3,000 at time zero to $5,038.50 at year 20. The two variables that determine net benefits for the poor are *RSSIP* and *RCIP* (columns 3 and 5 of Table 5-2). The annual increase in services supplied to the poor (column 3 of Table 5-2) rises from $44.92 in year one to $112.45 in year 20. Annual costs for the poor (column 7 of Table 5-2), after year 1,[a] rise from $.90 in year 2 to $1.59 in year 20.

[a]In the first year, the model requires the distribution of some $3.3 million of initial municipal costs; therefore, the first-year costs for the poor are $16. Thereafter, *RCIP* shows only increases to property taxes. The same holds for the affluent; a typical affluent family begins with a property-tax levy of $537.50 (column 6 of Table 5-2) and that levy is considered an increase in year 1 (since we move from zero to $537.50 in year 1).

A close look at the numbers at time zero in Table 5-2 produces what at first appears to be an anomalous situation. Certain variables (e.g., *RSSIA* and *RSSIP*) have values at time zero, whereas others (e.g., *RCIA* and *RCIP*) do not. This is a necessity, since DYNAMO computes values for rate equations at time zero by using values of level equations that are, at time zero, set equal to initial conditions. Most auxiliary variables (e.g., *MCA* and *MCP*, on which *RCIA* and *RCIP* depend) have zero values at time zero, since they depend on other auxiliary equations which do not have values until the first year.

Table 5-2
Secondary Variables of the Basic Model

(1) *Year*	*(2)* *RSSIA*	*(3)* *RSSIP*	*(4)* *RCIA*	*(5)* *RCIP*	*(6)* *MCA*	*(7)* *MCP*	*(8)* *AH*	*(9)* *PH*
0	−13.800	720.00	0	0	0	.000	6000.0	4000.0
1	−14.656	44.42	537.49	16.045	537.5	16.045	6000.0	4004.5
2	−15.564	46.80	33.03	.902	570.5	16.946	6000.0	4009.1
3	−16.531	49.06	35.11	.890	605.6	17.836	5999.9	4016.9
4	−17.654	51.64	37.62	.903	643.2	18.739	5996.9	4024.9
5	−18.754	53.90	39.64	.977	682.9	19.716	5996.6	4033.0
6	−20.038	56.90	42.25	.981	725.1	20.697	5993.3	4041.4
7	−21.298	59.39	44.73	1.067	769.9	21.764	5992.6	4050.0
8	−22.770	62.71	47.68	1.067	817.5	22.831	5989.0	4058.8
9	−24.216	65.45	50.48	1.162	868.0	23.993	5988.0	4067.9
10	−25.908	69.11	53.82	1.157	921.8	25.150	5984.1	4077.3
11	−27.574	72.14	56.98	1.260	978.8	26.401	5982.7	4086.9
12	−29.523	76.18	60.75	1.249	1039.6	27.660	5978.3	4096.9
13	−31.447	79.51	64.33	1.362	1103.9	29.021	5976.5	4107.1
14	−33.702	83.98	68.59	1.342	1172.5	30.364	5971.7	4117.7
15	−35.932	87.64	72.64	1.464	1245.1	31.827	5969.4	4128.6
16	−38.551	92.57	77.45	1.433	1322.6	33.260	5964.0	4139.9
17	−41.147	96.60	82.04	1.563	1404.6	34.823	5961.2	4151.5
18	−44.203	102.03	87.48	1.518	1492.1	36.341	5955.2	4163.5
19	−44.241	106.46	92.68	1.657	1584.8	37.998	5951.7	4176.0
20	−50.827	112.45	98.82	1.593	1683.6	39.591	5945.1	4188.9

The total family population of the municipality (the sum of columns 6 and 7 of Table 5-1) grows from 10,000 at time zero to 11,474 (approximately) at time 20. The population mix, however, changes drastically over that same time period. The composition of municipal family population changes from 40% poor at time zero to 53% poor at time 20. Poor-family population grows from 4,000 at time zero to 6,078 at time 20; affluent population decreases from 6,000 at time zero to 5,396 at time 20.

The number of housing units and their quality are functions of family population and mix. Quality, however, increases or decreases fully only after an 11-year lag; the filtering process is assumed to take an average of 11 years, so that the results of urban migration are not visible immediately. Housing stock and quality (columns 8 and 9 of Table 5-2) begin to change in year 2. This process continues and urban blight increases, but at a rate slower than the rate of poor-family arrivals. At time 20, 53% of municipal families are poor, but only 41% of municipal housing is of poor quality.

Sensitivity Analysis of the Basic Model

In this section, we subject the basic model to an extensive sensitivity

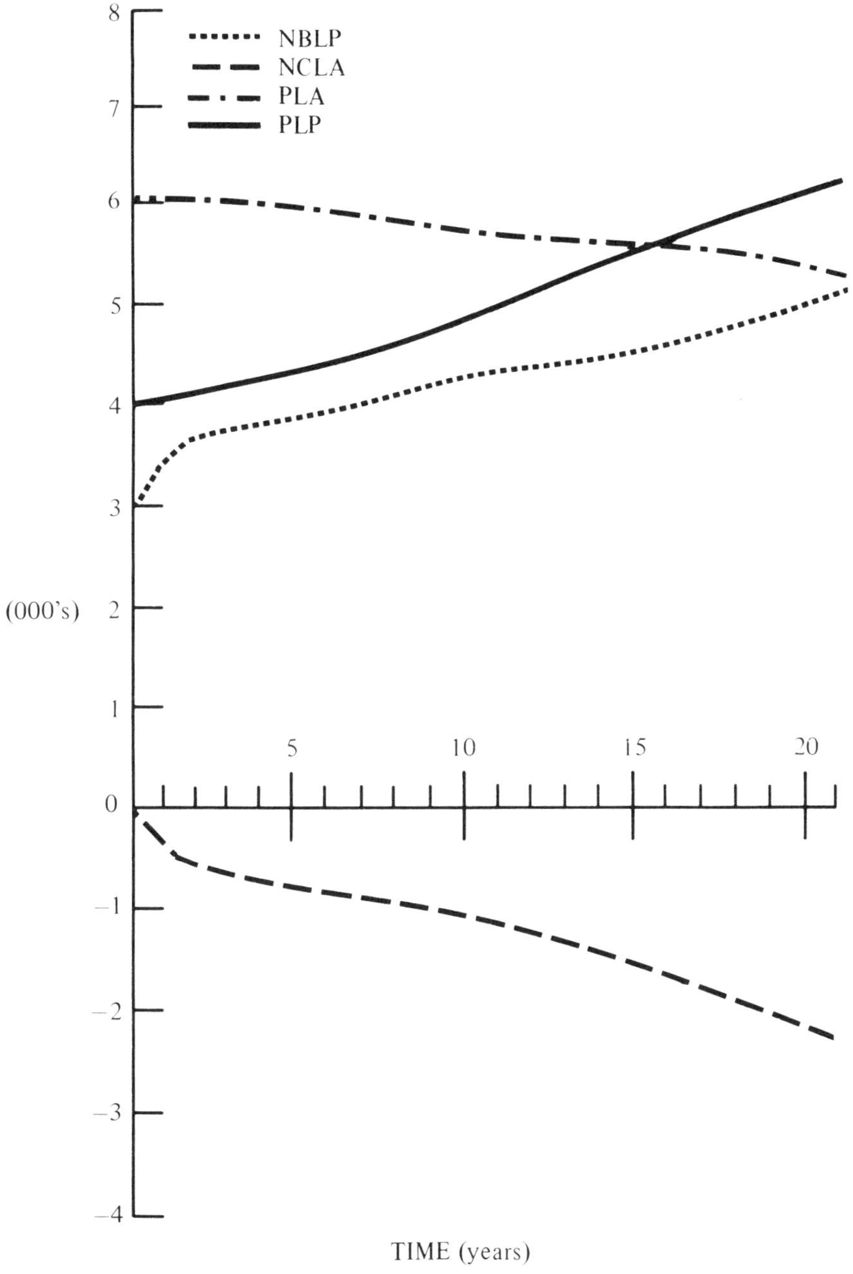

Figure 5-1. The Basic Model.

analysis by altering, systematically, the values of each parameter, many of which are now uncertain. This procedure will allow us to identify the parameters that influence key variables most significantly, and to determine the effect of changes in the values of parameters on the key variables. It will thus provide useful information about the effects of possible changes in parameter values.

To begin, we will subject the key variables of the model to plus and minus 10% and 25% changes in each of the parameter values, and summarize the results in Tables 5-3 through 5-6. We will then subject the key variables to some other plausible values of parameters outside this range.

In Chapter 6, each benefit-cost evaluation will be subjected to a range of values for each of the parameters found, in this chapter, to be crucial to an accurate assessment of the key variables of the model. In this manner, the amount of uncertainty present in the final evaluation of a project can be ascertained.

Sensitivity of Key Variables to a ±10% Change in Parameter Values

Table 5-3 is a summary of the results of varying, independently, each of the 14 constant parameters of the model by 10%. The sensitivity of key variables to changes in each parameter is measured by the values of the elasticity coefficients, which appear in columns 7, 10, 13, and 16.

Net costs, including opportunity loss, for a typical affluent family (columns 5 and 6) are completely insensitive (column 7) to all but five parameters: *NPPI, EØP, PNPEM, NSDA*, and *NPME*.[b] In addition, affluent net costs are relatively insensitive to changes in *NSDA* and *NPME*: they have elasticity coefficients of only .2, indicating an inelastic sensitivity of these key variables to 10% changes in affluent services forgone (*NSDA*) and in the proportion of affluent family income spent for education (*NPME*). Affluent net costs are most sensitive to changes in the rate of growth of progressive-sector productivity (*NPPI*) and to the inflation factor (*EØP*). These two variables have unitary elasticity coefficients; a 10% change in either of these two parameters will result in a 10% increase in net costs for a typical affluent family. The proportion of nonprogressive-sector employees employed in the municipality (*PNPEM*) has an elasticity coefficient of .63, indicating a modest (but inelastic) sensitivity of affluent net costs to a 10% change in its value.

[b]These parameters, defined in Chapters 3 and 4, are as follows: the normal growth in progressive-sector productivity (*NPPI*), an inflation factor (*EØP*), the percentage of nonprogressive workers of the municipality employed by the municipality (*PNPEM*), the percentage of services forgone by the affluent (*NSDA*), and the normal percentage of affluent income spent on education (*NPME*).

All other key variables of the model are even less sensitive to a 10% change in the value of each key parameter, as we see from columns 10, 13, and 16. Only the variable *NBLP* (net benefits for a typical poor family) is even modestly sensitive (column 13) to a 10% increase in progressive-sector productivity (*NPPI*) and inflation (*EØP*).

In Table 5-4, the results of varying each of the 14 parameters by −10% are summarized. They are very similar to those in Table 5-2, as we would suspect. The variable *NBLA* is sensitive (i.e., has a unitary elasticity) to a −10% change in productivity (*NPPI*) and inflation (*EØP*), and is somewhat less sensitive to the portion of income spent on education (*NPME*). All other key variables are completely insensitive to independent −10% changes to each of the 14 parameters.

Sensitivity of Key Variables to a ±25% Change in Parameter Values

Table 5-5 is a summary of the results of an independent 25% change in each of the 14 parameters of the model. Although there are a few minor changes in the elasticity coefficients when compared with the ±10% sensitivity analyses of Tables 5-3 and 5-4, the results remain quite similar. The parameters that were found to be most important in influencing key variables in Tables 5-3 and 5-4 are those found to be most influential in the 25% sensitivity analysis, as illustrated by a comparison of Tables 5-3 and 5-4 to Table 5-5.

Table 5-6 contains a summary of the results of the −25% sensitivity analysis. With minor exceptions, no change occurs from the 25% sensitivity analysis.

Sensitivity of Key Variables to Systematic Changes in the Values of the Two Tables

In order to complete the sensitivity analysis of all parameters, we must see just how sensitive the key variables of the model are to systematic changes in the values of the two tables—values given by equations (26, T) and (31, T) of Chapter 4. Although these functions are very difficult, if not impossible, to estimate accurately, we can determine their importance to key variables of the model, and come to a better qualitative understanding of their influence.

The results of the sensitivity analysis performed on each of the two table functions are summarized in Table 5-7. We see in Table 5-7 that in no case do the absolute values of the elasticity coefficients exceed .4, implying that

Table 5-3
Sensitivity of Key Variables to a +10% Change in Parameter Values

(1) No.	*(2)* Parameter	*(3)* Original Value	*(4)* New Value	*(5)* Original Time-20 NCLA	*(6)* New Time-20 NCLA	*(7)* Elasticity Coefficient	*(8)* Original Time-20 PLA	*(9)* New Time-20 PLA	*(10)* Elasticity Coefficient
1	*NPPI*	.031	.0341	\$ 2125	\$−2338	1.0	5396	5396	−.1
2	*EØP*	2.0	2.3	\$ 2125	\$−2339	1.0	5396	5363	0
3	*PNPEM*	.0537	.05907	\$−2125	\$−2284	.6	5396	5348	.1
4	*PPEM*	.0056	.00616	\$−2125	\$−2187	0	5396	5395	0
5	*NSDA*	−.06	−.066	\$−2125	\$−2180	.2	5396	5385	0
6	*AMD*	.50	.55	\$−2125	\$−2125	0	5396	5407	0
7	*DAHF*	11	12.1	\$−2125	\$−2124	0	5396	5396	0
8	*NPISP*	.10	.11	\$−2125	\$−2126	0	5396	5396	0
9	*PMD*	1.	1.1	\$−2125	\$−2125	0	5396	5396	0
10	*NMAAVH*	1000	1100	\$−2125	\$−2128	0	5396	5395	0
11	*NAVPH*	30	33	\$−2125	\$−2123	0	5396	5397	0
12	*NPPA*	.60	.60	\$−2125	\$−2128	0	5396	5395	0
13	*NPME*	.023	.023	\$−2125	\$−2180	.2	5396	5385	0
14	*PHFD*	11	11	\$−2125	\$−2125	0	5396	5396	0

(1) No.	(2) Parameter	(3) Original Value	(4) New Value	(11) Original Time-20 NBLP	(12) New Time-20 NBLP	(13) Elasticity Coefficient	(14) Original Time-20 PLP	(15) New Time-20 PLP	(16) Elasticity Coefficient
1	*NPPI*	.031	.0341	$5039	$5296	.4	6078	6138	.1
2	*EØP*	2.0	2.3	$5039	$5263	.5	6078	6139	.1
3	*PNPEM*	.0537	.05907	$5039	$5037	0	6078	6076	0
4	*PPEM*	.0056	.00616	$5039	$5039	0	6078	6078	0
5	*NSDA*	−.06	−.066	$5039	$5039	0	6078	6078	0
6	*AMD*	.50	.55	$5039	$5039	0	6078	6078	0
7	*DAHF*	11	12.1	$5039	$5039	0	6078	6078	0
8	*NPISP*	.10	.11	$5039	$5240	0	6078	6186	0
9	*PMD*	1.	1.1	$5039	$5239	0	6078	6069	0
10	*NMAAVH*	1000	1100	$5039	$5042	0	6078	6079	0
11	*NAVPH*	30	33	$5039	$5035	0	6078	6076	0
12	*NPPA*	.60	.60	$5039	$5042	0	6078	6079	0
13	*NPME*	.023	.023	$5039	$5039	0	6078	6078	0
14	*PHFD*	11	11	$5039	$5039	0	6078	6078	0

Table 5-4
Sensitivity of Key Variables to a −10% Change in Parameter Values

(1) No.	*(2)* Parameter	*(3)* Original Value	*(4)* New Value	*(5)* Original Time-20 NCLA	*(6)* New Time-20 NCLA	*(7)* Elasticity Coefficient	*(8)* Original Time-20 PLA	*(9)* New Time-20 PLA	*(10)* Elasticity Coefficient
1	*NPPI*	.031	.0279	$2125	−1932	1.0	5396	5427	.1
2	*EØP*	2.0	1.8	$2125	−1931	1.0	5396	6019	.1
3	*PNPEM*	.0537	.04833	$−2125	−1966	.7	5396	5445	.1
4	*PPEM*	.0056	.00504	$−2125	−2123	0	5396	5397	0
5	*NSDA*	−.06	−.054	$−2125	−2071	.2	5396	5407	0
6	*AMD*	.50	.45	$−2125	−2122	0	5396	5145	−.5
7	*DAHF*	11	9.9	$−2125	−2127	0	5396	5396	0
8	*NPISP*	.10	.09	$−2125	−2125	0	5396	5396	0
9	*PMD*	1.	.9	$−2125	−2125	0	5396	5396	0
10	*NMAAVH*	1000	900	$−2125	−2125	0	5396	5397	0
11	*NAVPH*	30	27	$−2125	−2128	0	5396	5395	0
12	*NPPA*	.60	.54	$−2125	−2122	0	5396	5397	0
13	*NPME*	.023	.0217	$−2125	−2095	.1	5396	5403	0
14	*PHFD*	11	9.9	$−2125	−2125	0	5396	5396	0

(1) No.	(2) Parameter	(3) Original Value	(4) New Value	(11 Original Time-20 NBLP	(12) New Time-20 NBLP	(13) Elasticity Coefficient	(14) Original Time-20 PLP	(15) New Time-20 PLP	(16) Elasticity Coefficient
1	*NPPI*	.031	.0279	$5039	4840	−.4	6078	6020	−.1
2	*EØP*	2.0	1.8	$5039	4836	−.4	6078	6019	−.1
3	*PNPEM*	.0537	.04833	$5039	5040	0	6078	6079	0
4	*PPEM*	.0056	.00504	$5039	5039	0	6078	6078	0
5	*NSDA*	−.06	−.054	$5039	5039	0	6078	6078	0
6	*AMD*	.50	.45	$5039	5035	0	6078	6078	0
7	*DAHF*	11	9.9	$5039	5039	0	6078	6078	0
8	*NPISP*	.10	.09	$5039	4836	−.4	6078	5069	−.2
9	*PMD*	1.	.9	$5039	5039	0	6078	6087	0
10	*NMAAVH*	1000	900	$5039	5034	0	6078	6075	0
11	*NAVPH*	30	27	$5039	5042	0	6078	6079	0
12	*NPPA*	.60	.54	$5039	5034	0	6078	6075	0
13	*NPME*	.023	.0217	$5039	5038	0	6078	6078	0
14	*PHFD*	11	9.9	$5039	5039	0	6078	6078	0

Table 5-5
Sensitivity of Key Variables to a +25% Change in Parameter Values

(1) No.	*(2)* Parameter	*(3)* Original Value	*(4)* New Value	*(5)* Original Time-20 NCLA	*(6)* New Time-20 NCLA	*(7)* Elasticity Coefficient	*(8)* Original Time-20 PLA	*(9)* New Time-20 PLA	*(10)* Elasticity Coefficient
1	*NPPI*	.031	.3875	$2125	$−2698	1.0	5396	5309	.1
2	*EØP*	2.0	2.5	$2125	$−2701	1.0	5396	5309	.1
3	*PNPEM*	.0537	.067125	$−2125	$−2523	.9	5396	5275	.1
4	*PPEM*	.0056	.0070	$−2125	$−2130	0	5396	5394	0
5	*NSDA*	−.06	.075	$−2125	$−2262	.3	5396	5368	0
6	*AMD*	.50	.6250	$−2125	$−2125	0	5396	5411	0
7	*DAHF*	11	13.75	$−2125	$−2123	0	5396	5397	0
8	*NPISP*	.10	.125	$−2125	$−2126	0	5306	5396	0
9	*PMD*	1	1.25	$−2125	$−2125	0	5396	5396	0
10	*NMAAVH*	1000	1.250	$−2125	$−2131	0	5396	5394	0
11	*NAVPH*	30	37.5	$−2125	$−2118	0	5396	5398	0
12	*NPPA*	.60	.75	$−2125	$−2131	0	5396	5394	0
13	*NPME*	.023	.02875	$−2125	$−2262	.3	5396	5368	0
14	*PHFD*	11	13.75	$−2125	$−2126	0	5396	5396	0

(1) No.	(2) Parameter	(3) Original Value	(4) New Value	(11) Original Time-20 NBLP	(12) New Time-20 NBLP	(13) Elasticity Coefficient	(14) Original Time-20 PLP	(15) New Time-20 PLP	(16) Elasticity Coefficient
1	*NPPI*	.031	.3875	$5039	$5626	.5	6078	6218	.1
2	*EØP*	2.0	2.5	$5039	5645	.5	6078	6221	.1
3	*PNPEM*	.0537	.067125	$5039	5034	0	6078	6073	0
4	*PPEM*	.0056	.0070	$5039	5038	0	6078	6078	0
5	*NSDA*	−.06	.075	$5039	5039	0	6078	6078	0
6	*AMD*	.50	.6250	$5039	5038	0	6078	6075	0
7	*DAHF*	11	13.75	$5039	5039	0	6078	6078	0
8	*NPISP*	.10	.125	$5039	5541	0	6078	6029	.2
9	*PMD*	1.	1.25	$5039	5040	0	6078	6055	0
10	*NMAAVH*	1000	1.250	$5039	5046	0	6078	6082	0
11	*NAVPH*	10	37.5	$5039	5029	0	6078	6073	0
12	*NPPA*	.60	.75	$5039	5046	0	6078	6082	0
13	*NPME*	.023	.02875	$5039	5039	0	6078	6078	0
14	*PHFD*	11	13.75	$5039	5039	0	6078	6078	0

Table 5-6
Sensitivity of Key Variables to a −25% Change in Parameter Values

(1) No.	(2) Parameter	(3) Original Value	(4) New Value	(5) Original Time-20 NCLA	(6) New Time-20 NCLA	(7) Elasticity Coefficient	(8) Original Time-20 PLA	(9) New Time-20 PLA	(10) Elasticity Coefficient
1	*NPPI*	.031	.02325	$2125	−1674	.9	5396	5470	0
2	*EØP*	2.0	1.50	$2125	−1672	.9	5396	5470	0
3	*PMPEM*	.0537	.040275	$−2125	−1728	.4	5396	5518	0
4	*PPEM*	.0056	.0042	$−2125	−2120	0	5396	5398	0
5	*NSDA*	−.06	−.045	$−2125	−1989	.2	5396	5424	0
6	*AMD*	.50		$−2125				5396	
7	*DAHF*	11	8.25	$−2125	−2130	0	5396	5396	0
8	*NPISP*	.10	.0875	$−2125	−2125	0	5396	5396	0
9	*PMD*	1	.75	$−2125	−2125	0	5396	5396	0
10	*NMAAVH*	1000	750	$−2125	−2116	0	5396	5399	0
11	*NAVPH*	30	22.5	$−2125	−2132	0	5396	5394	0
12	*NPPA*	.60	.45	$−2125	−2116	0	5396	5399	0
13	*NPME*	.023	.01725	$−2125	−1989	.2	5396	5424	0
14	*PHFD*	1.1	8.25	$−2125	−2125	0	5396	5396	0

(1) No.	(2) Parameter	(3) Original Value	(4) New Value	(11) Original Time-20 NBLP	(12) New Time-20 NBLP	(13) Elasticity Coefficient	(14) Original Time-20 PLP	(15) New Time-20 PLP	(16) Elasticity Coefficient
1	*NPPI*	.031	.02325	$5039	4576	−.4	6078	5941	−.1
2	*EØP*	2.0	1.50	$5039	4567	−.4	6078	5939	−.1
3	*PNPEM*	.0537	.040275	$5039	5043	0	6078	6082	0
4	*PPEM*	.0056	.0042	$5039	5039	0	6078	6078	0
5	*NSDA*	−.06	−.045	$5039	5038	0	6078	6077	0
6	*AMD*	.50		$5039			6078		
7	*DAHF*	11	8.25	$5039	5038	0	6078	6078	0
8	*NPISP*	.10	.0875	$5039	4785	−.1	6078	5941	−.1
9	*PMD*	1	.75	$5039	5037	0	6078	6100	0
10	*NMAAVH*	1000	750	$5039	5026	0	6078	6071	0
11	*NAVPH*	30	22.5	$5039	5047	0	6078	6083	0
12	*NPPA*	.60	.45	$5039	5026	0	6078	6071	0
13	*NPME*	.023	.01725	$5039	5038	0	6078	6077	0
14	*PHFD*	1.1	8.25	$5039	5039	0	6078	6077	0

Table 5-7
Sensitivity of Key Variables to ± 10% and ± 25% in Table Values.

(1) No.	*(2)* Percent Change	*(3)* Table		*(4)* Original Values	*(5)* New Values
1	−10	*PADAT*	=	−300/−150/0/150/300	−270/−135/0/135/270
2	+10	*PADAT*	=	−300/−150/0/150/300	−3301/−165/0/165/300
3	−25	*PADAT*	=	−300/−150/0/150/300	−225/−112.5/0/112.5/225
4	+25	*PADAT*	=	−300/150/0/150/300	−375/−187.5/0/187.5/375
5	−10	*PADPT*	=	−100/150/200	−90/135/180
6	+10	*PADPT*	=	−100/150/200	−110/165/220
7	−25	*PADPT*	=	−100/150/200	−75/112.5/150
8	+25	*PADPT*	=	−100/150/200	−125/187.5/250

(1) No.	*(2)* Percent Change	*(3)* Table		*(4)* Original Values	*(5)* New Values
1	−10	*PADAT*	=	−300/−150/0/150/300	−270/−135/0/135/270
2	+10	*PADAT*	=	−300/−150/0/150/300	−3301/−165/0/165/300
3	−25	*PADAT*	=	−300/−150/0/150/300	−225/−112.5/0/112.5/225
4	+25	*PADAT*	=	−300/150/0/150/300	−375/−187.5/0/187.5/375
5	−10	*PADPT*	=	−100/150/200	−90/135/180
6	+10	*PADPT*	=	−100/150/200	−110/165/220
7	−25	*PADPT*	=	−100/150/200	−75/112.5/150
8	+25	*PADPT*	=	−100/150/200	−125/187.5/250

the key variables of the model are relatively *insensitive* to systematic changes in the table functions. A logical inference from this fact is that only rough estimates of the values of these functions are necessary for us to proceed with confidence in our model. Unfortunately, we don't have even *rough* estimates for these values at this time.

Sensitivity of Key Variables to Other Plausible Parameter Values

Although we assume nonprogressive-sector productivity growth (*NPINPS*) to be zero, sporadic increases in productivity are indeed possible, and probable, in these activities. I have, therefore, subjected the model to two additional values for *NPINPS*, .5% and 1.0%, to observe the

(6) Original Time-20 NCLA	(7) New Time-20 NCLA	(8) Elasticity Coefficient	(9) Original Time-20 PLA	(10) New Time-20 PLA	(11) Elasticity Coefficient
$-2125	$-2122	0	5396	5457	−.1
−2125	−2128	0	5396	5336	.1
−2125	−2178	.1	5396	5548	−.1
−2125	−2133	0	5396	5244	.1
−2125	−2125	0	5396	5396	0
−2125	−2126	0	5396	5396	0
−2125	−2125	0	5396	5396	0
−2125	−2126	0	5396	5396	0

(12) Original Time-20 NBLP	(13) New Time-20 NBLP	(14) Elasticity Coefficient	(15) Original Time-20 PLP	(16) New Time-20 PLP	(17) Elasticity Coefficient
5038	5036	0	6077	6077	0
5038	5041	0	6077	6078	0
5038	5033	0	6077	6077	0
5038	5044	0	6077	6078	0
5038	5051	0	6077	5872	.3
5038	5027	0	6077	6283	.4
5038	5069	0	6077	5562	.4
5038	5010	0	6077	6590	.4

dynamic effects of these plausible values on the key variables of the model. The results are illustrated in Tables 5-8 and 5-9.

To determine just how sensitive the model is to increases in nonprogressive-sector productivity, we must compare the results shown in Tables 5-8 and 5-9 with the basic model (i.e., with Table 5-1) at time 20. Since the affluent bear most of the municipal costs, any increase in nonprogressive-sector productivity must result in a saving for the affluent, and this is borne out in column 2 of Tables 5-8 and 5-9. The .5% productivity growth results in an annual reduction of $140 in costs to the affluent at time 20 when compared to the basic model; the 1.0% growth rate, shown in Table 5-9, results in a $378 cost reduction for the affluent in year 20. The major results of these new plausible values is to reduce departures of the affluent; 22 fewer families depart with the .5% productivity rate, while 44 fewer depart with the 1.0% rate.

Table 5-8
Sensitivity of Key Variables to .5% Annual Growth of Nonprogressive-Sector Productivity

(1) Time E+00	(2) NCLA E+00	(3) NBLP E+00	(4) TNCLA E+06	(5) TNBLP E+06	(6) PLA E+00	(7) PLP E+00
.0	.0	3000.0	.000	12.000	6000.0	4000.0
1.	−13.8	3720.0	−.083	15.066	6000.0	4050.0
2.	−565.9	3748.4	−3.396	15.368	6000.0	4100.0
3.	−611.9	3794.2	−3.671	15.882	5999.2	4186.0
4.	−660.5	3842.0	−3.941	16.419	5966.0	4273.4
5.	−712.5	3892.3	−4.248	16.982	5962.5	4363.1
6.	−767.1	3944.4	−4.546	17.573	5926.4	4455.2
7.	−825.1	3999.3	−4.884	18.196	5919.7	4549.8
8.	−886.4	4056.3	−5.213	18.850	5880.4	4647.0
9.	−951.6	4116.3	−5.586	19.540	5870.2	4747.0
10.	−1020.5	4178.6	−5.947	20.266	5872.2	4849.6
11.	−1093.7	4244.2	−6.358	21.033	5813.1	4955.6
12.	−1171.1	4312.3	−6.752	21.840	5766.0	5064.6
13.	−1253.3	4384.0	−7.203	22.695	5747.5	5176.8
14.	−1340.3	4458.4	−7.634	23.596	5695.7	5292.4
15.	−1432.8	4536.8	−8.127	24.551	5672.3	5411.6
16.	−1530.5	4618.2	−8.594	25.559	5615.3	5534.5
17.	−1634.6	4703.8	−9.131	26.630	5586.3	5661.3
18.	−1744.6	4792.8	−9.636	27.761	5523.4	5792.3
19.	−1861.8	4886.4	−10.218	28.964	5488.2	5927.4
20.	−1985.7	4983.5	−10.760	30.236	5418.8	6067.1

It was shown previously (in Tables 5-3 through 5-7) that the model is relatively insensitive to changes in the assessed-valuation parameters *NMAAVH* and *NAVPH*. We now equalize these two valuation parameters at $500 to observe the impact of this possible policy move on the key variables. The results are shown in Table 5-10.

Equalizing assessed valuations for the affluent and poor results, as we would expect, in a sharp reduction in both the rate of poor arrivals and the rate of affluent departures. Annual costs for a typical affluent family decrease by $575 at time 20, while annual costs for a typical poor family increase (i.e., net benefits are reduced) by approximately $800. Affluent *departures* are reduced at time 20 by 184, while poor arrivals are reduced by 420.

Sensitivity of the Model to Municipal Expenditures

In equation (12,L) of Chapter 4, we assumed that the sole reason for increases in municipal expenditures was employee-wage increases. This certainly simplified the municipal-expenditure equation, but it also gave

Table 5-9
Sensitivity of Key Variables to 1.0% Annual Growth of Nonprogressive-Sector Productivity

(1) Time E+00	(2) NCLA E+00	(3) NBLP E+00	(4) TNBCLA E+06	(5) TNBCLP E+06	(6) PLA E+00	(7) PLP E+00
.0	.0	3000.0	.000	12.000	6000.0	4000.0
1.	−13.8	3720.0	−.083	15.066	6000.0	4050.0
2.	−565.9	3748.4	−3.396	15.368	6000.0	4100.0
3.	−609.3	3794.1	−3.655	15.882	5999.2	4186.0
4.	−654.9	3841.6	−3.907	16.417	5966.0	4273.4
5.	−703.6	3891.3	−4.195	16.978	5962.6	4363.1
6.	−754.5	3942.7	−4.472	17.566	5926.7	4455.2
7.	−808.4	3996.6	−4.786	18.184	5920.4	4549.8
8.	−865.2	4052.4	−5.089	18.831	5881.5	4646.9
9.	−925.4	4110.8	−5.434	19.513	5871.9	4746.7
10.	−988.7	4171.1	−5.764	20.227	5829.6	4849.3
11.	−1055.8	4234.4	−6.141	20.981	5816.4	4054.9
12.	−1126.5	4299.9	−6.500	21.772	5770.2	5063.4
13.	−1201.3	4368.5	−6.911	22.608	5753.0	5175.1
14.	−1280.1	4439.4	−7.300	23.485	5702.6	5290.1
15.	−1363.6	4513.7	−7.747	24.413	5630.9	5408.6
16.	−1451.6	4590.6	−8.166	25.388	5625.8	5530.5
17.	−1544.8	4671.1	−8.650	26.421	5599.1	5656.2
18.	−1643.0	4754.3	−9.100	27.507	5538.7	5785.7
19.	−1747.1	4841.6	−9.620	28.659	5506.4	5919.3
20.	−1856.8	4931.7	−10.101	29.871	5440.1	6057.0

prime emphasis to unbalanced productivity growth as an explanation of the fiscal pressures experienced by central cities. This significant source of pressure has been ignored totally by Campbell and Sacks. Their regression results [30, p. 51] indicate that six independent variables (density, percent urban, per capita income, per capita state aid, per capita federal aid, and local-expenditures assignment) explain to a high degree (R = .956 and R^2 = .914) the level and variation of per capita local expenditures. Although the predictive power of this multiple-regression equation may be high, it certainly does not indicate cause and effect.

We must admit, however, that equation (12,L) of Chapter 4 is incomplete. The most significant omission is a variable relating income and expenditures explicitly. Various estimates of income elasticity of demand for state and local services appear in the literature. Fuchs estimated [63, p. 42] an income elasticity of state and local expenditures of 1.07 for 1942-1957. Fabricant [54, p. 125] estimated an income elasticity for state and local expenditures of .92 for 1942. Campbell and Sacks [30, p. 52] have estimated an income elasticity of .606 for local expenditures for the year 1962.

Although estimates of income elasticity may attribute too much ex-

Table 5-10
Sensitivity of Key Variables to an Assessed-Value Ratio of 1.0

Time E+00	*NCLA* E+00	*NBLP* E+00	*TNCLA* E+06	*TNBLP* E+06	*PLA* E+00	*PLP* E+00
.0	.0	3000.0	.0	12.000	6000.0	4000.0
1.	−13.8	3720.0	−82.8	15.066	6000.0	4050.0
2.	−357.9	3436.6	−2147.3	14.090	6000.0	4100.0
3.	−394.2	3464.5	−2364.8	14.502	5999.2	4186.0
4.	−433.2	3494.5	−2589.9	14.879	5978.5	4257.8
5.	−474.8	3525.8	−2837.5	15.270	5975.5	4331.0
6.	−518.9	3558.2	−3088.7	15.677	5952.5	4405.8
7.	−566.0	3592.8	−3366.2	16.103	5947.0	4482.1
8.	−616.0	3628.5	−3647.5	16.546	5921.4	4560.0
9.	−669.5	3666.6	−3958.7	17.011	5913.1	4639.6
10.	−726.2	3705.9	−4273.1	17.496	5884.4	4721.0
11.	−786.9	3748.0	−4621.6	18.007	5872.9	4804.3
12.	−851.3	3791.5	−4972.5	18.539	5840.9	4889.6
13.	−920.4	3838.0	−5361.8	19.102	5825.7	4977.0
14.	−993.6	3886.2	−5752.7	19.690	5789.8	5066.6
15.	−1072.2	3937.8	−6186.8	20.313	5770.4	5158.5
16.	−1155.5	3991.1	−6621.2	20.965	5730.2	5252.8
17.	−1245.0	4048.4	−7103.9	21.658	5706.1	5349.7
18.	−1339.9	4107.7	−7585.2	22.384	5660.8	5449.3
19.	−1442.0	4171.5	−8120.4	23.159	5631.4	5551.7
20.	−1550.4	4237.6	−8651.8	23.972	5580.4	5657.1

planatory power to the income variable, our form of the municipal-expenditure equation is likely to attribute too much explanatory power to unbalanced productivity growth. Therefore, it might seem prudent to create another variant of the basic model which includes the highest income-elasticity estimate (i.e., the 1.07 estimated by Fuchs) to run side-by-side with the first basic model.[c] The only change in the basic model necessary to accomplish this is a modification to equation (12,L) of Chapter 4, which was

$$MC.K = MC.J + DT * MECI.JK \qquad (12,L)$$

and now becomes

$$MC.K = MC.J + DT * (MECI.JK + IRE.JK) \qquad (12,L)$$

where *IRE.JK* represents the income-related expenditures of the municipality. Income-related expenditures are given by

[c]The original treatment is, however, supported by the strong presumption that expenditure increases that arise from increasing costs of supplying the same quantity and quality of municipal services will be less acceptable to existing citizens than expenditure increases that arise from more and better municipal services. Expenditures of the latter category are likely to accompany increasing municipal income levels, and are not as likely to trigger cumulative departures of citizens from the municipality as are expenditure increases for the same services.

Table 5-11
The Second Basic Model

Time E+00	*NCLA* E+00	*NBLP* E+00	*PLA* E+00	*PLP* E+00
.0	.0	3000.0	6000.0	4000.0
1.	−13.8	3000.0	6000.0	4050.0
2.	−565.9	3028.4	6000.0	4100.0
3.	−645.5	3073.4	5999.2	4150.0
4.	−729.9	3120.7	5966.0	4201.4
5.	−819.6	3170.6	5960.4	4255.1
6.	−914.3	3223.0	5922.2	4311.1
7.	−1014.5	3278.5	5911.3	4369.6
8.	−1120.9	3336.6	5867.4	4430.8
9.	−1233.6	3398.2	5850.4	4494.7
10.	−1353.2	3462.8	5800.1	4561.5
11.	−1480.0	3531.4	5776.4	4631.4
12.	−1614.7	3603.2	5718.9	4704.6
13.	−1757.7	3679.4	5687.6	4781.1
14.	−1909.5	3759.3	5622.1	4861.3
15.	−2070.9	3844.1	5582.1	4945.3
16.	−2242.3	3933.0	5507.5	5033.2
17.	−2424.6	4027.4	5457.8	5125.4
18.	−2618.4	4126.4	5372.9	5222.1
19.	−2824.7	4231.6	5312.4	5323.5
20.	−3044.1	4341.7	5215.8	5429.8

$$IRE.KL = \{(WSLM.K - WSLM.J)/[(WSLM.K + WSLM.J)/2]\} * K * (WSLM.K - WSLM.J) \qquad (36,R)$$

where $(WSLM.K - WSLM.J)$ = the annual change in municipal income

K = the income elasticity of municipal expenditures

In words, equation (36,R) states that income-related municipal expenditures increase as a function of the relative change in income $\{(WSLM.K - WSLM.J)/[(WSLM.K + WSLM.J/2)]\}$ multiplied by the income elasticity of expenditures (K) and the annual change in income ($WSLM.K$ − WSLM.J). We assume K to equal 1.07, which is Fuchs's estimate of the income elasticity of municipal expenditures.

The results for this *second* basic model appear in Table 5-11. At time 20 in this new basic model, costs increase above the original level for both typical affluent and typical poor families. This is the result of the additional municipal expenditures now assumed to be incurred by the municipality. Costs rise by approximately $900 for a typical affluent family and $700 for a typical poor family. The cost increase for the poor results partly from increased affluent family departures and partly from the generally increased level of expenditures.

It is possible to conduct benefit-cost evaluations using two or more basic models in turn. In order not to complicate the analysis further, we will employ only the first of the preceding models in the next chapter.

Summary of Results

The extensive sensitivity analysis of this chapter has identified the parameters to which the model is most sensitive. These parameters, changes in whose values cause significant changes in the behavior of the model, are the following:

1. *NPIPS*—normal productivity growth in the progressive sector.
2. *EØP*—earnings over productivity.
3. *PNPEM*—the percentage of nonprogressive-sector employees employed by the central city.
4. *NSDA*—the opportunity loss in services experienced by affluent families in central cities.
5. *NPME*—the normal percentage of affluent income allocated to education.

The parameters *EØP* and *NPIPS* were shown to have unitary elasticity coefficients for the key variable *NCLA*. They are, therefore, the most sensitive parameters.

We are indeed fortunate to have an abundance of data to approximate these two most crucial parameters. The average value of *NPIPS*, over a long period of time, is likely to be close to 3.1%. Time series data necessary to estimate an average value of *EØP* are quite accessible for any given economy. Therefore, the most sensitive parameters are just those for which we have the best data!

The model was found to be relatively sensitive to the parameter *PNPEM*, although its elasticity coefficient never reached unity. It is very difficult to arrive at one estimate for this parameter; cities differ significantly in the kinds of services provided, and in the distribution of responsibility for providing these services between them and their state governments. Data, however, should be available for most cities to estimate this parameter closely. For example, detailed data concerning city employment are provided by the Bureau of the Census [151]. Because of the obvious importance of this parameter, we will subject the results of our benefit-cost analysis to a range of plausible values for this parameter.

The key variables of the model were shown to be far less sensitive to changes in *NSDA* and *NPME*, although their elasticity coefficients were shown to be positive (but under .5) for some key variables. Since we do not have extensive data on these parameters, we must subject all our evaluations to many plausible values for these parameters.

Fortunately, the discounting process of benefit-cost analysis reduces all elasticity coefficients even further, making the inelastic coefficients for these last two parameters even more inelastic. The difference between key variables of the basic model and key variables of any modified model will be narrower after discounting than before; the higher the discount rate, the narrower the difference.[d] The impact on net-present values of small errors in estimates of *NSDA* and *NPME* is, therefore, likely to be very small.

Although variations in the values of the two tables and in the parameters representing movement delays (i.e., *AMD* and *PMD*) were found to have only a slight effect on key variables of the model, no knowledge is available regarding even approximate values for such table functions and parameters. We have only one recourse for the selection of such values that seems reasonable; we must let the model tell us what values are indeed realistic. This can be done only by finding values that are capable of producing the historical behavior experienced in reality. Fortunately, even large errors in these values are not likely to influence discounted values significantly.

Unlike changes in parameters of the model, alterations to the form of certain equations are likely to generate major absolute alterations in the values of key variables. This was observed in the last section when we altered the equation for municipal costs. When equation forms are not known fully, we must create separate models with these alternative equation forms. New projects should be evaluated as they influence each model before a project is selected for implementation.

We now turn to the procedure for dynamic benefit-cost analysis, and use the results of this chapter to deal with the uncertainty that is likely to characterize the evaluation of projects that affect complex systems.

---

[d]For example, a $1,000 difference at year 20 between the value of a key variable in the basic model and its value in the modified model, when discounted at an interest rate of 10%, is only $149.

6 Dynamic Benefit-Cost Analysis

This chapter describes a comparative-dynamic procedure for benefit-cost analysis in models of complex nonlinear social systems. The partial urban model described in Chapters 3 and 4 and analyzed in Chapter 5 is an example of such a model; it will be used in this chapter to illustrate the procedure.

The procedure will be illustrated by examining the incremental effects of four independent hypothetical projects on the dynamic time path of the urban system. The discounted present value of net benefits will be the criterion utilized to evaluate the desirability of each project.

Because much uncertainty remains about the validity of the relationships of the model, we will subject each benefit-cost evaluation to *cumulative* changes in the five parameters whose values were identified as crucial to the values of key variables. If the recommendations produced by the system are invariant to *worst-case* cumulative values of these crucial parameters, we may be more confident of the validity of the benefit-cost evaluations, i.e., uncertainty in estimates of benefits and costs will be reduced.

Finally, we will present a summary indicating the likely success (using a benefit-cost criterion) of each proposed project under alternative assumptions about the real world. This summary will be the ultimate output of the analysis, and will constitute our basis for decision making in the public domain.

Dynamic Benefit-Cost Analysis: An Introduction

As we saw in Chapter 5, the dynamic time path of the basic model produces its own fluctuating net benefits for each typical group over the 20-year period. We must consider this time path of net benefits when evaluating new projects that influence the basic system, in order to determine the discounted net benefits of proposed projects properly.

The time path of net benefits for the existing system is ignored by static benefit-cost analysis. Although secondary or induced effects are often included in static analysis, they are considered normally as though the system existing at time zero (i.e., at the time of the benefit-cost calculation) is stable, rather than unstable. The static procedure will produce adequate results only when the interdependent relationships of the problem area produce a time-invariant (approximately) system state, or when the dynamic time path of the problem area is understood so well that the dynamic effects of proposed (i.e., superimposed) projects can be evaluated properly.

The correct procedure for benefit-cost analysis in cases that involve complex dynamic effects is (1) to identify the dynamic relationships and (2) to compare the dynamic net benefits produced by the modified model with the net benefits produced by a basic model. The comparative-dynamic procedure operates in exactly that way. It is illustrated here in the evaluation of four independent projects, each of which modified the basic system by affecting its established dynamic relationships.

For each program, we will measure net benefits separately for the following *three* typical groups over a 25-year period:

1. The affluent families residing in the municipality at a given moment in time.
2. The poor families residing in the municipality at a given moment in time.
3. The affluent families that resided in this municipality formerly, but now reside in its suburbs.

Since we assumed in Chapter 3 that the filtering process takes 11 years, the affluent who depart are assumed to continue to bear some costs over at least part of the 11-year period. These costs are simply the property taxes (*MCA.K*) on the excess of the total stock of affluent housing (*AH.K*) over the portion of that stock occupied at present by affluent families (*HPLA.K*). The variable *HPLA.K* is equal to the number of affluent families who reside in the municipality (*PLA.K*). The costs incurred by affluent families who depart are given by

$$MCEA.K = (AH.K - HPLA.K) * MCA.K \qquad (37,A)$$

Finally, annual net benefits are discounted at a social discount rate of 10% in each of the programs to be evaluated. The appropriateness of this rate will be discussed in Chapter 7. For now, it is used simply to illustrate the basic procedure.

Project No. 1: A Municipal Productivity Program

The first program is a municipal productivity-improvement program in which a 1% annual productivity gain, measured as a 1% reduction in municipal costs (i.e., $32,890 in year 1), is instituted at an annual incremental cost of $45,000 per year.[a] The program is assumed to be financed by

[a]This could result, for example, from a program of computerization of certain municipal

municipal revenue. The annual monetary value of the improvement in productivity is computed as follows:

$$MPIP.K = MPI * MC.K * CLIP(SWT1, TIME.K) \quad (38,A)$$

where MPI = the percentage cost reduction that results from the productivity program

$MC.K$ = the level of municipal costs at time K

$CLIP$ = a DYNAMO function that attaches the program to the basic model at a specified point in time

$SWT1$ = the time at which the program is to be attached to the basic model (i.e., year 1)

$TIME.K$ = a variable that simply counts time and attaches this program at the proper time

As stated above, the program is assumed to result in an annual reduction of municipal costs of 1% (i.e., $MPI = .01$). Annual program costs are assumed to be given by

$$MCPI.K = MCCP * CLIP(SWT1, TIME.K) \quad (38.1,A)$$

where $MCCP$ is the annual level of costs incurred as a result of this program.

The municipal cost reduction ($MPIP$) that results from equation (38,A) is subtracted from municipal costs. The annual costs of the program ($MCPI$) are added to municipal costs. The equation for municipal costs now becomes

$$MC.K = MC.J + DT * (MECI.JK + MCPI.J - MPIP.J) \quad (10,L)$$

The results of the municipal productivity program are illustrated in Table 6-1 and Figure 6-1; the benefit-cost evaluation appears in Table 6-3. To facilitate comparison of the modified model with the basic model, the basic model is reproduced, but this time for a 25-year period, in Table 6-2.

Just as one would expect, Table 6-3, which is a comparison of Tables 6-1 and 6-2, indicates that incremental benefits are obtained primarily by the affluent. The incremental benefits, however, are sufficient to induce only nine additional affluent families to remain over the 25-year period. There are only slight benefits for the poor. Total annual costs (column 9 in Table

---

functions that increases average output per man of municipal employees by 1% per year. The costs of such a program are assumed to grow at $45,000 per year, which might reflect an increasing commitment to computerization of municipal functions.

This formulation of the productivity program assumes that it is in effect for the entire 25-year period. This assumption, however, is only a convenient one; the program could be eliminated or reduced in any year. Therefore, this approach to dynamic benefit-cost analysis allows us considerable flexibility in devising programs.

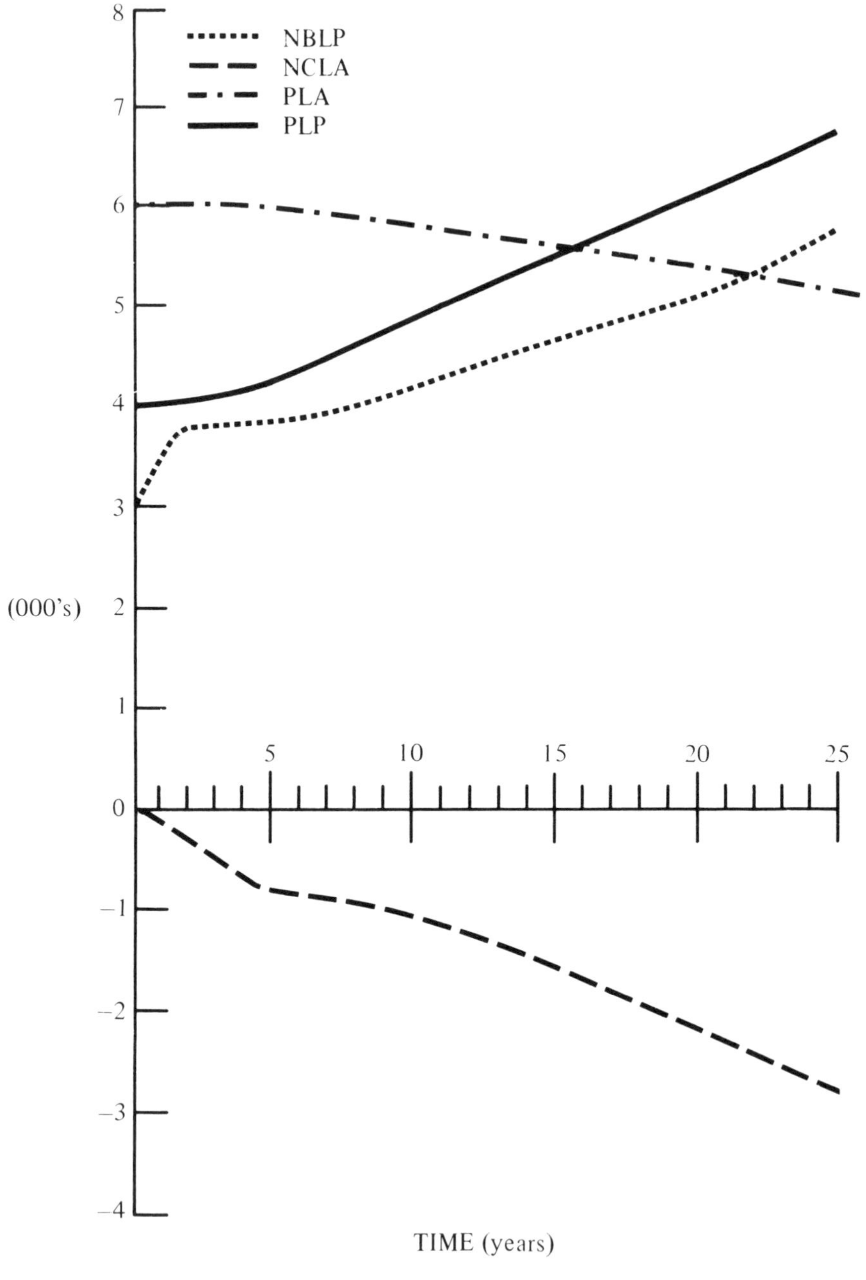

Figure 6-1. The Basic Model Modified by the Municipal Productivity Program.

Table 6-1
The Basic Model Modified by the Municipal Productivity Program

(1) *Time* *E+00*	*(2)* *NCLA* E+00	*(3)* *NBLP* E+00	*(4)* *TNCLA* E+06	*(5)* *TNBLP* E+06	*(6)* *PLA* E+00	*(7)* *PLP* E+00	*(8)* *MCEA* E+03
.0	.0	3000.0	.000	12.000	6000.0	4000.0	.0
1.	-13.8	3720.0	−.083	15.066	6000.0	4050.0	.0
2.	−565.9	3748.4	−3.396	15.368	6000.0	4100.0	.0
3.	−614.5	3794.3	−3.687	15.883	5999.2	4186.0	.5
4.	−667.8	3842.4	−3.984	16.420	5966.0	4273.4	19.9
5.	−724.4	3893.1	−4.319	16.986	5962.3	4363.1	23.5
6.	−783.7	3946.0	−4.644	17.580	5926.0	4455.2	49.1
7.	−846.5	4001.9	−5.010	18.208	5918.8	4549.9	57.1
8.	−912.6	4060.2	−5.365	18.869	5878.9	4647.2	90.4
9.	−982.6	4121.9	−5.766	19.568	5868.0	4747.3	104.5
10.	−1056.5	4186.2	−6.153	20.304	5824.2	4850.3	147.6
11.	−1134.9	4254.2	−6.593	21.085	5809.1	4956.4	169.9
12.	−1217.6	4325.1	−7.014	21.910	5760.8	5065.7	225.5
13.	−1305.5	4400.1	−7.495	22.786	5741.0	5178.4	258.7
14.	−1398.3	4478.3	−7.953	23.711	5687.7	5294.6	330.3
15.	−1497.0	4561.1	−8.477	24.697	5662.6	5414.7	377.8
16.	−1601.3	4647.4	−8.974	25.740	5603.8	5538.6	469.8
17.	−1712.4	4738.6	−9.543	26.852	5572.8	5666.6	536.2
18.	−1829.9	4833.8	−10.079	28.031	5507.7	5799.0	654.2
19.	−1955.2	4934.4	−10.695	29.290	5470.1	5935.9	745.4
20.	−2087.9	5039.4	−11.270	30.628	5397.9	6077.6	896.5
21.	−2229.4	5150.4	−11.933	32.058	5352.8	6224.3	1020.1
22.	−2379.5	5266.2	−12.546	33.570	5272.7	6374.7	1213.5
23.	−2539.7	5388.6	−13.255	35.167	5219.0	6526.2	1379.3
24.	−2709.8	5516.3	−13.901	36.842	5129.9	6678.9	1626.8
25.	−2891.7	5651.4	−14.651	38.615	5066.6	6832.8	1847.4

6-3) increase from $9,973 in year 4 to $27,033 in year 8, and then decrease until year 13, when benefits begin. Total annual benefits increase from $13,548 in year 13 to $563,345 at year 25. The present value of the net-benefit stream at a social discount rate of 10% is $408,840. Hence the program does pass our benefit-cost test. The internal rate of return (i.e., the rate of return equating the present value of the cash flows to zero) is approximately 24%.

Although this productivity program produces a very high net-present value, it fails to reverse the population movement of the affluent—it simply delays departures for a short time. Other projects may be designed, possibly at the same cost, that reverse the deterioration process, thereby producing a higher return. If we operate in a world of relatively fixed capital budgets (as is most often the case), we must consider not only the acceptability of a project, but the opportunities forgone as a result of passing up other public projects.

Table 6-2
The Basic Model for 25 Years

(1) *Time* *E+00*	*(2)* *NCLA* E+00	*(3)* *NBLP* E+00	*(4)* *TNCLA* E+06	*(5)* *TNBLP* E+06	*(6)* *PLA* E+00	*(7)* *PLP* E+00	*(8)* *MCEA* E+03
.0	.0	3000.0	.000	12.000	6000.0	4000.0	.0
1.	−13.8	3720.0	−.083	15.066	6000.0	4050.0	.0
2.	−565.9	3748.4	−3.396	15.368	6000.0	4100.0	.0
3.	−614.5	3794.3	−3.687	15.883	5999.2	4186.0	.5
4.	−662.2	3842.4	−3.974	16.420	5966.0	4273.4	19.9
5.	−721.4	3893.2	−4.301	16.986	5962.3	4363.1	23.4
6.	−779.8	3946.1	−4.621	17.581	5926.1	4455.2	48.7
7.	−842.1	4002.0	−4.985	18.209	5919.0	4549.9	56.7
8.	−908.2	4060.3	−5.339	18.869	5879.3	4647.2	89.7
9.	−978.7	4122.0	−5.743	19.568	5868.5	4747.3	103.8
10.	−1053.3	4186.3	−6.135	20.305	5824.8	5850.3	146.8
11.	−1133.0	4254.2	−6.583	21.086	5809.7	4956.4	169.3
12.	−1217.6	4325.1	−7.015	21.901	5761.6	5065.7	225.3
13.	−1307.9	4400.0	−7.509	22.785	5741.8	5178.4	259.1
14.	−1403.6	4478.2	−7.985	23.711	5688.5	5294.7	332.0
15.	−1505.9	4560.8	−8.529	24.695	5663.3	5414.7	381.1
16.	−1614.5	4647.0	−9.048	25.738	5604.3	5538.6	475.8
17.	−1730.5	4738.1	−9.644	26.849	5572.9	5666.6	545.3
18.	−1853.7	4833.2	−10.209	28.027	5507.4	5799.0	668.1
19.	−1985.4	4933.7	−10.858	29.286	5469.1	5935.9	764.9
20.	−2125.3	5038.5	−11.469	30.622	5396.2	6077.5	924.1
21.	−2275.0	5149.3	−12.171	32.051	5350.0	6224.2	1056.8
22.	−2434.1	5264.9	−12.824	33.562	5268.7	6374.6	1263.2
23.	−2604.4	5387.2	−13.578	35.157	5213.5	6526.1	1443.1
24.	−2785.6	5514.6	−14.269	36.831	5122.6	6678.7	1710.4
25.	−2979.7	5649.6	−15.069	38.602	5057.2	6832.6	1952.6

While the productivity program is acceptable on a benefit-cost criterion, it does not yield as high a discounted net benefit-cost ratio as would a project that reverses the urban deterioration process, nor does it slow the deterioration process as much as another program with a nearly identical internal rate of return. For example, Tables 6-4 and 6-5 illustrate the results of a program that doubles productivity improvement from 1% to 2% of municipal costs, at a cost that is double the $45,000 assumed for the 1% program, i.e., at a cost of $90,000 per year. The internal rate of return is 24% (approximately), but the larger positive dollar returns in the later years produce a rate of affluent departure that is slower (nine more affluent families remain at year 25) than that experienced by the first program. The second productivity program may, therefore, be deemed (by some criterion) superior to the first, although the internal rates of return for both projects are almost identical.

This project also illustrates the method whereby the comparative-dynamic procedure integrates the taxation (i.e., the initial incidence of

Table 6-3
Benefit-Cost Evaluation of the Municipal Productivity Program

(1) Year	*(2)* ΔNCLA	×	*(3)* PLA[a]	=	*(4)* ΔTNCLA	*(5)* ΔNBLP	×	*(6)* PLP[a]	=	*(7)* ΔTNBLP	*(8)* ΔMCEA	*(9)* Total Cash Flow
1												
2												
3												
4	−1.6		5966		−9,546	−.1		4273		−427		−9,973
5	−3.0		5962		−17,886	−.1		4363		−436		−18,322
6	−3.9		5926		−23,111	−.1		4455		−486	−400	−23,957
7	−4.4		5918		−26,044	−.1		4549		−455	−400	−26,899
8	−4.4		5879		−25,868	−.1		4647		−465	−700	−27,033
9	−4.0		5868		−23,472	−.1		4747		−475	−700	−24,647
10	−3.2		5824		−18,637	−.1		4850		−485	−800	−19,922
11	−1.9		5809		−11,037	0				0	−600	−11,637
12	0				0	0				0	−200	−200
13	+2.2		5741		+12,630	+.1		5178		+518	+400	+13,548
14	+5.3		5688		+30,146	+.1		5295		+530	+1,700	+32,326
15	+8.9		5663		+50,401	+.3		5415		+1,623	+3,300	+55,324
16	+13.2		5604		+73,973	+.4		5539		+2,216	+6,000	+82,189
17	+18.1		5773		+104,491	+.5		5667		+2,834	+9,100	+116,425
18	+23.8		5508		+131,090	+.6		5799		+3,479	+13,900	+148,469
19	+30.3		5470		+165,741	+.7		5936		+4,155	+19,500	+189,396
20	+37.4		5398		+201, 885	+.9		6078		+5,470	+27,600	+234,955
21	+45.6		5353		+244,097	+1.1		6224		+6,846	+36,700	+287,643
22	+54.6		5273		+287,906	+1.3		6375		8,484	+49,800	+346,190
23	+64.7		5219		+337,669	+1.4		6526		+9,136	+63,800	+410,605
24	+75.8		5130		+388,854	+1.7		6679		+11,354	+83,600	+483,808
25	+88.0		5067		+445,896	+1.8		6833		+12,299	+10,200	+563,345
								Net Present Value at Social Discount Rate of 10%				$408,840

[a]From Table 6-1

Table 6-4
The Basic Model Modified by the Second Municipal Productivity Program

(1) Time E+00	*(2)* NCLA E+00	*(3)* NBLP E+00	*(4)* TNCLA E+06	*(5)* TNBLP E+06	*(6)* PLA E+00	*(7)* PLP E+00	*(8)* MCEA E+03
.0	.0	3000.0	.000	12.000	6000.0	4000.0	.0
1.	−13.8	3720.0	−.083	15.066	6000.0	4050.0	.0
2.	−565.9	3748.4	−3.396	15.368	6000.0	4100.0	.0
3.	−614.5	3794.3	−3.687	15.883	5999.2	4186.0	.5
4.	−669.5	3842.3	−3.994	16.420	5966.0	4273.4	20.0
5.	−727.3	3893.0	−4.336	16.989	5962.3	4363.1	23.7
6.	−787.4	3945.9	−4.666	17.580	5925.9	4455.2	49.4
7.	−850.6	4001.8	−5.035	18.208	5918.7	4549.9	57.6
8.	−916.7	4060.1	−5.389	18.868	5878.6	4647.2	91.1
9.	−986.4	4121.8	−5.788	19.567	5867.6	4747.3	105.2
10.	−1059.3	4186.1	−6.169	20.304	5823.6	4850.3	148.3
11.	−1136.3	4254.2	−6.600	21.065	5808.4	4956.4	170.4
12.	−1217.1	4325.1	−7.011	21.910	5760.1	5065.7	225.6
13.	−1302.6	4400.2	−7.477	22.786	5740.2	5178.4	258.0
14.	−1392.5	4478.5	−7.919	23.712	5687.0	5294.6	328.4
15.	−1487.7	4561.3	−8.424	24.698	5662.1	5414.6	374.3
16.	−1588.0	4647.7	−8.898	25.742	5603.5	5538.6	463.7
17.	−1694.4	4739.1	−9.443	26.855	5572.8	5666.6	527.2
18.	−1806.7	4834.4	−9.951	28.035	5508.2	5799.0	640.5
19.	−1925.9	4935.2	−10.537	29.295	5471.2	5936.0	726.6
20.	−2052.0	5040.3	−11.080	30.633	5399.8	6077.7	870.1
21.	−2186.1	5151.5	−11.708	32.065	5355.6	6224.4	985.5
22.	−2328.0	5267.4	−12.284	33.579	5276.7	6374.8	1167.1
23.	−2479.2	5390.0	−12.952	35.177	5224.4	6526.3	1320.2
24.	−2639.5	5517.8	−13.559	36.853	5137.0	6679.0	1550.1
25.	−2810.5	5653.1	−14.265	38.627	5075.7	6832.9	1751.7

taxation) and expenditure decisions of proposed projects. These two decisions, usually treated separately in benefit-cost analysis, can be integrated by this procedure for any proposed project that is financed *internally*. Any project financed from general municipal revenue automatically has its costs allocated to property taxpayers. The incremental net benefits of a project to a typical group include provision for financing. The group that benefits may, and usually does, bear part of the costs.

Project No. 2: A Property-Tax Cut

The second proposed program to be evaluated consists of a $400 annual property-tax cut, beginning in year 5, for each affluent family of the municipality. It is computed as follows:

$$PTCAP.K = PTCA * CLIP(SWT5, TIME.K) \qquad (39,A)$$

Table 6-5
Benefit-Cost Evaluation of the Second Municipal Productivity Program

(1)	*(2)*		*(3)*		*(4)*	*(5)*		*(6)*		*(7)*	*(8)*	*(9)*
Year	*ΔNCLA*	×	*PLA*[a]	=	*ΔTNCLA*	*ΔNBLP*	×	*PLP*[a]	=	*ΔTNBLP*	*ΔMCEA*	*Total Cash Flow*
1			6000					4050				
2			6000					4100				
3			5999					4186				
4	−3.3		5966		−19,688			4273			−100	−19,788
5	−5.9		5962		−34,963	−.2		4363		−873	−300	−36,136
6	−7.6		5926		−45,038	−.2		4455		−891	−700	−46,629
7	−8.5		5919		−50,312	−.2		4550		−910	−900	−52,122
8	−8.5		5879		−49,972	−.2		4647		−928	−1,400	−52,300
9	−7.8		5868		−45,770	−.2		4747		−949	−1,400	−48,119
10	−6		5824		−34,944	−.2		4850		−970	−1,500	−37,414
11	−3.3		5808		−19,166			4956			−1,100	−20,266
12	+.5		5760		+2,880			5066			−300	+2,580
13	+5.3		5740		+30,422	+.2		5178		+1,036	+1,100	+32,558
14	+11.1		5687		+63,126	+.3		5295		+1,589	+3,600	+68,315
15	+18.2		5662		+103,048	+.5		5415		+2,708	+6,800	+112,556
16	+26.5		5604		+148,506	+.7		5539		+3,877	+12,100	+164,483
17	36.1		5573		+201,185	+1		5667		+5,667	+18,100	+224,952
18	+47.0		5508		+258,876	+1.2		5799		+6,959	+27,600	+292,275
19	+59.5		5471		+325,525	+1.5		5936		+8,904	+38,300	+372,729
20	+73.3		5400		+395,820	+1.8		6078		+10,940	+54,000	+460,760
21	+88.9		5356		+476,148	+2.2		6224		+13,693	+71,300	+561,141
22	+106.9		5277		+559,890	+2.5		6375		+15,938	+96,100	+671,928
23	+125.2		5224		+654,045	+2.8		6526		+18,273	+122,900	+795,218
24	+146.1		5137		+750,516	+3.2		6679		+21,373	+160,300	+932,189
25	+169.2		5076		+858,859	+3.5		6833		+23,916	+200,900	+1,083,675
								Net Present Value at Social Discount Rate of 10%				$803,893

[a]From Table 6-4.

Table 6-6
The Basic Model Modified by the Property-Tax Cut Program

(1) Time E+00	(2) NCLA E+00	(3) NBLP E+00	(4) TNCLA E+06	(5) TNBLP E+06	(6) PLA E+00	(7) PLP E+00	(8) MCEA E+03
.0	.0	3000.0	.000	12.000	6000.0	4000.0	.0
1.	−13.8	3720.0	−.083	15.066	6000.0	4050.0	.0
2.	−565.9	3748.4	−3.396	15.386	6000.0	4100.0	.0
3.	−614.5	3794.3	−3.687	15.883	5999.2	4186.0	.5
4.	−662.2	3842.4	−3.974	16.420	5966.0	4273.4	19.9
5.	−721.4	3893.2	−4.301	16.986	5962.3	4363.1	23.4
6.	−779.8	3946.1	−4.621	17.581	5926.1	4455.2	21.9
7.	−442.1	4002.0	−2.617	18.209	5919.0	4549.9	27.2
8.	−508.2	4060.3	−2.988	18.869	5879.3	4647.2	45.8
9.	−578.6	4122.0	−3.409	19.568	5892.5	4747.3	45.7
10.	−652.9	4186.2	−3.819	20.304	5848.8	4850.3	71.7
11.	−732.5	4254.1	−4.291	21.085	5857.7	4956.4	74.8
12.	−816.6	4324.7	−4.744	21.907	5809.6	5065.7	110.6
13.	−906.6	4399.5	−5.271	22.783	5813.8	5178.4	119.0
14.	−1001.8	4477.1	−5.771	23.705	5760.6	5294.6	167.9
15.	−1103.7	4559.5	−6.357	24.688	5759.4	5414.6	184.6
16.	−1211.4	4645.0	−6.906	25.726	5700.5	5538.5	250.9
17.	−1326.8	4735.7	−7.554	26.835	5693.2	5666.5	279.8
18.	−1448.8	4829.7	−8.154	28.006	5627.7	5798.7	369.0
19.	−1579.6	4929.6	−8.867	29.260	5613.6	5935.5	415.5
20.	−1718.0	5033.1	−9.519	30.586	5540.9	6077.0	534.9
21.	−1866.3	5143.1	−10.300	32.008	5518.8	6223.4	606.3
22.	−2023.4	5257.1	−11.003	33.507	5437.8	6373.8	765.4
23.	−2191.9	5378.2	−11.851	35.904	5406.8	6525.2	871.1
24.	−2370.5	5503.7	−12.602	36.753	5316.4	6677.8	1082.2
25.	−2562.1	5637.2	−13.517	38.511	5275.3	6831.6	1235.0

where *PTCA* is the size of the annual property-tax cut (now assumed to be $400). The parameter *SWT5* indicates that the program is to be attached in year 5.

The property-tax cut is subtracted from annual affluent costs, which were given by equation (18,A) of Chapter 4, and which now become

$$MCA.K = [(MTR.K * AVAH.K)/AH.K)] - PTCAP.K. \quad (18,A)$$

The municipal deficit generated by this tax cut is assumed to be financed by a revenue-sharing program instituted by a higher unit of government. The annual cost to the higher unit of government is found by subtracting municipal revenues from municipal costs. The results of the tax cut are illustrated in Tables 6-6 and 6-7 and Figure 6-2. Column 8 of Table 6-7 gives the external financing required for the tax cut.

The tax cut is sufficient between years 9 and 25 to induce 222 additional affluent families to remain in the urban area who would have left without tax relief. This is illustrated by a comparison of column 6 of Table 6-6 with

Table 6-7
Benefit-Cost Evaluation of the Property-Tax Cut Program

(1) Year	(2) ΔNCLA	×	(3) PLA[a]	=	(4) ΔTNCLA	(5) ΔNBLP	×	(6) PLP[a]	=	(7) ΔTNBLP	(8) MR−MC	(9) ΔMCEA	(10) Total Cash Flow
1													
2													
3													
4													
5													
6													
7	+400		5919		+2,367,600						−2,398,000	+26,800	−3,600
8	+400		5879		+2,351,600						−2,397,000	+29,500	−15,900
9	+400		5893		+2,357,200						−2,396,000	+43,900	+5,100
10	+400.4		5849		+2,341,900	−.2		4850		−970	−2,396,000	+58,100	+3,030
11	+400.5		5858		+2,346,100	−.1		4956		−496	−2,395,000	+75,100	+25,700
12	+401		5810		+2,329,800	−.4		5066		−2,026	−2,394,000	+94,500	+28,300
13	+401.3		5814		+2,333,200	−.5		5178		−2,589	−2,393,000	+114,700	+52,300
14	+401.8		5761		+2,314,800	−1.1		5295		−5,825	−2,393,000	+140,100	+56,100
15	+402.2		5759		+2,316,300	−1.3		5415		−7,040	−2,391,000	+164,100	+82,400
16	+403.1		5701		+2,298,000	−2.0		5539		−11,078	−2,392,000	+196,500	+91,400
17	+403.7		5693		+2,298,300	−2.4		5667		−13,600	−2,389,000	+224,900	+120,600
18	+404.8		5628		+2,278,200	−3.5		5799		−20,227	−2,386,000	+265,500	+137,500
19	+405.8		5614		+2,278,200	−4.1		5936		−24,338	−2,386,000	+299,100	+167,000
20	+407.3		5541		+2,256,900	−5.4		6077		−32,816	−2,384,000	+349,400	+189,500
21	+408.7		5519		+2,255,600	−6.2		6223		−38,583	−2,382,000	+389,200	+224,200
22	+410.7		5438		+2,233,400	−7.8		6374		−49,717	−2,379,000	+450,500	+255,183
23	+412.5		5407		+2,230,388	−9.0		6525		−58,725	−2,379,000	+497,800	+290,463
24	+415.1		5316		+2,206,672	−10.9		6628		−72,790	−2,375,000	+572,000	+330,882
25	+417.6		5275		+2,202,840	−12.4		6832		−84,717	−2,374,000	+628,200	+372,323
										Net Present Value at Social Discount Rate of 10%			$616,045

[a]From Table 6-4.

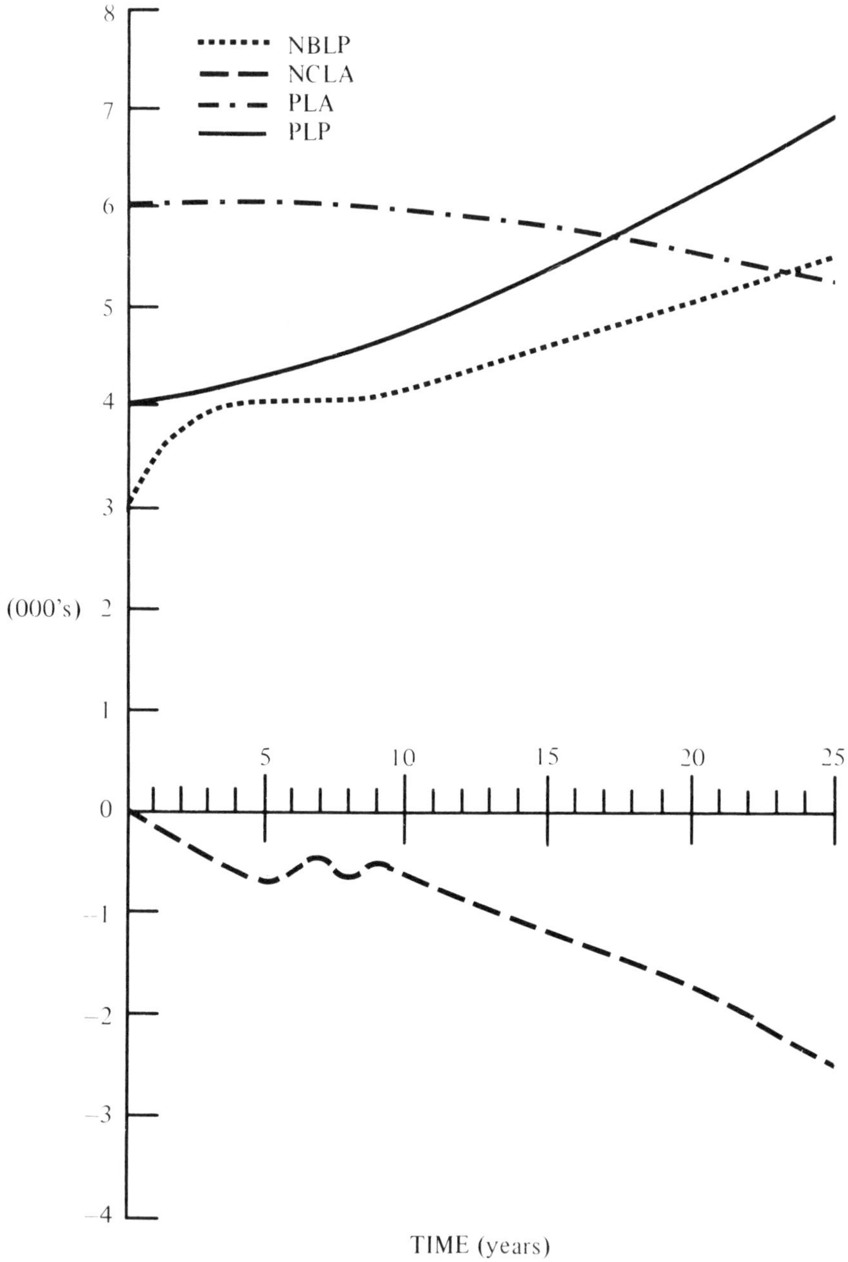

Figure 6-2. The Basic Model Modified by the Property-Tax Cut Program.

column 6 of Table 6-2. The rate of affluent population departure is reduced, but not reversed.

The incremental benefits of $400 for each affluent family in year 7 are the cause of the reduced rate of affluent departures, which in turn raises annual affluent benefits even further, so that by year 25 affluent benefits rise by $417. This occurs even though the size of the property-tax cut remains at $400 per year.

This provides an example of beneficial dynamic pecuniary effects: the reduced rate of affluent departures, as compared with that prevailing in the basic model, reduces annual property taxes for each affluent family by an amount greater than the $400 tax cut provided by this project.

The analysis of this program is correct only insofar as no additional costs or benefits accrue to other municipalities or suburbs within the higher unit of government providing the revenue-sharing. The higher unit of government, however, must include incremental costs (and benefits) incurred by other lower-level units of government as a result of this program. This does not mean that the positive net benefits of this program are offset exactly by incremental costs to other relevant units of government. The possibility of a net gain or loss does exist, but can be determined precisely only by extending the analysis to the various municipalities and suburbs likely to be affected.

The property-tax cut project produces positive incremental benefits for the affluent, but reduces the benefits enjoyed by the poor. The political power enjoyed by the poor is reduced relative to what it was under the basic model because the poor now represent a smaller percentage of the electorate. This results in higher property taxes for the poor than those found from the basic model, because of the assumptions underlying equation (34,A) of Chapter 4. The municipal assessed-value ratio for the affluent is reduced, thereby shifting more of the property-tax burden to the poor. This produces detrimental dynamic effects for the poor.

The property-tax cut has an overall net-present value of $616,045, as illustrated in Table 6-7, and an internal rate of return of 74%. On a pure benefit-cost criterion, the program appears to be desirable. The distribution of benefits, however, is quite detrimental to the poor, even though the per capita family income increases in the municipality (i.e., fewer affluent families depart) as a result of the program, and this in itself leads to increases in benefits for the poor—since, by equation (15,R), benefits to the poor are a function of per capita income. In this case, however, the effect of the program on benefits for the poor is swamped by increases in property taxes paid by the poor.

In summary, the program appears to be desirable on any allocation criterion at any reasonable discount rate. It may be found undesirable on some distribution criterion. The procedure does provide information regarding the distribution of benefits so that decision makers at least know the dynamic effects of the property-tax cut program on income distribution.

Project No. 3: A Program to Equalize Assessed Values

Not all programs instituted by the municipality involve a direct expenditure of funds. Some simply involve administrative changes in the structure of parameters of the urban system. Even these programs, however, exhibit dynamic streams of benefits and costs—benefits and costs that are by no means obvious intuitively. We turn to an example of such a program presently.

Let us assume that this municipality is considering a program that equalizes, at $500, the assessed values of typical affluent and poor family homes.[b] Such a program involves no major expenditure of funds, but is likely to generate a fluctuating benefit and cost stream for affluent and poor families. The results of such a program are presented in Tables 6-8 and 6-9 and Figure 6-3.

As we expect, the costs for a typical poor family rise (i.e., net benefits decline) and the in-migration rate of poor families drops considerably. There are approximately 600 fewer poor families at year 25 (column 5 of Table 6-8 versus column 7 of Table 6-2) than were present in the original model.

On a benefit-cost criterion, the program should be rejected; costs over time to the poor exceed significantly the benefits to the affluent. The net-present value at a social discount rate of 10% is −$2,697,259 (column 9 of Table 6-9). Since the costs exceed the benefits by an increasing amount in each year, the discount rate selected (provided it is positive) would not influence the decision.

If we look at the results of this program further, we may arrive at a different conclusion. If we are interested only in how our original 10,000 families fare as a result of this proposed project, then we will have to multiply the incremental time-varying costs to the poor by 4,000 (the original number of poor families). We can see intuitively from Table 6-8 that such a procedure for measuring benefits and costs will produce a more favorable evaluation of this project. Political decision makers may place more weight on how the original families of the municipality fare over time,

---

[b]Since poor families live in homes that have market values considerably below those of the affluent, this proposed program is not likely to be an attractive idea to the poor. However, if the affluent gain political control of the municipality, they might seek such a program to force the poor out of the central city. This might be done in an attempt to reduce detrimental neighborhood effects (i.e., externalities) created by the current poor housing stock.

Table 6-8
The Basic Model Modified by a Program that Equalizes the Assessed-Value Ratio

(1) *Time* *E+00*	*(2)* *NCLA* *E+00*	*(3)* *NBLP* *E+00*	*(4)* *PLA* *E+00*	*(5)* *PLP* *E+00*	*(6)* *MCEA* *E+03*
.0	.0	3000.0	6000.0	4000.0	.00
1.	−13.8	3720.0	6000.0	4050.0	.00
2.	−357.9	3436.6	6000.0	4100.0	.00
3.	−394.2	3464.5	5999.2	4186.0	.28
4.	−433.2	3494.5	5978.5	4257.8	7.74
5.	−474.8	3525.8	5975.5	4331.0	9.39
6.	−518.9	3558.2	5952.5	4405.8	19.38
7.	−566.0	3592.8	5947.0	4482.1	23.02
8.	−616.0	3628.5	5921.4	4560.0	36.36
9.	−669.5	3666.6	5913.1	4639.6	42.79
10.	−726.2	3705.9	5884.4	4721.0	60.57
11.	−786.9	3748.0	5872.9	4804.3	70.91
12.	−851.3	3791.5	5840.9	4889.6	94.55
13.	−920.4	3838.0	5825.7	4977.0	110.26
14.	−993.6	3886.2	5789.8	5066.6	141.64
15.	−1072.2	3937.8	5770.4	5158.5	164.69
16.	−1155.5	3991.1	5730.2	5252.8	206.29
17.	−1245.0	4048.4	5706.1	5349.7	239.29
18.	−1339.9	4107.7	5660.8	5449.3	294.35
19.	−1442.0	4171.5	5631.4	5551.7	340.80
20.	−1550.4	4237.6	5580.4	5657.1	413.63
21.	−1666.9	4308.8	5544.9	5764.6	478.16
22.	−1790.8	4382.6	5487.4	5877.5	574.44
23.	−1924.3	4462.2	5444.9	5993.0	663.27
24.	−2066.2	4544.9	5379.9	6112.1	790.54
25.	−2219.2	4634.4	5329.4	6235.2	911.95

than on the benefit and cost differences between the basic and revised models.

The preceding analysis does not lead us to any conclusions about the desirability of the equalization program on grounds of equity. The procedure *does not* contain a decision rule on matters of equity. It does, however, permit us to determine the probable effect of a proposed project upon various typical groups, thus facilitating comparisons of their interests.

The three programs evaluated thus far illustrate a significant and well-known characteristic of public projects: each project, whether or not acceptable on an objective benefit-cost basis, has distinct and possibly detrimental (by some criterion) distribution effects. Calculations of political benefits and opportunity costs must combine the allocation and distribution effects of proposed projects. It is not enough to calculate the total

Table 6-9
Benefit-Cost Evaluation of a Program that Equalizes the Assessed-Value Ratio

(1) Year	(2) ΔNCLA	×	(3) PLA[a]	=	(4) ΔTNCLA	(5) ΔNPLP	×	(6) PLP[a]	=	(7) ΔTNBLP	(8) ΔMCEA	(9) Total Cash Flow
1												
2	+208.0		6000		+1,248,000	−311.8		4100		−1,278,380	+220	−30,160
3	+220.3		5999		+1,321,580	−329.8		4186		−1,380,543	+220	−58,743
4	+233.0		5979		+1,392,874	−347.9		4258		−1,481,358	+12,160	−76,324
5	+246.6		5976		+1,473,682	−364.4		4331		−1,578,216	+14,010	−90,524
6	+260.9		5953		+1,553,138	−387.9		4405		−1,708,700	+29,320	−126,242
7	+276.1		5947		+1,650,802	−409.2		4482		−1,834,853	+33,680	−150,371
8	+292.2		5921		+1,730,116	−431.8		4560		−1,969,008	+53,340	−185,552
9	+309.1		5913		+1,827,708	−455.4		4639		−2,112,601	+61,010	−219,244
10	+327.1		5884		+1,924,656	−480.4		4721		−2,267,968	+88,230	−255,082
11	+346.1		5873		+2,032,645	−506.2		4804		−2,431,785	+98,390	−300,750
12	+366.3		5841		+2,139,558	−533.6		4890		−2,609,304	+130,750	−338,996
13	+387.5		5826		+2,257,575	−562.0		4978		−2,797,636	+148,840	−391,221
14	+410.0		5790		+2,370,390	−592.0		5067		−2,999,664	+190,360	−438,914
15	+433.7		5770		+2,502,449	−623.0		5159		−3,214,057	+216,410	−495,198
16	+459.0		5730		+2,630,070	−655.9		5253		−3,445,443	+269,510	−545,863
17	+485.5		5706		+2,770,263	−689.7		5350		−3,659,895	+306,010	−613,622
18	+513.8		5661		+2,908,622	−725.5		5449		−3,953,250	+373,750	−670,878
19	+543.4		5631		+3,059,885	−762.2		5552		−4,231,734	+424,100	−747,749
20	+574.9		5580		+3,207,942	−800.0		5657		−4,530,691	+510,470	−812,279
21	+608.1		5545		+3,271,915	−840.5		5766		−4,846,323	+578,640	−995,768
22	+643.3		5487		+3,529,787	−882.3		5878		−5,186,159	+688,760	−967,612
23	+680.1		5445		+3,703,145	−925.0		5993		−5,543,525	+779,830	−1,060,550
24	+719.4		5380		+3,870,372	−969.7		6112		−5,936,503	+919,860	−1,146,271
25	+760.5		5329		+4,052,705	−1015.2		6735		−6,329,772	+1,040,650	−1,230,182
										Net Present Value at a Social Discount Rate of 10%		\$−2,607,259

[a]From Table 6-8.

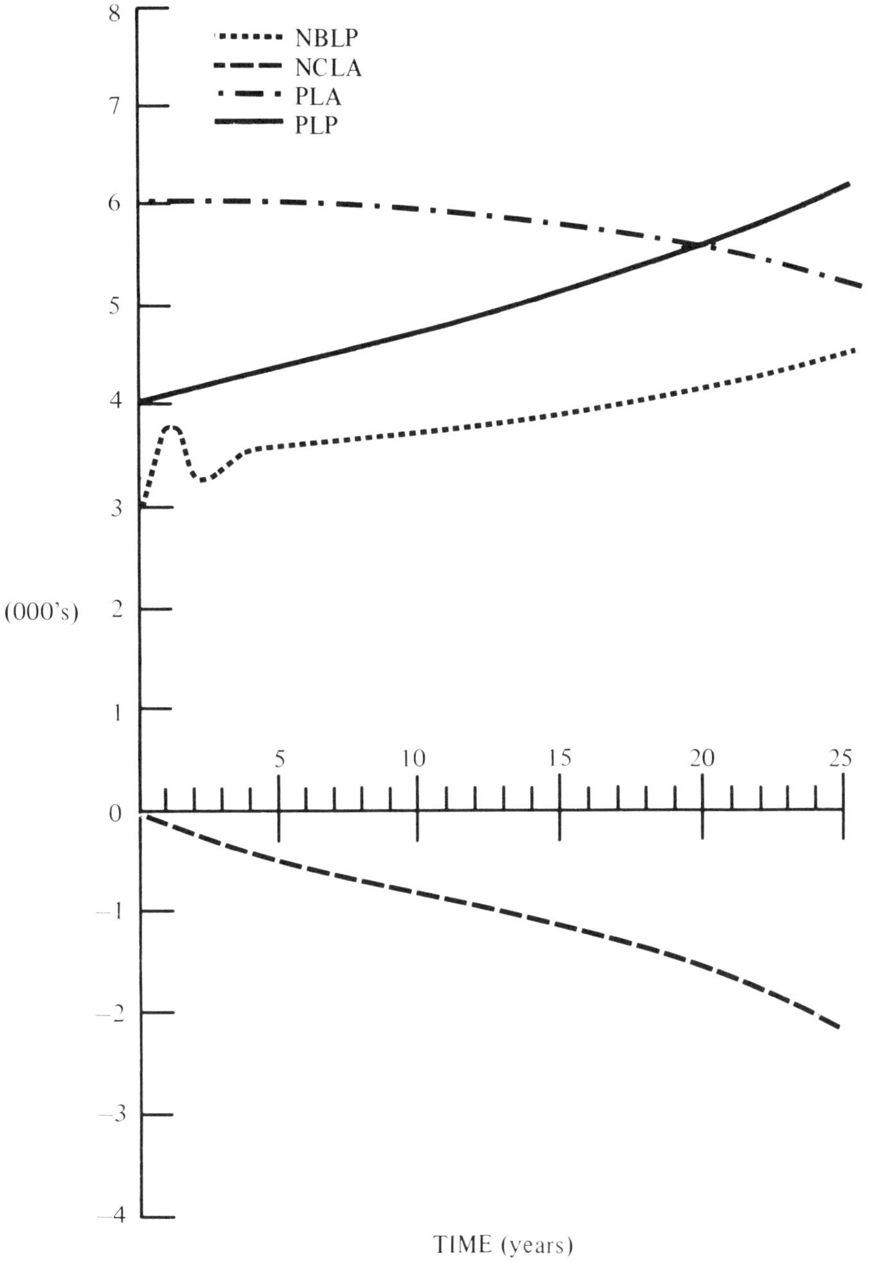

Figure 6-3. The Basic Model Modified by a Program that Equalizes the Assessed-Value Ratio.

objective benefits and costs, since the distribution of benefits and costs may be equally, or even more, important to the decision makers.

Project No. 4: A New Education Program

The fourth project to be evaluated is one that improves the educational quality of the public school system by reducing the difference in expenditures between it and suburban school systems.

Let us assume that a $100,000 *annual increase* in municipal expenditures will reduce the relative rate of deterioration of municipal schools from 6% (i.e., $NSDA = 6\%$ in the basic model) to 4%.

The annual increase in expenditures on education is given by

$$MEIP.K = AAEE * CLIP(SWT0, TIME.K) \qquad (40,A)$$

where $AAEE$ equals the additional annual expenditure on public education in the municipality. This annual expenditure simultaneously increases municipal costs and reduces the annual deterioration of educational services in this municipality relative to suburban schools.

Municipal costs are now given by

$$MC.K = MC.J + DT * (MECI.JK + MEIP.J) \qquad (12,L)$$

The equation for annual services forgone (by an affluent family) was given by

$$RSSIA.KL = NSDA * (NAS.K * NPME)/PLA.K \qquad (14,R)$$

and retains its form, but $NSDA$ now is assigned a value of 4%—down 2 percentage points from its original value.

The results of the new education program are illustrated in Tables 6-10 and 6-11 and Figure 6-4. Positive benefits accrue to affluent and poor families of the municipality in years 1 through 4, after which program costs begin to exceed benefits. The net-present value of the program is −3,016,033 at a social discount rate of 10%.

The education program, when both costs and benefits are considered, leads to a deterioration in net benefits for all families of the municipality. Additional costs of the program to a typical affluent family rise by an amount greater than program benefits, resulting in the departure of 52 additional affluent families at time 25, as illustrated by a comparison of Table 6-10 with Table 6-2. As additional affluent families depart, costs to those remaining increase, thus intensifying the exodus. Since the program affects both poor and affluent families adversely, it should be rejected on both benefit-cost and distribution criteria.

If it were possible for this municipality to invest an additional $100,000 annually in its public education system in such a manner as actually to make

Table 6-10
The Basic Model Modified by an Education Program

(1) *Time* *E+00*	*(2)* *NCLA* E+00	*(3)* *NBLP* E+00	*(4)* *TNCLA* E+06	*(5)* *TNBLP* E+06	*(6)* *PLA* E+00	*(7)* *PLP* E+00	*(8)* *MCEA* E+03
.0	.0	3000.0	.000	12.000	6000.0	4000.0	.0
1.	−9.2	3720.0	−.055	15.066	6000.0	4050.0	.0
2.	−556.5	3748.4	−3.339	15.386	6000.0	4100.0	.0
3.	−616.2	3793.8	−3.697	15.881	5999.4	4186.0	.3
4.	−678.7	3841.5	−4.049	16.416	5966.6	4273.4	21.0
5.	−744.4	3891.8	−4.439	16.980	5962.5	4363.1	25.5
6.	−813.0	3944.2	−4.817	17.572	5925.9	4455.2	54.4
7.	−885.0	3999.7	−5.237	18.198	5917.8	4549.8	64.9
8.	−960.3	4057.6	−5.644	18.855	5877.1	4647.0	104.1
9.	−1039.7	4118.8	−6.097	19.552	5864.7	4746.9	122.9
10.	−1122.8	4182.7	−6.534	20.285	5819.5	4849.8	175.5
11.	−1210.4	4250.3	−7.023	21.063	5802.3	4955.8	205.4
12.	−1302.3	4320.8	−7.491	21.884	5752.1	5064.9	275.0
13.	−1399.4	4395.4	−8.018	22.757	5729.7	5177.4	319.8
14.	−1501.3	4473.2	−8.518	23.679	5674.0	5293.4	410.9
15.	−1609.1	4555.6	−9.084	24.660	5645.7	5413.2	475.3
16.	−1722.4	4641.5	−9.618	25.699	5583.9	5536.9	593.9
17.	−1842.4	4732.5	−10.224	26.808	5549.2	5664.6	683.9
18.	−1968.7	4827.4	−10.790	27.983	5480.5	5796.5	837.3
19.	−2102.7	4927.8	−11.436	29.238	5438.6	5933.3	960.8
20.	−2243.9	5032.5	−12.033	30.571	5032.5	5362.4	1158.4
21.	−2393.8	5143.4	−12.717	31.998	5312.5	6221.1	1325.2
22.	−2552.0	5259.0	−13.341	33.508	5227.8	6371.4	1578.9
23.	−2720.2	5381.5	−14.060	35.102	5168.8	6522.8	1801.7
24.	−2897.9	5509.1	−14.706	36.776	5074.7	6675.4	2126.6
25.	−3087.1	5644.4	−15.453	38.547	5005.6	6829.2	2421.8

the municipal school system superior to suburban schools, say by 1% (i.e., to make *NSDA* equal to −.01), it would seem to be a very profitable investment on a benefit-cost criterion, as illustrated in Table 6-12. Benefits of such a program accrue to affluent and poor families throughout the life of the project. Positive annual net benefits for a typical affluent family increase continuously, from $11.50 in year 1 to $660 in year 25. Moreover, 159 fewer affluent families depart in year 25 than in the basic model.

If it is possible to find an education program that makes that sort of improvement at a cost that increases by no more than $100,000 per year, then the program is certainly justified on a benefit-cost criterion. This illustrates still another use for the comparative-dynamic procedure: to find projects that will be profitable if they produce the results expected of them. [c]

[c]It is not likely to be very easy to find such programs in reality, for in order to do so, we must know just what kinds of changes the affluent will consider as improvements. We do not require changes that actually improve the learning process, but rather those that are perceived by the affluent to improve the process. The latter types of changes are likely to be easier to find.

Table 6-11
Benefit-Cost Evaluation of an Education Program

(1) Year	(2) ΔNCLA	×	(3) PLA[a]	=	(4) ΔTNCLA	(5) ΔNBLP	×	(6) PLP[a]	=	(7) ΔTNBLP	(8) ΔMCEA	(9) Total Cash Flow
1	+4.6		6000		+27,600							+27,600
2	+9.4		6000		+56,400							+56,400
3	−1.7		5999		−10,198	+.5		4186		+2093	+2,000	−6,105
4	−12.5		5967		−74,588	+.9		4273		+3846	−1,100	−71,842
5	−23		5963		−137,149	−1.4		4363		−6,108	−2,100	−145,357
6	−34.2		5926		−202,669	−1.9		4455		−8,465	−5,700	−216,834
7	−42.9		5918		−253,882	−2.3		4550		−10,465	−9,200	−273,542
8	−52.1		5877		−306,192	−2.7		4647		−12,547	−15,400	−334,139
9	−61.1		5865		−358,352	−3.2		4,747		−15,190	−19,100	−392,642
10	−69.5		5820		−404,490	−3.6		4850		−17,460	−28,700	−450,650
11	−77.4		5806		−449,075	−3.9		4956		−19,328	−36,100	−504,503
12	−82.7		5752		−475,690	−4.3		5065		−21,780	−49,700	−547,170
13	−91.5		5730		−524,295	−4.6		5177		−23,814	−60,700	−608,809
14	−97.7		5674		−554,350	−5.0		5293		−26,465	−78,900	−659,715
15	−103.2		5646		−582,667	−5.2		5413		−28,148	−95,200	−706,015
16	−107.9		5584		−650,113	−6.5		5537		−35,991	−118,100	−804,204
17	−111.9		5549		−620,933	−5.6		5665		−31,724	−138,600	−791,257
18	−115.0		5481		−630,315	−5.8		5797		−33,623	−169,200	−833,138
19	−117.3		5439		−637,995	−5.9		5933		−35,005	−195,900	−866,860
20	−118.6		5362		−635,933	−6.0		6075		−36,450	−234,300	−906,683
21	−118.8		5312		−631,066	−5.9		6221		−36,704	−268,400	−936,170
22	−117.9		5228		−616,381	−5.9		6371		−37,589	−315,700	−969,670
23	−115.8		5169		−598,570	−5.7		6523		−37,181	−358,600	−994,351
24	−112.3		5075		−569,923	−5.5		6675		−36,713	−416,200	−1,022,836
25	−107.4		5006		−537,644	−5.2		6829		−35,563	−469,200	−1,042,407
								Net Present Value at a Social Discount Rate of 10%				$−3,016,033

[a]From Table 6-10.

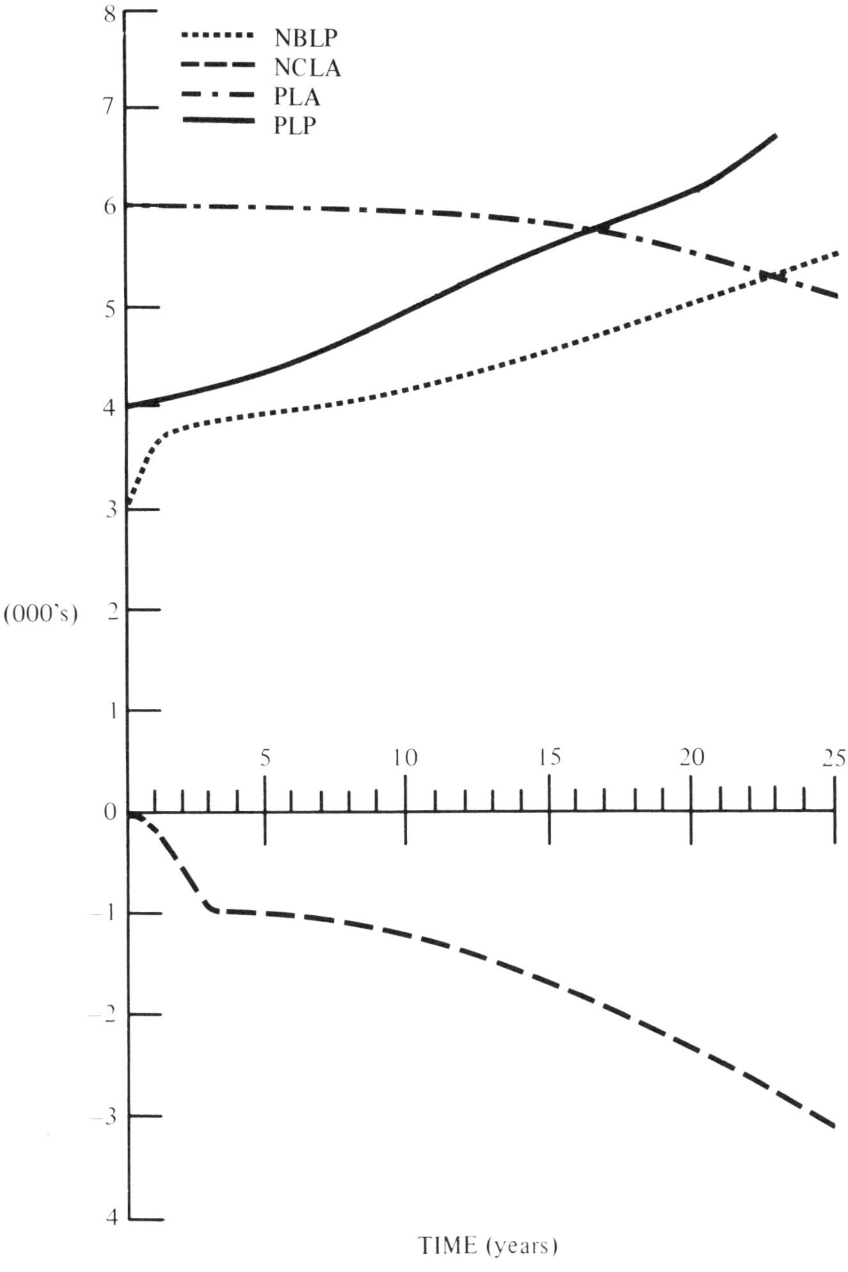

Figure 6-4. The Basic Model Modified by an Education Program.

Table 6-12
The Basic Model Modified by a Second Education Program

(1) *Time* *E+00*	*(2)* *NCLA* *E+00*	*(3)* *NBLP* *E+00*	*(4)* *PLA* *E+00*	*(5)* *PLP* *E+00*	*(6)* *MCEA* *E+03*
.0	.0	3000.0	6000.0	4000.0	.0
1.	2.3	3720.0	6000.0	4050.0	.0
2.	−532.7	3748.4	6000.0	4100.0	.0
3.	−563.2	3794.3	6000.1	4186.0	−.1
4.	−611.9	3842.0	5968.0	4273.4	19.6
5.	−662.9	3892.2	5966.3	4363.1	22.4
6.	−715.8	3944.7	5931.3	4455.2	49.4
7.	−771.1	4000.1	5926.6	4549.8	56.9
8.	−828.6	4058.0	5888.4	4647.1	92.9
9.	−888.9	4119.1	5880.3	4747.1	106.9
10.	−951.8	4182.9	5838.6	4850.0	154.4
11.	−1017.8	4250.4	5826.9	4955.9	177.2
12.	−1086.6	4320.8	5781.5	5065.1	239.0
13.	−1158.9	4395.2	5765.9	5177.6	273.3
14.	−1234.5	4472.9	5716.3	5293.6	353.2
15.	−1314.1	4555.0	5696.3	5413.4	402.6
16.	−1397.2	4640.6	5642.3	5537.0	504.9
17.	−1484.9	4731.2	5617.5	5664.8	574.2
18.	−1576.6	4825.6	5558.4	5796.8	704.6
19.	−1673.5	4925.5	5528.4	5933.3	799.4
20.	−1774.9	5029.6	5463.8	6074.6	965.1
21.	−1882.0	5139.7	5428.0	6220.9	1092.7
22.	−1994.3	5254.4	5357.3	6371.2	1302.7
23.	−2113.1	5375.8	5315.1	6522.6	1472.4
24.	−2237.7	5502.2	5237.7	6675.1	1737.8
25.	−2369.6	5636.0	5188.3	6828.9	1961.3

Sensitivity Analysis of Project Evaluations

In Chapter 5, we identified five parameters to which the key variables of the model were sensitive; two had unitary elasticity coefficients, and the remaining three had elasticity coefficients between .4 and .9 for certain key variables. The three parameters (*NPPI, EØP,* and *PNPEM*) to which the key variables of the model are most sensitive are those for which we have the best average data. The key variables of the model were shown to be only moderately sensitive to changes in the remaining two parameters (*NSDA* and *NPME*).

For purposes of benefit-cost analysis, what matters most is the sensitivity of net-present values to probable errors in the estimation of key parameter values. Here again, however, we are fortunate because the discounting process itself reduces further the sensitivity of key variables to possible errors in the estimates of crucial parameters.

This section examines the sensitivity of the results of the four previous projects to independent *and* cumulative changes in the five key parameters. If the results of this second sensitivity analysis do not affect the calculated estimate of the desirability or undesirability of each project, then we can be more confident of project evaluations produced by the model.

In order to test the sensitivity of the results of our four benefit-cost evaluations, we will subject each evaluation to a range of values for each of the five crucial parameters. The sensitivity of each evaluation to independent and cumulative changes in the parameters will be judged in the following manner:

1. The three crucial parameters (*NPPI*, *EØP*, and *PNPEM*) for which we have good average data will be varied by 10%; the two parameters for which we have the poorest data will be varied by 25%.
2. The changes will be cumulative, i.e., we will begin with the original program result and then add each parameter modification in succession.
3. Then we will compare each original program evaluation with the program evaluation that results from the same proposed project attached to a modified basic model (i.e., a model modified by cumulative alterations in crucial parameter values).
4. Finally, we will calculate again the net-present value of each program; after each of the five (cumulative) modifications, we will, as a result, be computing the *worst case* for comparison with the original program evaluation.

We will observe the effects of the 10% and 25% parameter modifications only. We should be able to estimate the results of −10% and −25% changes from the +10% and +25% changes, since the results of Chapter 5 lead us to believe that their effects will be of the same magnitude although opposite in direction.

Project No. 1: A Municipal Productivity Program

The original results of the municipal productivity program will now be compared to the results that would have been achieved if the five crucial parameters had been estimated incorrectly in the basic model. Five different modified basic models, each characterized by cumulative alterations in crucial parameter values, are used to evaluate the productivity program. The incremental net-present value of the productivity project, when attached to each *new* basic model, is reported in Table 6-13.

As we see readily from Table 6-13, the evaluation procedure for the municipal productivity program is most sensitive to small changes in the proportion of the total nonprogressive work force that is employed by the

Table 6-13
Benefit-Cost Evaluation of the Municipal Productivity Program under Alternate Cumulative Assumptions for Values of Key Parameters

	PROJECT NO. 1	*Original Evaluation: Net-Present Value = $408,840*			
Parameter Tested:	*NPPI*	*EØP*	*PNPEM*	*NSDA*	*NPME*
Original value	.031	2.0	.05370	.060	.023
New value	.034	2.2	.05907	.07500	.02875
Net-present value of cumulative change	$633,105	$773,548	$1,168,946	$1,171,048	$1,169,271

Table 6-14
Benefit-Cost Evaluation of the Property-Tax Cut Program under Alternate Assumptions for Values of Key Parameters

	PROJECT NO. 2	*Original Evaluation: Net-Present Value = $616,045*			
Parameter Tested:	*NPPI*	*EØP*	*PNPEM*	*NSDA*	*NPME*
Original value	.031	2.0	.05370	.060	.023
New value	.034	2.2	.05907	.07500	.02875
Net-present value of cumulative change	$645,624	$773,891	$868,807	$894,789	$900,338

municipality (*PNPEM*). The evaluation is also sensitive to relatively small (i.e., 10%) changes in progressive-sector productivity (*NPPI*) and earnings over productivity (*EØP*).

Only the values of *NPPI* and *PNPEM* seem to have a significant effect on net-present values and, therefore, on the uncertainty of this project evaluation. Our data on local government employment and average national productivity are, fortunately, good.

To summarize, although the project evaluation tends to be very sensitive to changes in the values for *NPPI* and *PNPEM*, these are parameters for which we have the best data. This implies that the uncertainty associated with the correctness of the original evaluation is low *if* we have a model with a valid *structure*.

Project No. 2: A Property-Tax Cut

The original results of the test of the property-tax cut for affluent families will now be compared to the results that would have been achieved under various assumptions regarding the values of each of the five crucial parameters. The results are shown in Table 6-14.

The value of *EØP* (i.e., earnings over productivity) most significantly influences net-present values of the property-tax cut program. The net-present value of the program increases from $645,624 to $773,891, an increase of $138,000, or approximately 21%, as the value of *EØP* changes from 2.0 to 2.2. The net-present value increases by approximately 12% as *PNPEM* changes from 5.37% to 5.907%. Other changes in net-present values that occur, because of modifications in parameters, are quite minor.

None of the cumulative changes are sufficient to change the recommendation of the benefit-cost criterion at a social discount rate of 10%. Cumulative changes in parameter values in the opposite direction (−10% and −25%) would have produced identical recommendations at social discount rates up to 20% (approximately).

We may conclude that the recommendation produced by the procedure for this program is relatively invariant to wide cumulative estimating errors in the model's most crucial parameters.

Project No. 3: A Program to Equalize Assessed Values

The original results achieved for the equalization program will now be compared to those that would have been produced had any or all of the five crucial parameters been estimated incorrectly. The results are shown in Table 6-15.

We see that net-present values are influenced significantly by the altera-

Table 6-15
Benefit-Cost Evaluation of the Tax Equalization Program under Alternate Cumulative Assumptions for Values of Key Parameters

	PROJECT NO. 3	*Original Evaluation: Net-Present Value = $2,607,259*			
Parameter Tested:	*NPPI*	*EØP*	*PNPEM*	*NSDA*	*NPME*
Original value	.031	2.0	.05370	.060	.023
New value	.034	2.2	.05907	.0075	.02875
Net-present value of cumulative change	−$2,440,453	−$2,569,478	−$2,509,822	−$2,435,888	−$2,472,450

Table 6-16
Benefit-Cost Evaluation of Education Program under Alternate Cumulative Assumptions for Values of Key Parameters

	PROJECT NO. 4	*Original Evaluation: Net-Present Value = $−2,718,159*			
Parameter Tested:	*NPPI*	*EØP*	*PNPEM*	*NSDA*	*NPME*
Original value	.031	2.0	.05370	.060	.023
New value	.034	2.2	.05907	.040	.02875
Net-present value of cumulative change	−$2,094,923	−$1,946,594	−$1,748,139	*	+$2,262,327

*The education program is directly concerned with this parameter and the original evaluation pertains to a change from − 6% to − 4%.

tion to *NPPI*; however, the alteration is not nearly enough to change the recommendation produced by the procedure. No other cumulative set of modifications has even this much influence on net-present values.

We can conclude that the recommendation produced by the procedure for this project is invariant to wide and cumulative changes to crucial parameter values.

Project No. 4: A New Educational Program

The results of the education program will be analyzed now to determine the effects of alternative cumulative values for the five crucial parameters. The results appear in Table 6-16.

In this case we see that the large negative present value is reversed by one parameter modification: the change in *NPME* from .023 to .02875. This reversal is explained quite easily. *NPME* represents the normal percentage of affluent-family income allocated to educational expenditures in the municipality. As the percentage rises (in this case by 25%), an education program that shaves 2 percentage points of the opportunity loss off this larger percentage *NPME* is likely to produce significant benefits, as it does in this case.

Summary

The lengthy analysis of this chapter demonstrates that the evaluations produced by a comparative-dynamic model with valid structural relationships will be invariant to rather wide estimating errors in *most* of the values of its crucial parameters. The type of program under consideration will determine the parameter to which the particular evaluation is most sensitive. The values of these crucial parameters must be ascertained accurately before we can feel secure about the validity of the benefit-cost evaluations. A prerequisite for ascertaintiing these values is a valid structural model.

In some proposed programs (e.g., No. 2 and No. 3), wide estimating errors have no effect on the validity of the recommendations. In all proposed programs, one or two parameters require additional scrutiny to ensure good evaluations.

7 Fundamental Issues of Benefit-Cost Analysis

In this chapter, some controversial and interrelated issues of benefit-cost analysis will be examined in light of the comparative-dynamic procedure. We will examine only those issues for which the procedure can add significant insights beyond those now obtainable from the literature. Important unsettled matters and shortcomings of the comparative-dynamic procedure are discussed throughout the chapter.

Provision for Uncertainty

1. Introduction

The extent and method of providing for uncertainty in estimates of benefits and costs is not clear from the literature on benefit-cost analysis.[a] There is no consensus on how and to what extent it should be done.

I believe it is useful in benefit-cost studies to continue to adhere to Knight's [87] distinction between risk and uncertainty. An investment whose outcome, by his definition, is considered "risky" is one for which we have many historical data on the actual returns of similar investment projects. On the other hand, an investment whose outcome is defined as "uncertain" is one for which we have no such historical data on similar projects.

For risky projects whose outcomes are independent of one another, the government may act like an insurance company and pool many risks. Expected returns and costs of proposed projects may be incorporated into benefit-cost studies as certainty equivalents. The deviations of actual returns from expected returns on individual projects are offset in the *aggregate* by deviations in the opposite direction by other projects. Since literally thousands of projects are being undertaken at any one time, each expected return is considered riskless. This is simply an application of the

[a]That uncertainty should be taken into account in welfare studies has been recognized in the literature of welfare economics. For example, Graaff [65, p. 119] argues that among the reasons why men fail to agree on the "desirability of a particular event" is that they "may disagree on the probable consequences of the event, or on the likelihood of those consequences—either because their own estimates of the situation differ or because they evaluate differently the reliability of the estimates of others."

insurance principle that draws support from the Law of Large Numbers.

However, for investments whose outcomes are considered uncertain, the Law of Large Numbers does not apply. For these projects, there are no such historical data for similar projects upon which we may base our expectations. If there are no data for similar projects, we cannot arrive at a probability distribution to attach to possible outcomes of the group. Therefore, we cannot infer an expected mean value that may be treated as certain for the costs and benefits of a project directly under consideration.

I believe that the studies reviewed in Chapter 2 illustrate that we are likely to encounter much uncertainty when we evaluate projects that affect complex social systems that are themselves poorly understood. Few data are likely to be available on similar projects. Furthermore, we must be suspicious of whatever evidence is put forth in justification of such projects unless this evidence is supported by a reasonable analysis of the system affected by the project.

Moreover, we must not confuse the type of uncertainty associated with the specification of the relationships underlying a problem area (i.e., the underlying social production function) with the uncertainty associated with construction costs. While we may agree with Turvey [150, p. 7] that probability distributions associated with construction costs are frequently skewed, and that these skewed distributions should be estimated for construction projects in order to compute expected mean costs correctly, the uncertainty associated with estimates of construction costs for government projects is far different (and easier to cope with) from the uncertainty associated with relationships underlying a complex social system. For example, it is a far more difficult task to estimate the benefits and costs of urban renewal projects to a municipality than it is to estimate the costs of construction for the buildings contained in such projects.

I further believe that provision for uncertainty must be made through a realistic assessment of benefits and costs, rather than by increasing the social discount rate by an arbitrary factor to allow for uncertainty. As Samuelson points out [133, p. 96]:

> If I thought that bureaucrats made rotten estimates of future benefits, I'd adjust their benefit estimates since it would be accidental in principle if I could achieve the optimal correction by stepping up the time discount factor. . . indeed, raising the interest rate on optimistic fools hampers them little, since they promise you pie in the sky tomorrow!

In Chapters 5 and 6, we illustrated a method whereby one could identify those parameters of a model of a complex system to which the key variables of the model were most sensitive. Errors in the estimation of these parameters produced uncertainty in the accuracy of estimates of benefits and costs for some projects. We now review the procedure described in Chapters 5 and 6 for dealing with uncertainty in benefit-cost evaluations.

2. Sensitivity Analysis in a Dynamic Model

The sensitivity analysis conducted in Chapters 5 and 6 illustrates the *method* whereby the amount of uncertainty present in a project evaluation is ascertained (subjectively) and reduced.[b] First, we isolate the most crucial parameters, and then we observe how possible errors in the estimation of these parameters influence the validity of a recommendation produced by the procedure. If the recommendation is not altered by potential errors in estimation, then the chance of a poor recommendation is reduced significantly. If the recommendation is altered by such potential errors, we must estimate the parameters more closely in order to reduce the uncertainty surrounding the validity of project evaluations.

Even if estimates of key parameters have been refined to a point where little uncertainty remains, we still have uncertainty present, since these parameters may, and probably will, change over time in a manner that is likely to be quite unpredictable or random. These unpredictable movements in parameters are likely to produce actual results that deviate from those expected. If we can specify the statistical characteristics of the "noise" or *random* elements, and if the model is identical in structure, parameters, and noise characteristics with the real-world problem area, we can expect the model to produce a dynamic behavior similar to the real system *over long periods of time*. Because it is unlikely that a model will represent the real system exactly, and because the values of noise inputs are likely unknown, the model will probably diverge from the real system at any given point in time.

If a large number of independent projects are undertaken, we can expect that actual net benefits will approximate expected net benefits accurately, given that we have minimized *technological uncertainty*. The Law of Large Numbers cannot be of much help when technological uncertainty, as contrasted with the uncertainty generated by random elements, is present in benefit-cost analysis.

Of course, sensitivity analysis can be carried out in ordinary benefit-cost analysis also. An extensive sensitivity analysis was conducted in the Sacramento Transit Authority case discussed in Chapter 2 (see also Appendix C). Multiple values were assigned to travel time in order to measure the sensitivity of benefit-cost ratios to this parameter.

However, if we do not describe accurately the intricate feedback relationships that produce benefits and costs to citizens of an urban area, no amount of sensitivity testing will improve confidence in the evaluations produced by the model. A model of the dynamic structure that produces observed symptoms must be available before effective sensitivity studies

[b]Of course, sensitivity analysis cannot *in itself* reduce uncertainty, but it can provide a procedure or method for reducing uncertainty in project evaluations.

of proposed projects can be carried out. Essential structural components to the relationships underlying the problems analyzed are missing from the benefit-cost studies reviewed in Chapter 2.

I do not mean to imply by the preceding discussion that a dynamic model produces good recommendations automatically or, for that matter, recommendations that are always superior to those of static models. The relevant point is that, in many social systems, the underlying dynamic relationships critically affect the expected returns of new projects. Static models must, by definition, omit these dynamic relationships. As a result, some cost-benefit studies have omitted important relationships.

Furthermore, all operational models of reality, including the partial urban model described in Chapters 3 and 4, omit some structural relationships. The characteristic of a useful model, however, is that it captures those relationships that are crucial in producing the symptoms of a problem that are observed in reality.

3. Summary

Uncertainty (technological) is not only present in many public-expenditure decisions, but is no doubt the principal characteristic. Our conception of the manner in which a problem area is affected by a project may be in error. The absence of knowledge concerning the structural form of a problem area and the values of crucial parameters creates uncertainty in the validity of the estimates of benefits and costs for projects that affect the problem area.

The underlying technological uncertainty can be expected to vary, depending upon our knowledge of the components of the relationships present in a problem area. Since this uncertainty is caused by our absence of knowledge concerning the dynamic relationships underlying the relevant social production function, it is not reduced because of the large number of projects undertaken by government.

Sensitivity analysis provides a method for reducing this uncertainty by locating crucial parameters and subjecting recommendations to multiple values of these parameters. If the impact of errors in estimates of these parameters is small, we can proceed with confidence in our results. Otherwise, we must estimate such crucial parameters more closely.

The Selection of a Social Discount Rate

1. Introduction

A generally accepted procedure for determining the social discount rate at which public projects are to be evaluated is not currently in use. Two general approaches have been proposed: the opportunity-cost approach and the social-time-preference approach.

The opportunity-cost approach to the selection of the social discount rate, described by Baumol [12], is the most objective and operational procedure. It requires a discount rate that reflects the weighted average of rates of return earned in the private sectors (i.e., consumption and investment sectors) from which public funds are withdrawn. Resources used in public projects must be taken from private consumption and investment, where they would otherwise yield a positive rate of return. This positive weighted-average return represents what is forgone when public projects are undertaken, and is the *minimum* return required on projects of the public sector.

The social-time-preference approach to discount rate selection, described by Feldstein [57], Marglin [99], and Hirschleifer [74], places the emphasis exclusively upon *consumption* forgone. The social-time-preference discount rate reflects the time preference consumers assign to consumption now as against consumption in the future. If a project displaces investment, it is necessary to compute its yield in terms of the stream of consumption that would have followed if the investment had not been displaced. Similarly, the benefits of a project consist of the consumption yielded by the public project.

Although the social-time-preference approach to the discount rate may be correct theoretically (i.e., if consumption is assumed to be the ultimate objective of life), it is impossible to apply, since the data it requires are not available. We are forced to a second- or third-best procedure for selection of the discount rate, a procedure closer to the more operational opportunity-cost approach than to the social-time-preference approach.

Once we have settled upon the opportunity-cost approach to the selection of the discount rate, two practical problems remain to be solved:

1. We must estimate from which sectors of the economy funds will be withdrawn for the public projects under evaluation.
2. We must make allowances in the discount rate for social opportunities forgone.

In summary, a search for the optimal discount rate is, in fact, as Baumol [14] points out, a wild goose chase; we must settle for a second-, third- or fourth-best solution. Although we cannot find the optimal discount rate, we must guard against self-serving arguments for high or low discount rates —arguments that can destroy the objectivity that the discount rate and benefit-cost analysis are supposed to bring to public-expenditure analysis. With this background in mind, we now examine and evaluate the indirect approach to the social discount rate illustrated in Chapter 5.

2. *The Role of the Discount Rate in Dynamic Models*

In Chapter 5 we selected, quite arbitrarily, a discount rate of 10% in order to be able to use the present-value citerion. But then we found that the calculated values of three of the four projects evaluated were completely insensitive to interest-rate changes (see pp. 88-108). Only the net benefits of a municipal productivity program, which had an internal rate of return of approximately 24%, were found to be sensitive to changes in the interest rate. Even this project, however, normally would be considered acceptable simply because almost every economist would conclude that marginal opportunity costs in the private sector are lower than 24%.

The magnitude of the discount rate became slightly more important when we subjected each of our project *evaluations* to a range of new values for the parameters we considered crucial (see pp. 109-113). For example, if for the municipal productivity program (see pp. 109-111) we had altered the crucial parameters by −10% and −25% rather than by the original +10% and +25%, the net-present value would have been negative for the first modification (i.e., the parameter *NPPI* = .027) at discount rates slightly above 14%. However, our original data for the three parameters to which the benefit-cost evaluation was most sensitive (*NPPI, EØP,* and *PNPEM*) are likely to be good.

For the other three projects evaluated in Chapter 6, the size of the discount rate, so long as it remains within a reasonable range, is irrelevant to the evaluations. For example, the discount rate would have had to reach 74% before the net-present value of the property-tax cut became zero. In addition, the parameters to which the benefit-cost evaluation was most sensitive (*EØP* and *PNPEM*) were just those for which we had the best data. The remaining two projects produced an almost continuous and growing stream of negative cash flows (see pp. 111-113). Their evaluations were almost completely insensitive to the size of the discount rate.

Of course, we cannot conclude that *all* dynamic models are relatively insensitive to changes in the social discount rate; it is certainly not an inevitable consequence of such models, especially *nonlinear* dynamic models. Nonlinear models may alternate between reinforcing (positive feedback) and controlling (negative feedback) modes of operation.

The nature of a positive or reinforcing feedback loop, such as that appearing in the partial urban model, is to create a process that feeds upon itself over a period of time. Any proposed project that reinforces the loop further is very likely to produce an increasing stream of costs if it contributes to a cumulative deterioration process; or an increasing stream of benefits if it contributes to a cumulative revival process. In either case, the net-present value of such a project is likely to be insensitive to interest rates; i.e., such a project can be evaluated without concern about the appropriate size of the social discount rate.

For example, the partial urban model contains a positive feedback loop that produces a stream of *increasing* costs for the affluent population. The dynamic effects of a program, such as the education program (see p. 104), that adds more costs than benefits for the affluent will simply intensify the cumulative deterioration process. On the other hand, if a project actually reverses the out-migration pattern of the affluent, it will produce enormous benefits. Projects that have these characteristics can be evaluated without concern for the appropriate size of the discount rate. If a project is a mere palliative, as is the case for the municipal productivity program, it will slow down the rate of departure of the affluent, but will produce only moderate returns. A project of this latter type is more likely to be sensitive to movements in the discount rate.

A nonlinear model, as stated previously, may contain controlling or negative feedback mechanisms that reverse cumulative processes, i.e., may cause the model to switch to the opposite mode of operation. If the reinforcing loop gives way to a controlling or equilibrium-seeking loop within a relatively short period of time, the *size* of the discount rate becomes critical for any evaluation. Again, however, the need for an accurate approximation to the discount rate can be determined only by a dynamic evaluation of the feedback structure underlying a problem area.

Finally, the comparative-dynamic procedure allows us to treat many alternative allocation programs and select those that are most profitable, thus taking into account some social opportunities that must be forgone. Since, in reality, most units of government have relatively fixed capital budgets, a procedure that evaluates many programs and rations available capital among the programs yielding the highest internal rates of return is likely to provide a satisfactory solution to the discount-rate problem, so long as the rate of return earned on the least profitable project is well above a relevant range of rates representing the true marginal opportunity cost of funds in the private sector.

In summary, we can expect to find in reality many projects that can be evaluated on allocation grounds without a precise assessment of the social discount rate, simply because dynamic models of reality, such as the partial urban model, may be relatively insensitive to discount-rate changes, at least over the relevant range of rates.

Dynamic Effects in the Partial Urban Model

1. Introduction

The partial model captures a cumulative deterioration process that feeds upon itself over time. The deterioration is displayed in the model by the cumulative decay in the quality of the housing stock. The departure of affluent families from the central city instigates a vicious deterioration process which is detrimental to all families that remain—a process that each family in the municipality would like to prevent, but is powerless to do so by itself.

As each affluent family departs, it contributes, unwillingly and without compensation to those who remain, to (1) a declining average per capita income in the central city, (2) a rising property-tax level for the affluent families remaining, (3) a deterioration in housing quality accompanied by detrimental neighborhood effects, and (4) a general decline in services and the quality of life in the central city.

Each departure of an affluent family aggravates the situation further. Because each departing affluent family makes its decision to leave in order to serve its interests best, the welfare of those remaining falls below the level they enjoyed previously, and this accelerates the movement of the affluent families remaining.

The progressive deterioration of the housing stock over time produces undesirable neighborhood effects which provide examples of detrimental technological externalities. The social costs of providing for a poor family in the municipality, including these detrimental neighborhood effects, exceed the private costs borne by the poor. As each affluent family departs, the housing it occupied formerly is assumed in the model to filter down to a poor housing unit; this also produces detrimental externalities even if it is not followed by the migration of a poor family. Therefore, the social benefits provided by the decision of an affluent family to reside in the central city must exceed the private benefits it enjoys in the city.

The cumulative deterioration process, therefore, provides an example of *external effects*, an example where, in Baumol's words [16, p. 11], "the individuals involved cannot extract themselves by their own uncoordinated efforts." The desires of affluent families to slow or reverse the cumulative deterioration process can be realized only by governmental action. Each family is powerless to stop the cumulative process which they all obviously dislike because of its cumulative detrimental effects on their welfare.

The government should intervene in this case in order to carry out the desires of its citizens. The comparative-dynamic procedure provides a tool for determining just where government intervention should take place; for government should intervene only where the benefits of intervention exceed the costs, i.e., it should intervene only when the benefit-cost criterion is met, provided of course that the resultant distribution effects are acceptable (by some criterion!).

The analysis of Chapter 6 illustrates that some proposed projects (e.g., the productivity program) may be mere palliatives—they pass the benefit-cost criterion but do not reverse or significantly arrest the cumulative deterioration process. Only the tax-cut and equalization programs of Chapter 6 arrest the process in a significant manner. Neither of these programs, however, actually reverses it.

Programs that reverse the process are likely to be those requiring drastic departure from current practices. An example of such a program is a massive revenue-sharing grant to a municipality for the purpose of improving its services to the affluent so that the affluent are relatively better off in the central city than in the adjacent suburbs.

Finally, the type of government intervention illustrated in Chapter 6 dealt only with programs that affected municipal costs, property taxes, and municipal services. In reality, there are many more programs that may be considered by government for arresting or reversing the cumulative deterioration process. In any simple model such as ours, however, we are limited in the kinds of programs that can be evaluated.

2. *Dynamic Pecuniary Externalities*

The comparative-dynamic procedure described in Chapter 6 *measures* many pecuniary externalities that are captured by the partial urban model. The departure of affluent families from the municipality produces detrimental dynamic effects for the citizens (affluent and poor) that remain. The departure of affluent families raises per-family costs to those affluent families remaining for the same level of urban services, and increases the opportunity loss they suffer relative to affluent families in the suburbs. In addition, services supplied to the poor are at least partially a function [e.g., equation (15,R) of Chapter 4] of the average per capita income of municipal families.

The detrimental effects upon the affluent citizens who remain in the municipality are simply manifestations of decreased scale economies as some affluent residents drop out of the municipality. Therefore, there is no reason to expect that increased benefits that result for affluent families of suburb Y, as a direct result of the relocation of affluent families of municipality X to suburb Y, will offset exactly the increased costs to the remaining affluent families of municipality X. How these pecuniary externalities resulting from migration patterns balance one another for citizens of the two political units depends upon many variables, such as population size and income characteristics; quality and size of the housing stock; assessed valuations and property taxes; and municipal costs. In order to evaluate properly the possibility of net gain or loss in real income resulting from these pecuniary externalities, however, the model would have to be extended to include multiple municipalities and multiple suburbs.[c]

We assumed in Section IV of the model that the affluent make decisions to depart based upon increases in property taxes and in the services they must forgo in the central city. By our specification of the model, educational services are assumed to be inferior in the central city relative to such services in the adjacent suburb, and they are assumed to deteriorate progressively over time. Equation (14,R) of Chapter 4 attempts to measure the annual increases in services forgone by a typical affluent family in the central city by measuring the difference between the services received by these affluent families and those received by affluent families in the adjacent suburb. Therefore, the procedure does capture, in a crude way, the decline in services as well as the increase in property taxes set off by the cumulative deterioration process. However, the procedure does not measure the *value* of the detrimental neighborhood effects (technological externalities) and other elements of the general decline in the quality of life in central cities.

To summarize, the model illustrates a case of dynamic external effects, where the uncoordinated efforts of individuals and businesses are bound to fail to reverse or arrest the cumulative deterioration process confronting central cities. The procedure measures some of the many detrimental effects to citizens of the municipality as the cumulative process intensifies.

Income-Distribution Effects

The comparative-dynamic procedure improves our ability to give advice to decision makers on the likely effects of proposed projects on income distribution. Typical groups of citizens are represented in the model, and proposed projects are evaluated as they affect these typical groups over time.

Rothenberg [126] illustrates how static urban models also can be used to determine income-distribution effects of urban renewal projects. In urban areas, however, as in many other social areas, consideration of the dynamic effects of proposed projects on the problem area is crucial for determining the initial, intermediate, and ultimate income-distribution effects. Without a valid model of urban deterioration and revival, how can we be sure of the income effects (or any effects, for that matter) of urban redevelopment projects? How do we obtain future values to discount?

[c]Professors Kadanoff and Weinblatt of the Urban Analysis Group at Brown University have constructed such a model [84], using data from Providence, R.I. However, the model has not been tested empirically. In addition, its lack of a choice criterion makes is impossible to approximate net gain or loss.

The dynamic urban model also illustrates the importance of careful analysis of proposed projects that have income redistribution as their *primary* goal. If these projects are financed by the municipality in a way that affects net benefits to its affluent population adversely, relative to net benefits attainable in the adjacent suburbs, the welfare of each affluent family may be advanced significantly by a move. Departure of affluent families generates detrimental dynamic effects for those affluent families who remain, and may result ultimately in lower, rather than higher, net benefits for the poor—this as a *direct result* of programs designed to improve the net benefits of the poor.

For example, consider the following two programs that have income redistribution as their primary objectives:

1. *A welfare program for the poor, beginning in year 10, and consisting of annual payments of $200 for each poor family.* The program increases the rate of affluent departures so that 65 fewer affluent families remain at year 25 than were present in the basic model.

   As a comparison of Table 7-1 with Table 6-2 illustrates, the increase in annual affluent family costs of $152 in year 10 rises to $160 in year 25 as a direct result of the increased rate of departures of affluent families, an increase that is itself an effect of *this* welfare program. The difference of $8 is an example of detrimental effects for each affluent family remaining in year 25.

   In addition, annual incremental poor family benefits fall from $200 at the inception of the program to $192 in year 25, even though $200 per poor family continues to be spent in year 25. This reflects the effect of a falling per capita municipal income that itself is the effect of *incremental* departures of affluent families caused by this program.
2. *A housing program for the poor that adds 10% additional poor housing each year at a cost of $10,000 per new house.* A comparison of Table 7-2 illustrates that annual poor benefits per family rise $840 in year 11 and slowly dwindle to $718 by year 25, while annual costs to affluent families increase from $666 to $696 in the same time period as a result of the program. Both cases provide examples of detrimental pecuniary effects. On the one hand, new decisions of affluent families to depart from the municipality increase annual costs for each affluent family remaining. On the other, the resultant drop in average family income produced in the municipality reduces benefits for poor families below those that would have been available had no new affluent departures taken place as a result of the new housing program.

Both of the above programs are examples of pure income-redistribution programs that create detrimental pecuniary effects for the affluent—detrimental effects that over a long period of time will both dribble away the

Table 7-1
The Basic Model Modified by a Welfare Program for the Poor

(1) *Time* *E+00*	*(2)* *NCLA* *E+00*	*(3)* *NBLP* *E+00*	*(4)* *PLA* *E+00*	*(5)* *PLP* *E+00*
.0	.0	3000.0	6000.0	4000.0
1.	−13.8	3720.0	6000.0	4050.0
2.	−565.9	3748.4	6000.0	4100.0
3.	−614.5	3794.3	5999.2	4186.0
4.	−666.2	3842.4	5966.0	4273.4
5.	−721.4	3893.2	5962.3	4363.1
6.	−779.8	3946.1	5926.1	4455.2
7.	−842.1	4002.0	5919.0	4549.9
8.	−908.2	4060.3	5879.3	4647.2
9.	−978.6	4322.0	5868.5	4747.3
10.	−1205.7	4382.1	5824.6	4850.3
11.	−1285.5	4450.1	5809.7	4966.4
12.	−1370.1	4520.9	5752.4	5085.5
13.	−1460.8	4595.9	5732.6	5208.0
14.	−1556.7	4673.9	5670.2	5334.1
15.	−1659.4	4756.5	5645.0	5463.9
16.	−1768.2	4842.4	5576.8	5597.6
17.	−1884.7	4933.4	5545.4	5735.4
18.	−2008.2	5028.1	5470.7	5877.5
19.	−2140.5	5128.3	5432.3	6024.2
20.	−2280.9	5232.6	5350.2	6174.4
21.	−2431.4	5343.1	5303.9	6325.7
22.	−2591.1	5458.0	5213.4	6478.0
23.	−2762.5	5579.8	5158.0	6631.5
24.	−2944.5	5706.6	5057.9	6786.1
25.	−3139.9	5841.1	4992.2	6941.8

incremental net benefits of each program for poor families and expedite the cumulative deterioration process.

The above analysis seems to suggest that, whenever a proposed project creates a significant disparity in net benefits provided by different (but competing) local governments, such a project should, ideally, be left to higher units of government for financing and implementation. Otherwise, the possibility exists of creating detrimental effects.

Boundary Conditions for Benefit-Cost Models

Although resource allocation is a problem for general equilibrium analysis, for obvious practical reasons we are forced to concentrate on only a small part of the general equilibrium system in our benefit-cost models. How do we define the boundaries for this small part of the general equilibrium

Table 7-2
The Basic Model Modified by a Housing Program for the Poor

(1) *Time* *E+00*	*(2)* *NCLA* *E+00*	*(3)* *NBLP* *E+00*	*(4)* *PLA* *E+00*	*(5)* *PLP* *E+00*
.0	.0	3000.0	6000.0	4000.0
1.	−13.8	3720.0	6000.0	4050.0
2.	−565.9	3748.4	6000.0	4100.0
3.	−614.5	3794.3	5999.2	4186.0
4.	−666.2	3842.4	5966.0	4273.4
5.	−721.4	3893.2	5962.3	4363.1
6.	−779.8	3946.1	5926.1	4455.2
7.	−842.1	4002.0	5919.0	4549.9
8.	−908.2	4060.3	5879.3	4647.2
9.	−978.6	4122.0	5868.5	4747.3
10.	−1053.3	4186.3	5824.8	4850.3
11.	−1133.0	5094.8	5809.7	4956.4
12.	−1883.8	5147.7	5761.6	5065.7
13.	−1974.6	5222.9	5741.8	5216.7
14.	−2070.7	5301.1	5648.5	5368.1
15.	−2175.2	5384.1	5623.3	5520.4
16.	−2284.4	5469.7	5524.3	5673.4
17.	−2402.6	5561.0	5492.8	5827.2
18.	−2526.8	5655.1	5387.2	5981.9
19.	−2661.2	5755.6	5348.6	6137.5
20.	−2802.7	5859.3	5235.6	6294.1
21.	−2955.8	5970.1	5188.9	6451.6
22.	−3117.2	6084.4	5067.4	6610.2
23.	−3291.8	6206.8	5011.6	6769.9
24.	−3476.2	6333.0	4880.4	6930.8
25.	−3675.8	6468.3	4814.1	7092.8

system? Obviously, the boundaries of our model must be large enough to save us from the worst evils of suboptimization; however, if the boundaries are too large, the task soon becomes unmanageable!

While there is no clear-cut answer to the above question, there are a few guidelines we can deduce from the comparative-dynamic procedure to help us in practice. These guidelines require us to:

1. Establish a political subdivision whose citizens are the main concern of the analysis.
2. Define the problem that is of major concern for the analysis as it influences the interests of the citizens.
3. Model the dynamic structural relationships that produce the observed symptoms.
4. Isolate the crucial parameters of the model, i.e., those parameters to whose values the key variables of the model are most sensitive.

5. Provide further detail for those parameters that are found to be crucial.[d]

Once we have captured the crucial structural relationships of the model, we can let *our parameters* define all the boundaries of the model. If the model is particularly sensitive to a few parameters, we can:

1. Attempt to "go behind" the "constants" to determine causal relationships producing their values.
2. Then proceed to detail the sensitive parameters further until the key variables do become relatively *insensitive* to all parameters.

This procedure may be quite feasible for some crucial parameters. For example, *PNPEM, NSDA,* and *NPME* were found to be three of the five crucial parameters. It is likely that upon further investigation we could elaborate the causal relations behind these constants; i.e., we would admit that they are variables and we would proceed in an attempt to find the functional relationships of the variables. For other crucial parameters, this procedure, for all practical purposes, may be impossible. For example, no easy functional relationships are likely to be found for the parameters *NPPI* (the rate of productivity growth in the progressive sector) and *EØP* (inflation) in the model. Here we would have to rely on time-series data to provide average long-run values.[e]

Although this procedure for determining the boundary of the model is crude, there do not seem to be many alternatives that are feasible to solve the problem. The procedure does seem to provide an alternative to the more normal piecemeal policy approach (i.e., an approach that looks at just, say, housing or fiscal pressures or migration).

Validation of Dynamic Benefit-Cost Models

The comparative-dynamic procedure relies on data of all kinds for model construction, and therefore should rely on many sources for its validation. One may object to such a model on the grounds that many estimates of values for parameters are crude. However, if we do not hypothesize quantitatively about structural relationships and parameter values that appear only in nonquantitative forms in reality, we may omit relationships from quantitative benefit-cost models that are crucial to the key variables of the model. If we relied exclusively on statistical analysis, we would not be able to locate a sufficient number of observations to estimate the values of most of the parameters for an urban model, at least not at this point in

[d]Steps 1, 2, 4, and 5 are, of course, equally applicable to those problem areas that can be represented accurately by static benefit-cost models.

[e]Exponential smoothing is another procedure that is compatible with our dynamic model for forecasting the values of *NPPI* and *EØP*, and any other parameter whose true value appears to be time related.

time. As a result, our quantitative models would be inadequate for purposes of benefit-cost analysis.

In a dynamic model, such as that described in Chapters 3 and 4, it is possible to isolate effectively the interdependence among all variables. For this reason, a feedback model is likely to produce better results than a regression model, where high multicollinearity is present among explanatory variables. [f] This is feasible because the data requirements for a feedback simulation model are not as stringent as for a multiple-regression model. The reason for this is now clear: a valid structure for a feedback model is far more important for producing accurate evaluations than is a precise assessment of the values of all but a few parameters.

This does not imply that parameters are unimportant to accurate evaluations. It simply implies that, for all but a few parameters (e.g., the five identified in Chapter 5), rough estimates will suffice. An accurate assessment of all remaining parameters (i.e., those that have zero elasticity coefficients) will not improve our evaluations very much, if at all.

Furthermore, even the parameters to whose values the key variables of the model are most sensitive may not be influential for all programs that are evaluated, as illustrated in Chapter 6 (see pp. 109-113). The values of only one or, at most, two of the five crucial parameters were found important for the evaluation of any one of the proposed programs in Chapter 6. However, the extent to which an accurate assessment of parameters matters, and the parameters whose values matter most, can be determined only by testing the sensitivity of parameters in a model of good structural relationships and plausible values for parameters.

Let us now describe the approach to model formulation and validation in complex problem areas. It is a flexible, iterative, and eclectic approach that requires us to:

1. Understand the problem area, including the quantitative findings on the problem.
2. Synthesize previous data and current thoughts, regardless of the quantitative or qualitative form of the data, in order to determine the "proper" structural relationships of the model.
3. Devise a "modular" concept for the model in which each logical part (e.g., sections of the partial urban model) can be analyzed separately in order to determine the reasonableness of the entire model.
4. Perform a sensitivity analysis of the model to determine crucial vari-

[f]It is well known that a high degree of multicollinearity between two or more independent variables in a multiple-regression model makes it extremely difficult, and in many cases impossible, to measure the *individual* influence of explanatory variables on the dependent variables. The multicollinearity problem has, for example, rendered attempts to explain differences in municipal expenditures less than satisfactory. This is illustrated by Masten and Quindry [102].

ables, and then locate further data, insights, and judgment to refine the estimates of crucial variables.

5. Analyze the dynamic properties of the model, and then compare the results of the model to actual results experienced in reality.
6. Perform a second sensitivity study subjecting each benefit-cost evaluation to extensive changes in the values of the parameters found most crucial in the first sensitivity study.
7. Subject the model and the results to the "expert" judgment of professionals experienced in the particular problem area.
8. Alter the model to incorporate new ideas generated by the analysis and by the synthesis of new data.
9. Utilize an efficient computer simulation program for the iterative procedure. [g]

Since a complex social system is likely to be very sensitive to *certain* key parameters, it is extremely useful to distill information from policy makers experienced in the problems affecting the social system under study. Experienced professionals are likely to know of plausible values for key parameters, values that are not obtainable from any other source. [h]

Before we leave the subject of validation, we must point out an inherent limitation of the comparative-dynamic procedure. Although certain dynamic effects are identified and quantified in the procedure, this is accomplished through the time behavior of a predetermined *static* structure. Once the values are set for the level equations and the constants, the dynamic behavior of the model is *determined.* It is this *time-invariant* underlying structure that makes the procedure a comparative-dynamic one. This, of course, makes prediction regarding distant benefits and costs very difficult, since in practice the "constants" and the form of the equations may themselves change over time.

In summary, problems of devising valid operational models of complex social systems are likely to be reduced by the comparative-dynamic procedure. This is possible because we can use many data that are essentially qualitative in form, and because plausible values should suffice for most of the parameters of the model. Such a model has limitations, however, limitations derived from its underlying static structure.

[g]This is the truly remarkable aspect of the DYNAMO Compiler program. All the computer iterations necessary to bring the partial model and the dynamic procedure to the state presented in this book required a budgetary commitment of approximately $800.

[h]Since many of the data required to construct such models are derived from subjective sources, a decision-theoretic approach might be useful after the first sensitivity study. We could solicit prior probabilities from policy makers regarding the many possible values a parameter could take in reality, in order to compute expected values for these parameters. We could revise our prior probabilities over time as new data appear.

Conclusion

In any real-world application of benefit-cost analysis, we must compromise with the exacting requirements of pure economic theory. Otherwise, we could do very little project evaluation, for benefit-cost analysis draws little support from welfare economics. The unmodified benefit-cost criterion meets the exacting requirements of welfare economics only in a world where the income distribution resulting from a project is considered ideal (by some criterion), where there is an omniscient economist who can carry out interpersonal utility comparisons, and where second-best problems are absent. Of course, these conditions are not met even remotely in reality.

Public projects, however, may be evaluated roughly in accordance with the exacting requirements of economic theory. The well-known caveats of welfare analysis should be heeded, and we should modify the results of the pure benefit-cost criterion when good common sense tells us that it is appropriate to do so. We should not allow these familiar warnings, however, to prevent any systematic economic analysis of public projects. A close examination of the results of recently enacted social programs discloses the dangers of relying on other, more subjective and nebulous, criteria for the evaluation of public expenditures. The only criterion that is certainly worse than the benefit-cost criterion is no allocation criterion whatsoever.

The comparative-dynamic procedure should be vastly superior to any rule-of-thumb procedure for the evaluation of public projects that affect complex social systems—systems whose main characteristic is that they produce behavior that is counterintuitive. It is well known that intuitively plausible solutions to problems in these complex systems may actually produce deterioration. These systems require more, and not less, analysis.

The comparative-dynamic procedure allows us to apply economic theory in the investigation of projects that affect complex systems by following roughly the prescriptions of welfare economics. The two most vexing theoretical problems posed by welfare economics for applied work are (1) the need to carry out interpersonal comparisons of utility and (2) the warning, posed by the theorem of second-best, that we should not optimize in a piecemeal manner.

To grapple with the first problem, we established typical groups whose interests were perceived as common in the political process. The procedure was then used to evaluate public projects as they affected the interests of each typical group. This procedure allowed us to determine the approximate effects on income distribution that each project produced.

The problems of second-best were addressed crudely when we attempted to define boundary conditions (see pp. 126-128) broadly enough to prevent the worst evils of suboptimization, while tackling a problem whose size was manageable. Since the urban model captured a system that was reasonably independent of other sectors of the economy, I believe we lessened the sting for our analysis that the theorem of second-best truly creates for other, more piecemeal applications of benefit-cost analysis.

In addition to these theoretical requirements posed for benefit-cost analysis by welfare economics, a benefit-cost study must deal with numerous analytical difficulties. The most serious analytical difficulties arise in:

1. Estimation of benefits and costs.
2. Selection of the discount rate.
3. Provision for uncertainty.

Each of these three problems was addressed by the comparative-dynamic procedure. Compromise (third- or fourth-best) solutions were proposed in Chapters 5 and 6 and reviewed earlier in this chapter. Many additional problems remain to be solved. As our experience with benefit-cost studies grows, compromise solutions to other problems are almost certain to appear. We should be careful not to set impossible standards for ourselves.

Now that we have completed the principal analytical task of this volume, we may turn to some important institutional questions that arise when benefit-cost analysis is applied to program evaluation within the context of the political decision-making process of a democracy. In order to breath life into the evaluation procedure, it must be employed systematically as an integral part of the decision-making process.

8 Is a Systematic Selection Procedure for Rational Public-Expenditure Decisions Possible?

The purpose of this chapter is to determine the extent to which it is possible to evaluate alternative public expenditures systematically in the real world. Before turning directly to answer this question, we must outline the institutional characteristics of the public budgeting process, where these decisions are typically made. This will allow us to define our concept of *rationality* for public-expenditure decision making. Given our definition of rationality, we then examine the extent to which benefit-cost analysis in general and the comparative-dynamic procedure in particular provide a systematic procedure for achieving this behavior in practice. Finally, we return to answer the question posed by the title of this chapter.

Institutional Characteristics of the Budget-Making Process

The budget-making process of democratic governments, within which all public-expenditure decisions are determined, has the following principal characteristics according to Lindblom [91]:

1. It is incremental and historical in nature. Previous budgets are accepted as starting points and are adjusted incrementally, in order to arrive at new budgets. The existing base is never evaluated thoroughly (i.e., zero-base budgeting is never performed).
2. Projects selected in the budget-making process differ only slightly from existing policies—only slightly different projects are relevant politically.
3. A multiplicity of conflicting interests are reconciled in the budgetary process. New policy often results from mutual adjustment of positions by participants. Conflicting interests of legislators, agency bureaucrats, and chief executives are resolved in the process. No one person possesses the unilateral ability to determine the makeup of any part of the budget. The projects and policies that result are generally different from those proposed at the beginning of the process. Actual projects, as a result, usually depart from any one person's ideal.
4. Each participant counts on past decisions for his new policy objectives. In this manner, objectives are defined as a by-product of the policy-making process. A rational decision within this process cannot be defined in terms of meeting a preconceived welfare function.

5. Important consequences of decisions are often overlooked because of self-interest or complexity.

This description of the policy-making process of a democracy makes it quite evident that we should not realistically expect the results of our benefit-cost studies to be translated directly into policy decisions, since actual policy decisions are made by reconciling many conflicting interests and values. Only a naive notion of the budget process could assume that an efficiency criterion such as ours could be dominant in such a process. Therefore, we should expect that the nature of the partisan mutual adjustment process of budget making in a democracy effectively precludes the use of benefit-cost analysis as the *sole* criterion for the selection of public expenditures.

What, then, can we expect as a rational decision-making process for the selection of public expenditures? What role should our procedures play in such a process? It is to these questions that we turn now.

Rationality in Public-Expenditure Decisions

We saw in Chapter 6 that none of the four projects evaluated could be considered value-free, regardless of the size of its discounted net benefits. Some of the proposed projects evaluated there (e.g., the municipal productivity program) should be expected to make both the poor and the affluent better off, although not necessarily by an equal amount. Other projects (e.g., the tax-equalization program) should be expected to benefit one group (the affluent) at the expense of the other (the poor). No final decision on a benefit-cost criterion alone, however, is possible for the latter type of program, since interpersonal comparisons of utility must be made before we can conclude that welfare (i.e., happiness) is increased.

Therefore, all benefit-cost evaluations must be accompanied by value premises regarding the desirability of the resultant state of the distribution of income. Although the procedure described in this volume provides a method for evaluating proposed projects as they affect each typical group, it comes with no set of rules for imputing virtue to the incremental income-distribution effects of each project. These value judgments must be supplied by political decisions in the budget-making process. Therefore, the value or ethical judgments required for virtually every public-expenditure decision are outside the scope of the benefit-cost criterion.

There is, however, a factual basis for each decision too, and it is here that our procedure and more conventional methods are useful. These factual questions include the direct and indirect effects of a potential project along with its effects upon the distribution of income. With this factual information in hand, the political process then can proceed to supply the value information necessary, but now on the basis of more accurate information regarding the allocational and distributional effects of proposed projects. Some welfare economists have suggested that this is the best we can expect. For example, after reviewing the weaknesses of welfare economics for normative purposes, Graaff [65, p. 170] concludes:

> I do feel very strongly that the greatest contribution economics is likely to make to human welfare, broadly conceived, is through positive studies—through contributing to our understanding of how the economic system actually works in practice. . . . If positive economics can provide people with an understanding of the various far-reaching indirect effects of particular policies, it will probably also provide them with a basis for drawing welfare conclusions, for themselves and according to their own lights. In my view the job of the economist is not to try to reach welfare conclusions for others, but rather to make available the positive knowledge . . . on the basis of which laymen can pass judgement.

The comparative-dynamic procedure is intended precisely for the purpose of uncovering the direct and indirect effects of alternative projects and seems to qualify on Graaff's criteria as a procedure for carrying out positive economic studies.

Graaff's requirements for rational public-expenditure decisions seem to complement those of Simon [143]. Simon, while adhering to the notion that evaluation decisions should be split into their factual and ethical components, notes [143, p. 179]:

> that this criterion [the economic efficiency criterion for factual decisions] while it supplies a common denominator for the comparison of administrative alternatives does not supply a common numerator. Even though all decisions be made in terms of alternative applications of the same resources, the problem still remains of comparing the values which are attained by the different courses of action. The efficiency criterion neither solves nor avoids this problem of comparability.

Simon believes that [143, p. 188]

> the portion of the decision-making process which is factual, which is amenable to scientific treatment, resolves itself into the determination of the production functions of administrative activities.

In addition, he believes that [143, p. 189]

> momentous decisions are made every day as to the allocation of resources to one or another competing purpose, and that, particularly in non-commercial organizations, the decisions are made in an almost complete absence of the evidence which would be necessary to validate them.

Rationality, therefore, in Simon's view requires that we uncover relevant social production functions in order to answer factual questions regarding benefits and costs of alternative public-expenditure projects.

Finally, Lindblom [91, pp. 309-310] believes that "the principal characteristic of the rational decision—perhaps the defining characteristic—turns on the accuracy of the decision maker's predictions about the outcome of his policies."

To summarize this discussion, we may say that the rational public-expenditure decision is one which is separated into its factual and value components. The factual component involves uncovering relevant social production functions and subjecting proposed projects, superimposed on these production functions, to the benefit-cost criterion while simultaneously identifying distributional effects. The presentation of these factual data regarding efficiency and distribution is about as far as analysis by economists can proceed. The remaining information required for a rational decision consists of value or ethical judgments, which are needed to supplement these factual data in order to select public projects. The value component of information is the output of the political process.

With these concepts of rationality in mind, we next examine additional realities of budget making and observe the extent to which our benefit-cost procedures may help.

Benefit-Cost Analysis, Incomplete Data, and Public Policy

Given the nature of the budget-making process in a democracy we can be sure that decisions will not ordinarily wait for full and complete analysis on any problem. A problem is identified and political pressures begin to build to enact legislation to solve the problem. Intuitive solutions which address the visible symptoms of a problem are often chosen, unless these "solutions" have been shown to be ineffective in the past. The search for solutions tends to be fairly simpleminded; solutions are often sought in the portion of the social system where the symptoms appear.

The one lesson we have learned from past experience is that social problems are often embedded within complex systems and the symptoms they exhibit are often unrelated in time and location to underlying causes. Public programs which attack these symptoms are often doomed at the outset. These are the lessons reviewed in Chapter 2.

The reasons why so many social programs fail to accomplish their stated objectives lie in the deficiency of information regarding the true nature of the social production functions upon which these programs are to act.

This deficiency of information means, in Fabricant's words [55, p. 160], that "too little is yet known about the connection between any given policy and its results." Often, in the case of social production functions, the underlying dynamics among the variables producing symptoms critically affect the dynamic time path of benefits and costs for projects that are offered as solutions. In other cases, the production functions may be relatively simple and the benefits and costs of a project itself may not be affected critically by the dynamic time path of the existing social production function. In the former case, the comparative-dynamic procedure is required. In the latter case, a static benefit-cost procedure will suffice.

As indicated in Chapter 2, I believe that many, perhaps most, of the programs affecting health, education, housing, welfare, and transportation require a dynamic evaluation procedure because of the internal dynamics of the relevant social production functions upon which they act.

I also believe that programs affecting the physical environment and the criminal-justice system fall into the same category. On the other hand, programs affecting water resources, the judiciary, foreign policy, defense, disease prevention, and safety may possibly be evaluated successfully by static methods. However, before we content ourselves with the static procedure, we should examine the dynamic variables in each production function. *Only after we have examined the dynamics* and found proposed projects to be relatively unaffected by the dynamic time path of the underlying production function can we be sure that the static procedure is correct. Furthermore, even when the static method is used, we must be sure we have uncovered the relevant social production function.

The comparative-dynamic procedure employing the simulation method allows us to assemble the relevant quantitative and qualitative research findings on a problem into one comprehensive, eclectic model. The model may then be employed to evaluate alternative projects as they affect our typical groups of citizens. Any portions of such models that are found crucial because of the sensitivity of project evaluations to their specification should be candidates for additional research.

Since the realities of the political decison-making process require programs to solve immediate problems, we are compelled to bring the best data available to the decision. Therefore, it is not valid to ignore analysis of a problem because of incomplete data, since, with or without analysis, decisions will be made!

To summarize this chapter to this point, benefit-cost analysis is the proper tool to use to answer the factual or positive questions regarding the direct and indirect economic effects of proposed projects. This factual information, including the distribution of benefits and costs, becomes the basis for decision making in the public domain. Value or ethical judgments are added in the political process once this factual information is made available. This combination of factual and value information in the decision-making process is the hallmark of a rational decision. Factual benefit-cost information should be compiled for each major decision, bringing together in the process all quantitative and qualitative findings available in an eclectic model to support the decision.

A dynamic procedure is required to evaluate those problem areas in which the dynamics of the variables in the relevant social production function affect, in a nontrivial way, the benefits and costs of new programs. Where this is not true, a static procedure will suffice.

Additional Requirements for a Systematic Selection Procedure

A systematic selection procedure must be capable of evaluating projects whose objectives are primarily distributional by the same methods used to evaluate projects whose objectives are primarily concerned with improving economic efficiency.

Income-distribution effects of proposed projects provide critical data for each public-expenditure decision. For example, the tax-equalization program evaluated in Chapter 6 is one that is highly beneficial for the affluent population of the central city and certainly is in accordance with their partisan self-interests, even though, when net costs to the poor are considered, the net-present value of the project is negative. In reality, the affluent may be able to muster sufficient political support to approve such a program. If we assume the poor to be aware of the detrimental effects of this program to their interests, their only recourse is to the political process, where they can seek to reverse the decision on tax equalization or seek an equally lopsided program in their behalf, such as the housing or welfare program illustrated in Chapter 7. This is the way the political budgetary process works.

Moreover, our evaluation of "pure" distributional programs, such as the tax-equalization program of Chapter 6 and the welfare program of Chapter 7, illustrates the impossibility of evaluating programs affecting the allocation of resources differently from programs affecting the distribution of income. Each type of program has effects upon the allocation of resources and upon the distribution of income. Each type of program, one justified primarily on the grounds of efficiency and the other justified primarily on the grounds of equity, promotes the economic interests of some and tramples upon the interests of others.

Each of these programs, one primarily affecting income distribution and the other primarily affecting the allocation of resources, is evaluated similarly by various partisan groups regardless of the primary intent of the program. They both are subject to similar factual questions and tests of rationality, and therefore should be subjected to benefit-cost analysis in order to assess their direct and indirect effects. Each type of program should be evaluated identically in the decision-making process.

At this point I should like to stress another requirement pertaining to the treatment of certain pecuniary externalities in benefit-cost analysis, since conventional methods of benefit-cost analysis have often ignored them completely. Citizens of the central city cannot estimate, on the basis of the existing tax and benefit structure of the municipality, the net benefits they can derive from remaining in or leaving the city, since those data depend upon the uncoordinated actions of other citizens. Therefore, although there is no strict interdependence of utility functions among these citizens, the market data alone fail to provide sufficient information to allow these citizens to individually arrive at optimum decisions in much the same way that the market fails to incorporate full social costs in the case of technological externalities. In both cases, government is justified in entering to remedy an otherwise nonoptimum distribution of resources.

The point here is that government intervention is required in the presence of certain pecuniary externalities which have the effect of frustrating consumer goals (or sovereignty). These goals are what Graaff [65, p. 104] calls "political," and may only be achieved by the coordinated action of the group. A systematic selection procedure should be capable of evaluating this type of public program, and here a dynamic evaluation procedure appears mandatory.

The final requirement for a systematic selection procedure involves programs designed to achieve objectives in the stabilization branch of public finance. In my view, the most serious deficiency in current macroeconomic models is the exclusion of any indication of "who" benefits and "who" is harmed by various policy alternatives to achieve stabilization objectives. Much of the current discussion regarding the effectiveness of various policies to curb inflation, for example, is to me quite sterile; for there seems to be widespread agreement on the overall qualitative effects of many alternative programs, but no indication of the appropriate distribution of benefits and costs of these programs—critical data to make the decision-making process rational (regarding these stabilization activities). Groups now support policies which, when their full effects are known, may be counter to the true interests they espouse in the partisan mutual-adjustment process. This problem may be corrected by adapting the dynamic benefit-cost procedure to macroeconomic models.

To summarize, in practice, benefit-cost analysis has an extremely important role to play in the selection of public expenditures in each of the three highly interrelated branches of public finance: allocation of resources, distribution of income, and stabilization of the economy. Its role is to supply the factual or positive information to decision makers so that the discounted net benefits of each proposed program and their distribution are known, at least approximately, before value judgments are added and decisions made. In each type of program, the selection procedure should include estimates of pecuniary externalities whenever these externalities prevent individuals from achieving optimum decisions because of the effects of uncoordinated actions of others.

Conclusion

At this point, the reader must feel that I have a strong preference for a systematic selection procedure anchored in benefit-cost analysis for most public expenditure decisions. Like most economists, I do indeed. An entire volume could be written citing the many public programs which have failed to achieve their objectives because such a systematic procedure was either not applied or applied incorrectly. A systematic benefit-cost procedure applied to the relevant social production functions could have led to much-improved decisions.

Clearly there are a number of theoretical problems, which have been reviewed in this volume, that beleaguer the benefit-cost criterion. However, in each case the sting of these theoretical problems is softened considerably when the realities of the budget process are considered. For example, even if we could carry out interpersonal comparisons of utility, we should not expect political decision makers to embrace our studies and make only those decisions which provide the greatest improvement to national welfare.

An interpersonal comparison of utility would merely provide more factual information concerning the program alternatives under consideration—information that would contribute to improved decisions. Policy makers would supplement this additional information with value information and arrive at their own decision. In other words, benefit-cost analysis provides certain factual information for the decision process which has value itself, notwithstanding the fact that is devoid of any interpersonal comparisons of utility, for even with such comparisons, the decision would be far from automatic. Only the factual basis would be improved.

Similarly, the theoretical difficulties posed by problems of second-best are not of great practical significance, so long as we are concerned with those public projects which produce relatively high social returns and displace only that private production and consumption which provides relatively low social returns.

The analytical problems encountered in a typical benefit-cost study and reviewed in Chapters 1 and 7 are numerous, but no more difficult than those confronting the national-income accountant. These problems require us to work for good second-or third-best compromise solutions, and to continue to improve our solutions.

Rationality in public-expenditure decisions requires us to uncover the likely effects of alternative projects before we choose among them. Benefit-cost analysis, so long as it is carried out properly, allows us to do precisely that. Value or ethical judgments must be made once this information is available. The political process of a democracy, however, is set up to supply just that kind of value information.

In conclusion, benefit-cost analysis used in conjunction with the political process constitutes a systematic procedure for rational decision making in the public domain. We must be careful, however, not to set impossible theoretical standards for such a procedure. If we do, we should be prepared to surrender at once!

Appendix A: The Basic Model

```
100   *
200   *
300   *
400   *   DYNAMIC BENEFIT-COST ANALYSIS
500   R   MWINPS.KL=NPPI*(LCNPS.K*PNPI.K) * EØP
600   C   NPPI=.031
700   R   MPINPS.KL=NPINPS*(LCNPS.K*PNPI.K)
800   C   NPINPS=.0
900   L   LCNPS.K=LCNPS.J+DT*(MWINPS.JK-MPINPS.JK)
1000  N   LCNPS=60000000
1100  A   PNPI.K=PLA.K/LEV4.K
1200  A   PPI.K=PLP.K/LEV5.K
1300  R   MWIPS.KL=NPPI*(LCPS.K*PPI.K)*(EOP)
1400  C   EOP=2.0
1500  R   MPIPS.KL=NPPI*(LCPS.K*PPI.K)
1600  L   LCPS.K=LCPS.J+DT*(MWIPS.JK-MPIPS.JK)
1700  N   LCPS=12000000
1800  A   WSLM.K=NAS.K+NPS.K
1900  R   MECI.KL=PNPEM*(LCNPS.K-LEV3.K) +PPEM*(LCPS.K-LEV2.K)
2000  C   PNPEM=.0537
2100  C   PPEM=.0056
2200  L   MC.K=MC.J+DT*MECI.JK+WPPAPF.J+ NEW.J+MEIP.J
2300  N   MC=0
2400  A   NEW.K=-MPIP.K+MCPI.K+PHCC.K
2500  L   NAS.K=NAS.J+DT*(MWINPS.JK)
2600  N   NAS=60000000
2700  R   RESDIA.KL=NSDA*(NAS.K*NPME)/PLA.K
2800  C   NSDA=-0.06
2900  R   RCIA.KL=MCA.K-LEV6.K
3000  L   NBCLA.K=NBCLA.J+DT*(RESDIA.JK-RCIA.JK)
3100  N   NBCLA=0
3200  R   PMA.KL=DELAY(PADA.JK,AMD)
3300  R   PADA.KL=TABHL(PADAT,NBCLA.K,-10000,10000,5000)
3400  T   PADAT=-300/-150/0/150/300
3500  C   AMD=.5
3600  C   NAFM=.10
3700  L   PLA.K=PLA.J+DT*(PMA.JK)
3800  N   PLA=6000
3900  N   AH=6000
4000  L   AH.K=AH.J+DT*(PMA.JK/DAHC)
4100  C   DAHC=11 YEARS
4200  R   RESDIP.KL=NPISDP*((WSLM.K-LEV1.K) /TPL.K)+PHCC.K/PLP.K
4300  C   NPISDP=.10
4400  R   RCIP.KL=(MCP.K-LEV7.K)
4500  L   NBCLP.K=NBCLP.J+DT*(RESDIP.JK- RCIP.JK)+WPPAPF.J/PLP.J
4600  N   NBCLP=3000
4700  R   PMP.KL=DELAY1(PADP.JK,PMD)
4800  R   PADP.KL=TABHL(PADPT,NBCLP.K,0,10000,5000)
4900  T   PADPT=-100/150/200
5000  C   PMD=1 YEAR
5100  C   NPFM=.10
```

```
5200   L   PLP.K=PLP.J+DT*(PMP.JK)
5300   N   PLP=4000
5400   N   PH=4000
5500   L   PH.K=PH.J+DT*(PMP.JK/PHAD)+PHCP.J
5600   L   TPL.K=TPL.J+DT*(PMP.JK+PMA.JK)
5700   N   TPL=10000
5800   A   MTR.K=MC.K/(AVAH.K+AVPH.K)
5900   A   MCA.K=((MTR.K*AVAH.K)/AH.K)-PTCAP.K
6000   A   AVAH.K=AH.K*NMAAVH*MAVR.K
6100   C   NMAAVH=1000
6200   A   AVPH.K=PH.K*NAVPH
6300   C   NAVPH=30
6400   C   NPPA=.60
6500   A   MAVR.K=NPPA/(PLA.K/TPL.K)
6600   A   AVP.K=AVAH.K+AVPH.K
6700   A   MR.K=(AVP.K)*(MTR.K)-PTCAP.K*AH.K
6800   A   MCP.K=((MTR.K*AVPH.K)/PH.K)
6900   L   LEV3.K=LCNPS.J
7000   N   LEV3=0
7100   L   LEV1.K=WSLM.J
7200   N   LEV1=0
7300   L   LEV2.K=LCPS.J
7400   N   LEV2=0
7500   L   LEV6.K=MCA.J
7600   N   LEV6=0
7700   L   LEV7.K=MCP.J
7800   N   LEV7=0
7900   L   LEV4.K=PLA.J
8000   L   LEV5.K=PLP.J
8100   N   LEV5=4000
8200   N   LEV4=6000
8300   A   PHCC.K=PULSE(HGHT1.K,FRST10,INTVL)
8400   C   FRST10=10
8500   A   HGHT1.K=PHCP.K*CPH
8600   A   PHCP.K=PULSE(HGHT2.K,FRST10,INTVL)
8700   A   HGHT2.K=PHCR*PH.K
8800   C   PHCR=0
8900   C   CPH=10000
9000   A   WPPAPF.K=PULSE(HGHT.K,FRST8,INTVL)
9100   C   FRST8=8
9200   A   HGHT.K=PLP.K*WPPF
9300   C   WPPF=000 DOLLARS YR. PER FAMILY
9400   C   INTVL=50
9500   A   TNBCLA.K=NBCLA.K*PLA.K
9600   A   MCEA.K=(AH.K-PLA.K)*MCA.K
9700   A   TNBCLP.K=NBCLP.K*PLP.K
9800   A   PTCAP.K=PTCA*CLIP (0,1,SWT5,TIME.K)
9900   C   PTCA=0
10000  C   SWT5=5 YEARS
10100  A   MPIP.K=MPI*MC.K*CLIP(0,1,SWT1, TIME.K)
10200  C   MPI=0 PER YEAR
10300  C   SWT1=1 YEAR
10400  C   MCPP=0
10500  A   MCPI.K=MCPP*CLIP(0,1,SWT1,TIME.K)
10600  L   NPS.K=NPS.J+DT*(MWIPS.JK)
10700  N   NPS=12000000
10800  A   NAMD.K=NAFM*(NAS.K/PLA.K)
```

```
10900  A     NPMD.K=NPFM*(NAS.K/PLP.K)
11000  C     NPME=.023
11100  C     PHAD=11
11200  A     MEIP.K=AAEE*CLIP(0,1,SWT1,TIME.K)
11300  C     AAEE=0
11400  NOTE
11500  PRINT NBCLA,NBCLP,PLA,PLP,MCEA
11600  PLOT  NBCLA=A,NBCLP=P,PLA=R,PLP=I
11700  SPEC  DT=1/LENGTH=25/PRTPER=1/PLTPER=0
11800  RUN BASIC
```

Appendix B: Tertiary Variables of the Basic Model

(1) Year	(2) LCNPS (Millions)	(3) LCPS (Millions)	(4) MECI (Thousands)	(5) WSLM (Millions)	(6) MC (Millions)	(7) MR (Millions)	(8) MTR ($/Thousand)	(9) MAVR	(10) NAMD	(11) NPMD
0	60	12	3289.2	72	0	0	0	1.0	1000	300
1	63.72	12.372	201.8	76.46	3.289	3.289	.5348	1.0050	1062	314.67
2	67.67	12.760	214.3	81.19	3.491	3.491	.5649	1.0100	1127.8	329.77
3	71.87	13.161	227.5	86.19	3.705	3.705	.5945	1.0187	1197.9	342.13
4	76.32	13.577	241.6	91.48	3.933	3.933	.6246	1.0298	1279.3	354.63
5	81.03	14.007	255.1	97.04	4.174	4.174	.6572	1.0391	1359.0	367.03
6	86.05	14.450	272.1	102.95	4.430	4.430	.6899	1.0511	1452.0	379.34
7	91.25	14.908	257.3	109.17	4.702	4.702	.7255	1.0612	1543.3	391.56
8	97.01	15.380	306.4	115.77	4.989	4.989	.7610	1.0743	1650.0	403.67
9	102.98	15.867	323.5	122.71	5.295	5.295	.7998	1.0854	1754.8	415.67
10	109.35	16.369	345.0	130.09	5.619	5.619	.8383	1.0996	1877.4	427.56
11	116.08	16.888	364.3	137.86	5.964	5.964	.8803	1.1119	1998.1	439.33
12	123.26	17.423	388.5	146.11	6.328	6.328	.9220	1.1275	2139.4	450.97
13	130.84	17.975	410.1	154.79	6.717	6.717	.9674	1.1411	2278.8	462.48
14	138.93	18.544	437.3	164.01	7.127	7.127	1.0121	1.1585	2442.2	473.84
15	147.46	19.132	461.5	173.72	7.564	7.564	1.0609	1.1737	2603.8	485.05
16	156.56	19.738	492.2	184.04	8.026	8.026	1.1087	1.1930	2793.6	496.10
17	166.17	20.364	519.3	194.89	8.518	8.518	1.1608	1.2101	2981.6	506.98
18	176.41	21.010	553.8	206.43	9.037	9.037	1.2114	1.2318	3203.2	517.68
19	187.22	21.677	584.2	218.57	9.591	9.591	1.2666	1.2512	3423.2	528.20
20	198.75	22.365	622.8	231.48	10.175	10.175	1.3197	1.2758	3683.1	538.53

Appendix C: Cost and Benefit Evaluation of the Sacramento Transit Authority *

Interim Technical Report No. 4
CAL - MTD - 10

October 1970

Milton S. Baum, Ph.D., Professor of Economics
Albert Gutowsky, Ph.D., Associate Professor of Economics
Gerald Rucker, Student Research Assistant

Benefits-Costs Model

Summary

The objective of this study is to estimate the benefits and costs of the Sacramento Transit Authority operation, not only to the patrons of the service but also to those using automobiles and the general public. This analysis is based on data developed from the on-bus survey of transit passengers riding regularly scheduled lines and conducted in May 1968. The purpose of this survey was to determine the destinations, origins, economic and sociological characteristics of the transit riders. Other data are based on the household survey of Sacramento residents made by the California State Division of Highways.

Benefits from the operation of the transit system accrue to automobile users in the form of less street and highway congestion, less smog, and lowered welfare costs. Some riders lacking other means of transportation would be unable to retain their employment and would change their status from producers and tax contributors to charges upon society if transit was not available. Revenues from fares, advertising, and charter operations have been less than the operating and indirect costs of the transit system since 1960, and declining revenues accompanied by deficit operations has

*Research initiated and completed under an Urban Mass Transportation Grant, Department of Transportation Contract No. DOT-UT-42 between the Transit Authority of the City of Sacramento, California and the United States of America, and under a subcontract between the Sacramento Transit Authority and the Sacramento State College Foundation.

been the typical transit situation throughout the country. This study attempts to put a money value on these other benefits so a more accurate assessment of the Sacramento Transit Authority may be made. Techniques used in this analysis should be useful in other cities.

Since World War II the national trend has been for riders to desert public transit in favor of automobiles which adds to street congestion and slows transit service. This diversion reduces transit revenues, increases congestion and transit system costs which in turn triggers a reduction in schedules motivating more transit patrons to substitute private autos; thus completing a vicious cycle with our cities suffering from the resultant smog, congestion and devotion of more and more land to the private automobile.

Local transit affords captive riders the opportunities to engage in social-cultural activities, as well as employment that would be impossible or impractical without public transportation. Most of the costs and benefits of the system may be estimated in dollars, but the social-cultural advantages, as well as the reduction in air pollution, do not lend themselves to this approach.

Air Pollution

Air pollution and ecology are popular subjects for discussion, but few positive steps have been taken to improve the situation. One expert has stated that motor vehicles are responsible for at least 90 percent of the nitrogen oxides, between 60 and 70 percent of the hydrocarbons, and approximately 50 percent of the particle matter that contaminate the atmosphere.[a] It is estimated in this study that if the transit system was not available the additional pollutants per year for the Sacramento area, excluding weekend traffic, would be approximately 1007 tons of carbon monoxide, 240 tons of hydrocarbons and 37 tons of oxides of nitrogen. These estimates assume the present 1.36 persons per automobile and a 20 percent reduction in travel by captive riders caused by the lack of transportation facilities.

Benefits

In estimating the costs and benefits a person's time is given a range of values from $1.55 to $3.75. Generally, the higher values of time increase the benefits from the transit system because the latter reduces auto congestion and saves time for the auto user.

[a]Sacramento Bee, July 27, 1968, p. D18, reporting on research of Dr. Lowell L. Coulson, Professor of Meteorology, University of California, Davis.

In this study, benefits and costs are estimated for peak, off-peak and the total for these two periods. Under the assumptions used in this study, the total benefits exceed costs from $2,660,999 to $3,912,090 for the system dependent upon the value of time utilized.[b] Included in the costs is an imputed interest rate of 6 percent applied to the city's net adjusted investment to the transit system of $1,912,064 (as of May 31, 1968). Although the city is not actually paying interest on this investment as the funds are not borrowed, there is nevertheless an opportunity cost, since the city is currently borrowing for parking lots and other purposes at 6 percent interest. The benefit-cost ratio for the system varies between 2.1 and 2.79 depending upon the value of time utilized and whether the imputed interest cost on the city's investment in the transit system is included or not.[c] Table I summarizes the costs and benefits under four different time valuations. The higher the time valuation the greater the benefits of the transit system due to the savings of time for the motorists through reduced traffic congestion.

Lines 6, 1, 5 and 3 were the leaders in producing net benefits as shown in Table VII. Weekend, charter and advertising revenues and expenses are not allocated to individual lines but are included in the benefit-cost analysis of the system as a whole.[d] Route 9 was not computed on the 1968 data as it was a brand new route at the time of the survey and needed time to build new clientele. It also serves as a connecting link between other lines thus increasing the utility of those lines. Data for 1969 operations indicate Line 9 costs exceeded benefits, but since that survey passenger traffic has been steadily increasing. This line should be carefully analyzed to see if increased promotion and route modification would improve its benefit-cost ratio.

In addition to the benefits measured in monetary terms the transit system also produces other important benefits such as reduced pollution and socio-cultural advantages that contribute to the quality of life. Without transit the increase auto congestion would create more problems for the police traffic details and financing problems for parking lots in the central business district. Increased congestion would no doubt result in more land being devoted to the automobile and take more real property off the tax rolls.

Many of the benefits both pecuniary and non-pecuniary are not limited to the City of Sacramento. The area served by the transit line includes parts

[b]Line 9 was excluded from this computation.

[c]The real costs of driving automobiles are customarily understated by disregarding the opportunity cost of interest and property taxes on the resources devoted to the road and highway system. This practice encourages the increase in use of private automobiles at the expense of transit.

[d]Weekend traffic was not sampled in the on-bus survey.

Table I
Summary Benefits and Costs, Sacramento Transit Lines, 1968[a]

	Values of Time			
	$1.55	*$1.80*	*$2.80*	*$3.75*
Benefits				
Increased congestion costs to auto users	$ 839,832	$1,006,751	$1,316,508	$2,090,923
Increased welfare costs and lost wages if bus not available	2,569,192	2,569,192	2,569,192	2,569,192
Revenue: weekday operations	1,233,824	1,233,824	1,233,824	1,233,824
Revenue: weekends	111,175	111,175	111,175	111,175
Revenue: charter operations	257,589	257,589	257,589	257,589
Revenue: advertising	17,367	17,367	17,367	17,367
Total benefits	5,028,979	5,195,898	5,505,655	6,280,070
Costs				
Operating costs: weekdays	1,780,006	1,780,006	1,780,006	1,780,006
Operating costs: weekends	286,676	286,676	286,676	286,676
Charter costs	186,574	186,574	186,574	186,574
Opportunity cost[b]	114,724	114,724	114,724	114,724
Total costs	2,367,980	2,367,980	2,367,980	2,367,980
Benefits minus costs	2,660,999	2,827,918	3,137,675	3,912,090
Cost-benefit ratio	2.123	2.194	2.325	2.652
Cost-benefit ratio without opportunity cost[b]	2.231	2.305	2.443	2.786
Line 9[a]				
Benefits	59,182			
Costs	90,745			
Benefit-cost ratio	.65			

[a]Line 9 was a new line when the 1968 survey was conducted and was not included in the system analysis. Separate benefit-cost ratios based on 1969 revenue and cost data are indicated above. The line has been showing an improvement in patronage and should be given an opportunity to prove itself.

[b]Opportunity cost referred to here is the estimated 6 percent interest on the city's net investment in the transit system. Although they are not paying interest to others on this investment, the city is paying 6 percent on other borrowed funds.

of Yolo, Placer, and Sacramento County in addition to the city. Thus, financial assistance from the people within the area served, rather than the present support from only the City of Sacramento is a logical approach to the financial problems of the Sacramento Transit Authority. More financial support making it possible to operate more frequent schedules would help reduce congestion and pollution caused largely by motorists. A change of attitudes causing a transfer of more people from the private automobile to the transit system would also help reduce these problems. An educational campaign led by the city and state officials pointing out the pollution reductions caused by the substitution of bus travel for the private automobile may be helpful.

Application of Benefit-Cost Analysis to the Sacramento Transit Authority

The important role of transportation in American cities is widely recognized for its economic importance and its impact upon the quality of life. Thus a comprehensive analysis of the impacts of our transportation system on urban living is very important. This benefit-cost analysis of the Sacramento Transit system attempts to quantify the influence of the system upon the community by estimating not only the revenues and expenditures of the system but also the externalities or benefits and costs to the community as a whole.

With-Without Comparisons

Without the transit system alternative means of transportation would be necessary and the additional costs and benefits of such facilities to the individual and society are estimated in this report. Important benefits of the system are reduced congestion, pollution and an improvement in the quality of life for those without alternate means of transport. More general use of transit would reduce traffic congestion, pollution and need for more street and parking facilities. Reduced traffic congestion would decrease the workload for traffic control officers allowing some reallocation of police time to other pressing problems. Without public transit some workers dependent upon such facilities to commute to their places of employment would lose their jobs and become dependent upon welfare for support.

Revenues

Revenues from fares, advertising and charters are also benefits. Fare revenues by line peak and off-peak are estimated for a year of weekday revenue in Table II. The system's advertising revenues for 1968 were $17,367 and net revenues from charter operations after expenses were $71,015.

Table II
Estimated Revenue From Weekday Operations, 1968

Line	*Peak*	*Off-Peak*	*Total*
1	$87,732	$66,168	$153,900
2	59,090	22,990	82,080
3	71,725	61,085	132,810
4	44,175	29,402	73,577
5	92,150	69,492	161,642
6	121,030	64,790	185,820
7	43,415	47,072	90,487
8	43,272	50,825	94,097
10	21,748	3,250	24,998
11, 12	40,560	17,420	57,980
13	17,428	20,020	37,448
14	22,100	22,165	44,265
15	23,545	22,620	46,165
16	3,510	2,990	6,500
17, 18	20,280	21,125	41,405
19[a]	650	—	650
Total	712,410	521,414	1,213,328

[a]Line 19 was discontinued on 9/6/70.

Impact upon Present Auto Users

Estimates were made of the increased cost to present auto users if congestion was increased as a result of present transit users substituting automobiles. Mr. Herbert Mohring has estimated the increase in time, operating and accident costs per vehicle mile on urban streets at various volume capacities.[e] Mr. Mohring used $1.55 and $2.80 per hour as time values. In the Sacramento study, additional time values of $1.80 and $3.75 per hour have been estimated by this staff. The volume capacity ratio on urban roads during the peak hours has been assumed to be .7. For short periods of time during the peak hours main traffic arteries in Sacramento were congested beyond capacity. Lacking data from traffic engineers on the percentage of capacity utilized throughout the peak periods judgment indicated that .7 of capacity was a reasonable factor. No consideration has been given to added congestion costs for off-peak and weekend traffic, as the impact of the transit system passengers during such periods is small.

Additional time values were added based upon Sacramento data for 1968 indicating an estimated hourly wage rate for workers of $3.75 per hour and $1.32 per hour average per person in the area, whether working or not. The latter figure multiplied by 1.36 persons per car equals $1.80 per hour.

[e]Herbert Mohring, *Urban Highway Investments*, Measuring Benefits of Government Investments, Brookings Institute (1965) 1.248.

Considerable differences of opinion exist as to whether time spent in an automobile should be valued at the same level as time on the job. Recent empirical studies estimate time spent commuting as worth between 33 and 50 percent of the wage rate.[f] On the other hand, researchers Dan Haney and Tom Thomas reported in a Stanford Research Institute study for the Bureau of Public Roads an estimate of $2.82 per hour for peak hour traffic. This figure is very close to the $2.80 value used in this study for Sacramento. Based upon a range of time values from $1.55 to $3.75 the increased costs to present auto users for one year are estimated in Table III.

Automobile Costs for Transit Patrons

When time is valued from $1.55 to $3.75 per hour transit riders would apparently decrease their own transportation costs by substituting automobiles because transit use typically involves more walking and waiting time. The fact that the transit riders did not substitute automobiles was due to one or more considerations. Some of these were non-availability of an automobile or inability to drive, convenience of the bus when parking is difficult, traffic congestion, a dislike for driving responsibilities and in some instances a low opportunity cost for time.[g]

Since the transit riders did not substitute automobiles for these trips it can be assumed that the use of automobiles would not have decreased their commuting cost or they would have utilized the automobile when possible to do so. In some instances transit may have had a considerably lower opportunity cost than automobile transportation but how much lower would be dependent upon personal factors not possible to calculate. It will be assumed here that the cost of using the automobile including parking and time cost is the same as the cost of using transit including time cost, although in some instances this may over-estimate the cost of transit.

Parking Facilities

Diversion of transit customers to automobiles would create demands upon the city for increased parking facilities with the attendant problem of selling

[f]Everett Johnston, *Valuation of Travel Time* (unpublished), paper presented at the Western Economic Association Meeting, August, 1970.

[g]The area served by the Sacramento Transit lines does not include all of the Sacramento Regional area, but the data indicates that the family income of the transit users is lower than that of the automobile users and probably the former have lower opportunity costs for time. Median family income for bus riders, 1968, was $6340 per year compared to $8116 for Sacramento Regional Area. The income figure for bus riders was obtained from the on-bus survey and the regional data from the Division of Highways' regional random sample of five percent of households.

Table III
Estimated Increased Congestion Costs to Auto Users from Elimination of Transit (Peak Only)

	Values of Time			
Line	*$1.55*	*$1.80*	*$2.80*	*$3.75*
1	71,408	84,391	110,358	175,275
2	70,896	83,786	109,567	174,018
3	50,120	59,233	77,458	123,021
4	31,378	37,083	48,494	77,020
5	46,963	55,507	72,579	115,272
6	95,804	113,223	148,060	235,155
7	24,813	29,324	38,347	60,904
8	32,872	38,853	50,808	80,695
10[a]				
11, 12	95,585	112,968	147,722	234,617
13	123,558	160,232	209,534	332,788
14	72,914	86,171	112,685	178,970
15	59,110	69,858	91,352	145,089
16	37,755	44,619	58,348	92,670
17, 18	26,656	31,503	41,196	65,429
19[b]				
Total	839,832	1,006,751	1,316,508	2,090,923

[a]Line 10 carried so few passengers that the congestion costs if automobiles were substituted would be insignificant.

[b]Line 19 did not travel on the highly congested roads or arterials.

bonds to finance the project. The costs of financing, construction and land acquisition are expected to be recovered from parking fees but lost property taxes from real estate taken off the tax roll are an additional factor to be considered. It is estimated that the lost property taxes would amount to approximately $30.00 per space per year and would increase over time as property becomes more valuable. The total amount of lost property taxes has not been computed in the benefit-cost ratios for the transit system as the number of increased spaces would be influenced by the ability of the present facilities to absorb the increased traffic and the length of time that the diverted transit users would be parking automobiles in such facilities. The avoidance of the financing problems for such facilities and the loss of property tax revenues on real estate that would have to be condemned for such additional parking facilities are additional factors in favor of transit facilities that are not included in the benefit-cost ratios computed in this paper.

Transit and Job Opportunity

Public transit is of great importance to the poor, the elderly and the infirm who for one reason or another cannot drive or cannot afford an automobile. The problem has been well stated by Mr. Charles M. Haar, as follows:

> In a highly differentiated and diffused urban society, transportation becomes vital to the economic and social welfare of individuals; it determines the nature and variety of opportunities available in jobs, housing, recreation, shopping, and entertainment. The McCone Commission, for example, found that an important factor in the hostility underlying the Watts riot was the sense of isolation due to the inadequate transportation system right spank in the middle of the most motorized city in the United States. The isolation was pervasive, extending even to services intended to benefit the inhabitants of the area; it required a bus ride of two hours to reach the County General Hospital and an hour and forty-five minutes to get to the Youth Employment Training Center.
>
> Transportation, therefore, has become a vital lifeline to jobs, education, and public services in American cities. Unfortunately, our present transportation system does not provide adequately for many persons most in need of the services it can perform; it has created a new "minority" in this country of those who cannot drive: the old, the young, the poor, and the handicapped.[h]

If public transit was not available, the existing transit users not having the use of a car would be forced to either move within walking distance of work, which is not practical in many instances, quit their jobs, drive themselves or obtain rides with other drivers. Some, however, would be forced to give up jobs which would be a loss to them, and also to society. The impact upon society would be reduced by some replacement by persons previously unemployed. The individuals faced with the loss of their jobs are likely to be poor or elderly, or both, as people in these groups are less likely to have automobiles available. Persons seeking work also frequently use transit service for this purpose. Consequently, the costs to society in lost production and welfare costs would increase if bus service was not available, subject to adjustments for those taken off welfare rolls and employed as a result of replacing workers without personal transportation (see Table IV). It is assumed that half of the workers losing their jobs will be forced on welfare. Some of the workers losing their jobs will have family incomes from other sources such as spouses employed, retirement or investments while others will have no other source of income and will be forced on welfare. The estimate is that half will fall in the latter category. Cost is based on average cost per welfare case, plus 19.72% administrative

[h]Charles M. Haar, "Transportation and Economic Opportunity," *Traffic Quarterly*, October 1967, p. 521.

Table IV
Estimated Increased Welfare Costs and Loss in Wages for Captive Riders

	Loss of Wages			*Increase in Welfare*		
Line	*Peak*	*Off-Peak*	*Total*	*Peak*	*Off-Peak*	*Total*
1	$73,125	$55,165	$128,290	$129,825	$97,938	$227,763
2	49,768	19,312	68,970	88,166	34,287	122,453
3	42,012	35,788	77,800	88,816	75,658	164,474
4	44,226	29,484	73,710	75,096	50,064	125,160
5	84,691	63,889	148,580	124,829	94,169	218,998
6	69,605	48,370	117,975	123,581	94,878	209,459
7	33,575	36,372	69,947	46,836	50,740	97,576
8	41,101	48,250	89,351	57,336	67,308	124,644
10	8,072	1,206	9,278	21,037	3,144	24,181
11, 12	30,866	13,229	44,095	70,920	30,394	101,314
13	6,722	7,890	14,612	14,586	17,123	31,709
14	14,514	14,513	29,027	23,137	23,137	46,274
15	20,290	19,495	39,785	27,807	26,717	54,524
16	2,513	2,140	4,653	6,543	5,573	12,116
17, 18	17,318	18,025	35,343	22,548	23,469	46,017
19	825	—	825	1,289	—	1,289
Total	539,113	413,128	952,241	922,352	694,599	1,616,951

average cost in Sacramento County.[i] Lost wages are based on conservative estimates of $1.65 per hour and an average of four hours per day.

Air Pollution

Data were utilized from the on-bus survey of the Sacramento Transit Lines by individual line including the passenger's point of origin, destination and other relevant information. Data were taken for a representative weekday, so the passenger miles were multiplied by 250 to obtain the total number of passenger miles for weekdays during a year. This figure was adjusted for 1.36 persons per vehicle, to obtain an estimate of the number of automobile miles that would be needed to substitute for the present transit patronage. From studies made for the United States Public Health Service, an estimate of the pollutants per mile for automobiles and buses caused by the use of transit is available and Table V indicates the reduction resulting from the local transit system operation.

Costs

Direct operating and indirect operating costs for the weekday services were

[i]The administrative overhead figure was obtained from the Sacramento County Welfare Office as an average figure for all programs.

Table V
Air Pollution Estimates in Pounds (Based on 1968 Passenger Traffic)

	Automobile[a]			*Bus Operations*			*Reduced Pollution from Bus Operations*		
Line	*CO*	*HC*	*NOX*	*CO*	*HC*	*NOX*	*CO*	*HC*	*NOX*
1	225,036	62,318	24,235	4,238	9,322	15,255	220,798	52,996	8,980
2	130,097	36,027	14,010	3,761	8,275	13,540	126,336	27,752	470
3	187,320	51,873	20,173	3,128	6,880	11,259	184,192	44,993	8,914
4	132,287	36,633	14,246	2,734	6,014	9,842	129,553	30,619	4,404
5	324,219	89,784	34,916	5,516	12,136	19,858	318,703	77,648	15,058
6	305,039	84,472	32,850	5,291	11,641	19,048	299,748	72,831	13,802
7	124,941	34,599	13,455	3,060	6,732	11,016	121,881	27,867	2,439
8	99,778	27,631	10,745	2,655	5,841	9,558	97,123	21,790	1,187
10	45,277	12,538	4,876	1,252	2,756	4,509	44,025	9,782	367
11, 12	125,855	34,852	13,554	2,321	5,107	8,352	123,534	29,745	5,202
13	117,817	32,626	12,688	1,628	3,580	5,859	116,189	29,046	6,829
14	117,867	32,640	12,693	1,954	4,298	7,034	115,913	28,342	5,659
15	67,899	18,803	7,312	1,365	3,003	4,914	66,534	15,800	2,398
16	11,546	3,197	1,243	420	924	1,512	11,126	2,273	(269)
17, 18	39,012	10,803	4,201	1,305	2,871	4,698	37,707	7,932	(497)
19	982	272	106	176	388	634	806	(116)	(528)
Total (lbs.)	2,054,972	569,068	221,303	40,804	89,768	146,888	2,014,168	479,300	74,415
Tons	1,027.49	284.53	110.65	20.40	44.88	73.44	1,007.08	239.65	37.21

Note: The pollutants are Carbon Monoxide (CO), Hydrocarbons (HC) and Nitrogen Oxides (NOX).
[a]Assumes a 20 percent reduction in travel by captive riders if the transit system was not available.

taken from the company's records and are shown in Table VI. Direct costs were assigned to routes and peak or off-peak on the basis of mileage. Indirect costs were assigned on the basis of passenger miles. All drivers' wages were assigned to the peak period, as drivers are guaranteed eight hours of pay per day upon reporting for work as requested. If off-peak operations were suspended, the drivers needed for peak operations would still have to be paid for eight hours under the working rule.

In addition to the costs summarized in Table VI weekend operations are estimated to have costs that exceed revenues by $175,550 for the year 1968. As previously explained in the introduction of this study an imputed interest charge of 6 percent on the $1,912,064 net investment (May 31, 1968) adds $114,724 to the costs of the bus operations. If imputed interest on highway and street investment and lost tax revenues were added to the automobile user costs on the same basis, the costs of automobile operations would be higher than those shown here. Table VII summarizes net benefits by route varying with time values. Net benefits were defined as total benefits minus costs. Benefits included such factors as transit revenues and estimates of the increased costs that would be borne by the motorists and community if the transit system was not available. Table VIII shows the benefit-cost ratio by line and for peak, off-peak and all operations. Route 9 is shown separately as it was a new service when the surveys were made in 1968. The data shown in the bottom line of Table VII for Line 9 were taken from a 1969 survey and reflect the unfavorable results.

Land Values

The start of service by Line 9 connecting several depressed areas to the rest of the system has had no apparent impact upon land values in those depressed areas. It is probably too soon after the institution of the service for people to adjust to the changed service. The county assessor's appraisal values for the Northgate and Strawberry Manor areas show no significant increases in market value, as compared to changes in the county as a whole.

Conclusions

In conclusion it can be said that the transit system, in addition to having an estimated favorable cost ratio of between 2.12 and 2.79 reduces the estimated pollution in the air by over 1283 tons per year (see Table I and V). The potential for greater reduction is present if more people can be induced to use buses instead of the private car. The transit system also improves the quality of life by allowing people without alternate means of transportation

Table VI
Estimated Operating Costs One Year, Weekdays Only, 1968

	Direct Operating Cost			*Indirect Operating Cost*			*Total Cost*		
Line	*Peak*	*Off-Peak*	*Total*	*Peak*	*Off-Peak*	*Total*	*Peak*	*Off-Peak*	*Total*
1	$111,174	$35,952	$147,126	$23,710	$14,178	$37,888	$134,884	$50,130	$185,014
2	101,644	28,947	130,591	20,476	5,908	26,384	122,120	34,855	156,975
3	82,608	25,979	108,587	18,537	13,292	31,829	101,145	39,279	140,416
4	69,958	24,957	94,915	14,872	9,157	24,029	84,830	34,114	118,944
5	148,615	42,909	191,524	34,702	29,095	63,797	183,317	72,004	255,321
6	150,095	33,617	183,712	32,978	20,529	53,507	183,073	54,146	237,219
7	78,318	27,925	106,243	11,424	12,554	23,978	89,742	40,479	130,221
8	70,678	20,503	92,181	8,837	10,634	19,471	79,515	32,137	111,652
10[a]	32,784	10,703	43,487	3,880	1,034	4,914	36,664	11,737	48,401
11, 12	70,328	10,265	80,593	14,010	4,431	18,441	84,338	14,696	99,034
13	48,042	8,465	56,507	9,699	6,794	16,493	57,741	15,259	73,000
14	50,077	17,757	67,834	10,993	8,566	19,559	61,070	26,323	87,393
15	34,744	12,649	47,393	6,682	7,089	13,771	41,426	19,738	61,164
16	11,080	3,503	14,583	1,078	738	1,816	12,158	4,241	16,399
17, 18	33,633	11,676	45,309	3,664	3,545	7,209	37,297	15,221	52,518
19	6,119	—	6,119	216	—	216	6,335	—	6,335
Total	1,099,897	316,807	1,416,704	215,758	147,544	363,302	1,315,655	680,109	1,780,006

[a]This system of assigning direct operating cost on a mileage basis may overstate such costs for the Number 10 Line as it is a high-speed line and drivers' wages are more directly related to time than distance on such a route. Fuel and some other costs will also be somewhat lower per mile on a high-speed operation.

Table VII

Net Benefits by Line (Weekday Operations)[a,b]

Line	Peak $1.55	Peak $1.80	Peak $2.80	Peak $3.75	Off-Peak	Total $1.55	Total $1.80	Total $2.80	Total $3.75
1	$277,206	$240,189	$266,156	$331,073	$165,141	$396,347	$409,330	$435,297	$500,214
2	145,800	158,690	184,471	248,922	41,624	187,424	200,314	226,095	290,546
3	151,528	160,641	178,866	224,429	133,260	284,788	293,901	312,126	357,689
4	110,045	115,750	127,161	155,687	74,836	184,881	190,586	201,997	230,523
5	165,316	173,860	190'932	233,625	155,546	320,862	329,406	346,478	389,171
6	226,947	244,366	279,203	366,298	144,892	371,839	389,258	424,095	511,190
7	58,897	63,408	72,431	94,988	93,705	152,602	157,113	166,136	188,693
8	95,066	101,047	113,002	142,889	134,246	229,312	235,293	247,248	277,135
10[d]	14,193	14,193	14,193	14,193	−4,137	10,056	10,056	10,056	10,056
11, 12	153,593	170,976	205,730	292,625	46,347	199,940	217,323	252,077	338,972
13	104,553	141,227	190,529	313,783	29,774	134,327	171,001	220,303	343,557
14	71,595	84,852	111,366	177,651	33,492	105,087			
15	89,326	100,074	121,568	175,305	49,094	138,420	149,168	170,662	224,399
16	38,163	45,027	58,756	93,078	6,462	44,625	51,489	65,218	99,540
17, 18	49,505	54,352	64,045	88,278	47,398	96,906	101,750	111,443	135,676
19[e]	−3,571	−3,571	−3,571	−3571	0	−3,571	−3,571	−3,571	−3,571

[a]Advertising, charter and weekend costs and benefits were allocated to the system but not to individual lines.

[b]Net benefits are equal to total benefits minus costs.

[c]Doesn't change with values of time because congestion costs don't affect the off-peak trips.

[d]Net benefits did not change with increases in the value of time as traffic congestion was not considered a significant factor for Lines 10, 19 and 9.

[e]Line 19 discontinued 9/6/70. Line 9 had benefit of minus $31,563 at all values of time because of low ridership. At the time of the 1969 survey Line 9 had been in operation six months. Ridership has been steadily increasing and shows approximately 33 percent increase in passengers over the 1969 corresponding period.

Table VIII
Benefit-Cost Ratio by Line (Peak Periods)

	Peak					*Total*			
Line	*$1.55*	*$1.80*	*$2.80*	*$3.75*	*Off-Peak*	*$1.55*	*$1.80*	*$2.80*	*$3.75*
1	2.68	2.78	2.97	3.45	4.37	3.14	3.21	3.33	3.70
2	2.19	2.30	2.51	3.04	2.19	2.19	2.28	2.44	2.85
3	2.50	2.59	2.77	3.22	4.39	3.03	3.09	3.22	3.55
4	2.30	2.36	2.50	2.84	3.19	2.55	2.60	2.70	2.94
5	1.90	1.95	2.04	2.27	3.16	2.26	2.29	2.36	2.52
6	2.24	2.33	2.52	3.00	3.68	2.57	2.64	2.79	3.15
7	1.66	1.71	1.81	2.06	3.31	2.17	2.21	2.28	2.45
8	2.20	2.27	2.42	2.80	5.18	3.05	3.11	3.21	3.48
10	1.39	1.39	1.39	1.39	0.65	1.21	1.21	1.21	1.21
11, 12	2.82	3.03	3.44	4.47	4.15	3.02	3.19	3.54	4.42
13	2.81	3.44	4.30	6.43	2.95	2.84	3.34	4.02	5.71
14	2.17	2.39	2.82	3.91	2.27	2.20	2.85	2.66	3.42
15	3.16	3.42	3.98	5.23	3.49	3.26	3.44	3.79	4.67
16	4.14	4.70	5.83	8.66	2.52	3.72	4.14	4.98	7.07
17, 18	2.33	2.46	2.72	3.37	4.11	2.85	2.94	3.12	3.58
19	0.44	—	—	—	—	0.44	—	—	—

to engage in social and cultural activities that would otherwise be unavailable. The transit system tends to reduce the injuries and loss of life from traffic accidents by reducing congestion. The benefits flowing to automobile users and the general public are large and justify considerable assistance by the greater community benefiting from the service. (See Tables III and IV for the benefits to auto users and the community.) This community is much greater than the City of Sacramento and includes parts of Sacramento, Yolo, and Placer County served by Sacramento Transit Lines. Property taxes are a poor tax base and are already close to the saturation point. Assuming constitutional problems are solved, a diversion of gasoline tax revenues or a sales tax on fuel for vehicles are possible sources of financial support. Another potential tax support is a diversion of federal or state income taxes.

This study was based on survey data gathered in 1968, and although costs of bus operations can be expected to increase in the future the same can be said for the costs of automobile operation and the value of time. Consequently it can be expected that the benefit-cost ratios will remain favorable for some years into the future although they can be expected to vary somewhat from the 1968 ratios. An improvement in passenger load factors through improved attitudes toward transit usage would increase revenues with small attendant increases in cost through more starts and stops for the increased patronage.

Glossary

Section I: Unbalanced Productivity Growth

LCPS = Labor costs in the progressive sector of the economy

MWIPS = Annual increase in money wages in the progressive sector of the economy

MPIPS = Monetary value of annual increases in productivity in the progressive sector

NPPI = Normal annual growth in productivity in the progressive sector

PPI = Percentage of poor families (engaged in progressive activities) residing in the municipality at time *J* that are residing in the municipality at time *K*

EØP = A factor that relates increases in wages to normal annual growth in productivity

PLP = Number of poor families residing in the municipality

LCNPS = Labor costs in the nonprogressive sector

MWINPS = Annual increase in money wages in the nonprogressive sector

MPINPS = Monetary value of annual increases in productivity in the nonprogressive sector

PNPI = Percentage of affluent families (engaged in nonprogressive activities) residing in the municipality at time *J* that are residing in the municipality at time *K*

PLA = Number of poor families residing in the municipality

NPINPS = Normal annual growth in productivity in the nonprogressive sector

WSLM = Income produced in progressive and nonprogressive activities within the boundaries of the municipality

NAS = Income produced in nonprogressive activities within the boundaries of the municipality

NPS = Income produced in progressive activities within the boundaries of the municipality

DT = Computation interval

Section II: Municipal Costs and Benefits

MC = Level of municipal expenditures

MECI = Annual increases in wages for municipal employees

PNPEM = Portion of nonprogressive employees that are employed by this municipality

RSSIA = Annual opportunity loss for a typical affluent family

NSDA = Annual rate of services forgone by affluent residents (as a percentage of income)

NPME = Annual percentage of income that the affluent normally spend for education

RSSIP = Annual benefits perceived in this municipality by a typical poor migrant

NPISP = A factor representing the relative attractiveness of this municipality for poor in-migration

TPL = Total number of families residing in this municipality

Section III: New Family Benefits

NCLA = Annual net costs, including opportunities forgone, for a typical affluent family

RCIA = Annual increases in costs for affluent residents of this municipality

MCA = Annual property taxes paid by the affluent

MTR = Municipal tax rate (dollars per thousand)

AVAH = Total assessed value of affluent housing

AH = Number of affluent housing units in the urban area

NBLP = Annual net benefits for a typical poor family

RCIP = Annual rate of increase in costs paid by a typical poor family

MCP = Annual property taxes paid by the poor

AVPH = Total assessed value of poor housing

PH = Number of poor housing units in the urban area

Section IV: Municipal Population and Housing

PMP = Number of poor families arriving or departing during the period *JK*

PMA = Number of affluent families arriving or departing during the period *JK*

*DELAY*1 = A DYNAMO function that calls an exponential delay subroutine

PADA = Number of arrival or departure decisions of the affluent

AMD = Average delay between decisions of affluent families to move and the actual move

TABHL = A function giving a table of values

PADAT = Table of arrival and departure decisions for the affluent

DAHF = Delay required for affluent housing to filter down after affluent departures

PADP = Number of arrival or departure decisions of poor families

PMD = Average delay between decisions of poor families to move and the actual move

PADPT = Table of arrival and departure decisions for the poor

PHFD = Delay required for poor housing to filter up after poor departures

Section V: Municipal Taxation and Revenue

MR = Municipal revenue raised by the municipality

AVP = Total assessed value of property in the municipality

NMAAVH = Normal assessed value for an affluent housing unit

MAVR = A factor relating assessed valuation of affluent property to the population mix in the municipality

NPPA = Normal percentage of affluent families residing in central cities

NAVPH = Normal assessed value of a typical poor housing unit

Bibliography

1. Advisory Commission on Intergovernmental Relations, Metropolitan Social and Economic Disparities, *Implications for Intergovernmental Relations in Central Cities and Suburbs,* Washington, D.C., U.S. Government Printing Office, January 1965.
2. Kenneth J. Arrow, "Political and Economic Evaluation of Social Externalities," in Julius Margolis (Ed.), *The Analysis of Public Output,* New York, National Bureau of Economic Research, 1970.
3. ____, *Social Choice and Individual Values,* Second Edition, New Haven, Yale University Press, 1963.
4. ____, and Tibor Scitovsky (Eds.), American Economic Association, *Readings in Welfare Economics,* Homewood, Illinois, Irwin, 1969.
5. R.U. Ayres and Allen Kneese, "Production, Consumption, and Externalities," *American Economic Review,* Vol. 59, June 1969.
6. Milton S. Baum and Albert Gutowsky, *Cost and Benefit Evaluation of the Sacramento Transit Authority, Interim Technical Report No. 4,* October 1970.
7. William J. Baumol, *Welfare Economics and the Theory of the State,* Second Edition, Cambridge, Massachusetts, Harvard University Press, 1965.
8. ____, *Economic Theory and Operations Analysis,* Third Edition, Englewood Cliffs, New Jersey, Prentice-Hall, 1972.
9. ____, *Economic Dynamics,* Third Edition, London, Macmillan, 1970.
10. ____, "External Economies and Second Order Optimality Conditions," *American Economic Review,* Vol. 59, June 1964.
11. ____, "Macroeconomics of Unbalanced Growth: The Anatomy of Urban Crisis," *American Economic Review,* Vol. 57, March 1967.
12. ____, "On the Social Rate of Discount," *American Economic Review,* Vol. 58, September 1968.
13. ____, "Informed Judgment, Rigorous Theory and Public Policy," *Southern Economic Journal,* Vol. 32, October 1966.
14. ____, "On the Social Rate of Discount," Comment on the Comments, *American Economic Review,* Vol. 59, December 1969.
15. ____, "On the Discount Rate for Public Projects," in the *Analysis and Evaluation of Public Expenditures: The PPB System,* Washington, D.C., U.S. Government Printing Office, 1969, Vol. 1.
16. ____, "Urban Services: Interactions of Public and Private Decisions," in Howard G. Schaller (Ed.), *Public Expenditures Decisions*

in the Urban Community, Washington, D.C., Resources for the Future Inc., 1963.

17. Gary S. Becker, *Human Capital: A Theoretical and Empirical Analysis with Special Reference to Education,* New York, Columbia University Press, 1964.
18. M. Blaugh (Ed.), *Economics of Education 1, Selected Readings,* Baltimore, Penguin Books, 1968.
19. Karl Hendrik Borch, *The Economics of Uncertainty,* Princeton, New Jersey, Princeton University Press, 1968.
20. Samuel Bowles, "Towards an Educational Production Function," in W. Lee Hansen (Ed.), *Education, Income, and Human Capital,* New York, National Bureau of Economic Research, 1970, pp. 11-61.
21. David F. Bradford, "Discussion: An Econometric Model of Intra-Metropolitan Housing Location: Housing, Business, Transportation, and Local Government," Papers and Proceedings, *American Economic Review,* Vol. 62, May 1972.
22. Phillip Brickman and Donald T. Campbell, "Hedonic Relativism and Planning the Good Society," in M.H. Appley (Ed.), *Adaptation Level Theory: A Symposium,* New York, Academic Press, 1971.
23. Eugene B. Brody (Ed.), *Behavior in New Environments, Adaptation of Migrant Populations,* Beverly Hills, Sage Publications, 1969.
24. James Buchanan, *The Demand and Supply of Public Goods,* Chicago, Rand McNally, 1968.
25. _____, *Cost and Choice, An Inquiry in Economic Theory,* Chicago, Markham, 1969.
26. _____, "Joint Supply, Externality and Optimality," *Economica,* Vol. 46, November 1966.
27. _____, "External Diseconomies, Corrective Taxes and Market Structure," *American Economic Review,* Vol. 59, March 1969.
28. _____, and William C. Stubblebine, "Externality," *Economica,* Vol. 42, November 1962.
29. Jesse Burkhead, *Input and Output in Large-City High Schools,* Syracuse, Syracuse University Press, 1967.
30. Alan K. Campbell and Seymour Sacks, *Metropolitan America, Fiscal Patterns and Governmental Systems,* New York, Free Press, 1967.
31. R.H. Coase, "The Problem of Social Costs," *Journal of Law and Economics,* Vol. 3, October 1960.
32. James S. Coleman, "The Concept of Equality of Educational Opportunity," *Harvard Educational Review,* Vol. 38, pp. 7-22.
33. R.M. Cyert and J.G. March, *A Behavioral Theory of the Firm*, Englewood Cliffs, New Jersey, Prentice-Hall, 1963.

34. R.A. Dahl, *Pluralist Democracy in the United States*, Chicago, Rand McNally, 1967.

35. R.A. Dahl and Charles E. Lindblom, *Politics, Economics and Welfare,* New York, Harper, 1953.

36. O.A. Davis, "Welfare Economics and the Theory of Second Best," *Review of Economic Studies,* Vol. 32, 1965.

37. _____, "On Externalities, Information and Government-Assisted Invisible Hand," *Economica,* Vol. 46, August 1966.

38. _____, "On the Distinction between Public and Private Goods," *American Economic Review,* Vol. 57, May 1967.

39. _____, "Piecemeal Policy, the Theory of Second Best," *Review of Economic Studies,* Vol. 34, July 1967.

40. _____, and Morton I. Kamien, "Externalities, Information and Alternative Collective Action," in Joint Economic Committee, *The Analysis and Evaluation of Public Expenditure: The PPB System,* Vol. 1, 1969.

41. _____, and Andrew B. Whinston, "Externalities, Welfare and the Theory of Games," *Journal of Political Economy,* Vol. 70, 1962.

42. Harold Demetz, "Toward a Theory of Property Rights," *American Economic Review,* Vol. 57, March 1967.

43. F. Trenery Dolbear, Jr., "On the Theory of Optimal Externality," *American Economic Review,* Vol. 57, March 1967.

44. Robert Dorfman (Ed.), *Measuring Benefits of Government Investment,* Washington, D.C., Brookings Institution, 1965.

45. Anthony Downs, *An Economic Theory of Democracy,* New York, Harper, 1957.

46. _____, "An Economic Theory of Political Action in a Democracy," *Journal of Political Economy,* Vol. 65, April 1957.

47. _____, *Inside Bureaucracy,* Boston, Little, Brown, 1967.

48. _____, "A Theory of Bureaucracy," *Proceedings of American Economic Association for 1964.*

49. Richard A. Easterlin, "Does Economic Growth Improve the Human Lot? Some Empirical Evidence," to be published in Paul A. David and Melvin W. Reder (Eds.), *Nations and Households in Economic Growth: Essays in Honor of Moses Abramovitz,* Palo Alto, California, Stanford University Press, forthcoming.

50. Otto Eckstein, Water Resources Development, *The Economics of Project Evaluation,* Cambridge, Massachusetts, Harvard University Press, 1965.

51. _____, "A Survey of the Theory of Public Expenditure Criteria," in *National Bureau of Economic Research, Public Finances: Needs,*

Sources and Utilization, Princeton, New Jersey, Princeton University Press, 1961.

52. Hope T. Eldridge and Dorothy S. Thomas, *Population Redistribution and Economic Growth, United States, 1870-1950,* Philadelphia, American Philosophical Society, 1964.
53. Robert F. Engle III, Franklin M. Fisher, John R. Harris, and Jerome Rothenberg, *An Econometric Simulation Model of Intra-Metropolitan Housing Location: Housing, Business Transportation, and Local Government,* Papers and Proceedings, *American Economic Review,* Vol. 62, May 1972.
54. Solomon Fabricant, *The Trend of Government Activity in the United States Since 1900,* New York, National Bureau of Economic Research, 1952.
55. _____, *A Primer on Productivity,* New York, Random House, 1969.
56. M.S. Feldstein, "Net Social Benefit Calculation and the Public Investment Decision," *Oxford Economic Papers,* Vol. 16, March 1964.
57. _____, "The Social Time Preference Discount Rate in Cost-Benefit Analysis," *Economic Journal,* Vol. 74, June 1964.
58. G.H. Fisher, "Cost Functions and Budgets," in Julius Margolis (Ed.), *The Analysis of Public Output,* New York, National Bureau of Economic Research, 1970.
59. Gene Fisher, "The Role of Cost-Utility Analysis," in D. Novick (Ed.), *Program Budgeting,* New York, Holt, Rinehart and Winston, 1969.
60. Jay W. Forrester, *Principles of Systems,* Second Preliminary Edition, Cambridge, Massachusetts, Wright-Allen Press, 1969.
61. _____, *Urban Dynamics,* Cambridge, Massachusetts, M.I.T. Press, 1969.
62. _____, *Industrial Dynamics,* Cambridge, Massachusetts, M.I.T. Press, 1961.
63. Victor R. Fuchs, *The Service Economy,* New York, National Bureau of Economic Research, Columbia University Press, 1968.
64. Harvey A. Garn and Robert H. Wilson, *A Critical Look at Urban Dynamics: The Forrester Model and Public Policy,* Washington, D.C., The Urban Institute, December 1970.
65. J. de V. Graaff, *Theoretical Welfare Economics,* London, Cambridge University Press, 1967.
66. Leo Grebler, *Housing Market Behavior in a Declining Area, Long-Term Changes in Inventory and Utilization of Housing on New York's Lower East Side,* New York, Columbia University Press, 1962.
67. Edward K. Hamilton, Allen Schick, and Charles L. Schultze, *Setting*

National Priorities: The 1971 Budget, Washington, D.C., Brookings Institution, 1970.

68. W.R. Hamilton, S.E. Goldstone, J.W. Milliman, A.L. Pugh III, E.R. Roberts, and A. Zellner, *Systems Simulation for Regional Analysis–An Application to River Basin Planning,* Cambridge, Massachusetts, M.I.T. Press, 1969.
69. Robert H. Haveman, "Public Expenditures and Policy Analysis: An Overview," in Robert H. Haveman and Julius Margolis (Eds.), *Public Expenditures and Policy Analysis,* Chicago, Markham, 1970.
70. Robert H. Haveman and John V. Krutilla, *Unemployment, Idle Capacity and the Evaluation of Public Expenditures: National and Regional Analysis,* Baltimore, Johns Hopkins Press, 1968.
71. Robert H. Haveman and Julius Margolis (Eds.), *Public Expenditures and Policy Analysis,* Chicago, Markham, 1970.
72. John R. Hicks, "The Four Consumer's Surpluses," *Review of Economic Studies,* Vol. 11, 1943.
73. Harley H. Hinrichs and Graeme M. Taylor, *Program Budgeting and Benefit Cost Analysis: Cases and Readings,* Pacific Palisades, California, Goodyear Publishing, 1969.
74. Jack Hirschleifer, *Investment, Interest and Capital,* Englewood Cliffs, New Jersey, Prentice-Hall, 1970.
75. ____, and Daniel Shapiro, "The Treatment of Uncertainty," in Robert H. Haveman and Julius Margolis (Eds.), *Public Expenditures and Policy Analysis,* Chicago, Markham, 1970.
76. ____, James C. DeHaven, and Jerome W. Millman, *Water Supply, Economics, Technology and Policy,* Chicago, University of Chicago Press, 1960.
77. Charles Hitch, "Sub-Optimization in Operations Problems," *Journal of the Operations Research Society of America,* May 1953.
78. Harold Hovey, *Planning-Programming-Budgeting System,* New York, Praeger, 1968.
79. Maynard Hufschmidt and Jacques Gerin, "Systematic Errors in Cost Estimating for Public Investment Projects," in Julius Margolis (Ed.), *The Analysis of Public Output,* New York, National Bureau of Economic Research, 1970.
80. Christopher Jenks, Mary Smith, Henry Acland, Mary Jo Bane, David Cohen, Herbert Gintis, Barbara Heyns, and Stephan Michelson, *Inequality: A Reassessment of the Effect of Family and Schooling in America,* New York, Basic Books, 1972.
81. Joint Economic Committee, 91st Congress, *The Analysis and Evaluation of Public Expenditures: The PPB System,* Washington, D.C., U.S. Government Printing Office, 1969, Vols. 1-3.

82. _____, *Planning-Programming-Budgeting,* Budget Bureau Guidelines of 1968, Washington, D.C., U.S. Government Printing Office.

83. Leo P. Kadanoff, "From Simulation Model to Public Policy: An examination of Forrester's Urban Dynamics," *Simulation,* Vol. 13, June 1971.

84. _____, and Herbert Weinblatt, "Public Policy Conclusions from Urban Growth Models," Unpublished Research Note 9, Urban Analysis Group, Brown University, 1971.

85. John F. Kain, "The NBER Urban Simulation Model and Urban Economics in the 1970's," in *Annual Report of the National Bureau of Economic Research,* New York, National Bureau of Economic Research, September 1971.

86. Allen Kneese and Ralph d'Arge, "Pervasive External Costs and the Response of Society," in Joint Economic Committee, *The Analysis and Evaluation of Public Expenditures: The PPB System,* Washington, D.C., U.S. Government Printing Office, 1969, Vol. 1.

87. Frank H. Knight, *Risk, Uncertainty and Profit,* New York, Hart, Schraffner and Marx, 1921.

88. Frank H. Knight, "Some Fallacies in the Interpretation of Social Cost," *Quarterly Journal of Economics,* Vol. 78, 1964, reprinted in Kenneth J. Arrow and Tibor Scitovsky (Eds.), American Economic Association, *Readings in Welfare Economics,* Homewood, Illinois, Irwin, 1969.

89. John V. Krutilla and Otto Eckstein, *Multiple Purpose River Development,* Baltimore, Johns Hopkins Press, 1958.

90. Charles Lindblom, *The Policy Making Process,* Englewood Cliffs, New Jersey, Prentice-Hall, 1968.

91. _____, "Decision Making in Taxation and Expenditures," in National Bureau of Economic Research, *Public Finances: Needs, Sources and Utilization,* Princeton, New Jersey, Princeton University Press, 1961, pp. 295-329.

92. R.G. Lipsey and K. Lancaster, "The General Theory of Second Best," *Review of Economic Studies,* Vol. 24, 1956.

93. I.M.D. Little, *A Critique of Welfare Economics,* New York, Oxford University Press, 1958.

94. Ira S. Lowry, *A Model of Metropolis,* Santa Monica, California, Rand Corporation, 1964.

95. _____, "Filtering and Housing Standards: A Conceptual Analysis," *Land Economics,* Vol. 36, No. 4, November 1960, p. 362.

96. Ronald N. McKean, *Efficiency in Government through Systems Analysis,* New York, Wiley, 1958.
97. Stephen A. Marglin, *Public Investment Criteria,* Cambridge, Massachusetts, M.I.T. Press, 1967.
98. ____, "The Opportunity Costs of Public Investment," *Quarterly Journal of Economics,* Vol. 77, May 1963.
99. ____, "The Social Rate of Discount and the Optimal Rate of Investment," *Quarterly Journal of Economics,* Vol. 77, New York, May 1963.
100. Julius Margolis (Ed.), *The Analysis of Public Output,* New York, National Bureau of Economic Research, 1970.
101. Julius Margolis, "Shadow Prices for Incorrect or Non-Existent Market Values," in Robert H. Haveman and Julius Margolis (Eds.), *Public Expenditures and Policy Analysis,* Chicago, Markham, 1970.
102. John T. Masten and Kenneth E. Quindry, "A Note on City Expenditure Determinants," *Land Economics,* Vol. 46, February 1970.
103. E.J. Mishan, *The Cost of Economic Growth,* New York, Praeger, 1967.
104. ____, *Cost-Benefit Analysis: An Introduction,* New York, Praeger, 1971.
105. ____, "Criteria for Public Investment: Some Simplifying Assumptions," *Journal of Political Economy,* Vol. 75, April 1967.
106. ____, "The Post-War Literature on Externalities," *Journal of Economic Literature,* Vol. 9, March 1971.
107. ____, *Welfare Economics, Ten Introductory Essays,* Second Edition, New York, Random House, 1969.
108. J.N. Morgan, M.H. David, W.J. Cohen, and H.F. Brazer, *Income and Welfare in the United States,* New York, McGraw-Hill, 1962.
109. Richard A. Musgrave, *The Theory of Public Finance,* New York, McGraw-Hill, 1959.
110. ____, "Cost-Benefit Analysis and the Theory of Public Finance," *Journal of Economic Literature,* Vol. 7, September 1969.
111. Richard F. Muth, *Cities and Housing: The Spatial Pattern of Urban Residential Land Use,* Chicago, University of Chicago Press, 1969.
112. ____, "Discussion: An Econometric Simulation Model of Intra-Metropolitan Housing Location: Housing, Business, Transportation and Local Governments," Papers and Proceedings, *American Economic Review,* Vol. 62, May 1972.
113. S.K. Nath, "Are Formal Welfare Criteria Required?" *Economic Journal,* Vol. 74, September 1964.

114. National Academy of Engineering, *Symposium and Workshop on Application of Technology to Improve Productivity in the Service Sector of the National Economy,* Washington, D.C., November 1971.
115. National Bureau of Economic Research, *Public Finances: Needs, Sources, Utilizations,* Princeton, New Jersey, Princeton University Press, 1961.
116. National Commission on Urban Problems, *Building the American City,* Washington, D.C., U.S. Government Printing Office, December 1968.
117. New York State Commission on the Quality, Cost and Financing of Elementary and Secondary Education, *Report of the Commission,* Vol. I, 1972.
118. *New York Times,* September 10, 1972, Section E.
119. Alan Nichols, "On the Social Rule of Discount: Comment," *American Economic Review,* Vol. 59, December 1969.
120. W.E. Oates, E.P. Howrey, and W.J. Baumol, "The Analysis of Public Policy in Dynamic Urban Models," *Journal of Political Economy,* Vol. 79, February 1971.
121. Charles R. Plott, "Externalities and Corrective Taxes," *Economica,* Vol. 46, February 1966.
122. The President's Commission on National Goals, *Goals for America,* Englewood Cliffs, New Jersey, Prentice-Hall, 1960.
123. A.R. Prest and R. Turvey, "Cost-Benefit Analysis: A Survey," in American Economic Association and Royal Economic Society, *Surveys in Economic Theory,* Vol. III, New York, St. Martin's Press, 1966.
124. Alexander L. Pugh III, *DYNAMO II User's Manual,* Cambridge, Massachusetts, M.I.T. Press, 1970.
125. David D. Ramsey, "On the Social Rate of Discount: Comment," *American Economic Review,* Vol. 59, December 1969.
126. Jerome Rothenberg, *Economic Evaluation of Urban Renewal,* Washington, D.C., Brookings Institution, 1967.
127. Henry Rowen, "Systematic Public Sector Decision Making," in Julius Margolis (Ed.), *The Analysis of Public Output,* New York, National Bureau of Economic Research, 1970.
128. Seymour Sacks, "Central City and Suburban Public Education: Fiscal Resources and Realities," in the National Society for the Study of Education *Yearbook,* 67th, Part I, 1968.
129. P.A. Samuelson, "Diagrammatic Exposition of a Theory of Public Expenditure," *Review of Economics and Statistics,* Vol. 37, November 1955.

130. ____, "Evaluation of Real National Income," *Oxford Economic Papers,* Vol. 2, N.S. II, January 1950.

131. ____, "The Pure Theory of Public Expenditures," *Review of Economics and Statistics,* Vol. 36, 1954.

132. ____, "Aspects of Public Expenditure Theories," *Review of Economics and Statistics,* Vol. 40, 1958.

133. ____, "Principles of Efficiency: Discussion," Papers and Proceedings, *American Economic Review,* May 1964.

134. ____, "Income Distribution: Theories and Facts," *Survey of Current Business,* Vol. 51, No. 7, Part II, July 1971.

135. Henry J. Schmandt and G. Ross Stephens, "Local Government Expenditure Patterns in the United States," *Land Economics,* Vol. 39, November 1963.

136. Charles L. Schultze, *The Politics and Economics of Public Spending,* Washington, D.C., Brookings Institution, 1970.

137. ____, Edward R. Fried, Alice M. Rivlin, and Nancy H. Teeters, *Setting National Priorities: The 1972 Budget,* Washington, D.C., Brookings Institution, 1971.

138. ____, Edward R. Fried, Alice M. Rivlin, and Nancy H. Teeters, *Setting National Priorities: The 1973 Budget,* Washington, D.C., Brookings Institution, 1972.

139. Tibor Scitovsky, "External Diseconomies in the Modern Economy," *Western Economic Journal,* Vol. 4, Summer 1966.

140. ____, "Two Concepts of External Economies," *Journal of Political Economy,* Vol. 62, 1954, reprinted in Kenneth J. Arrow and Tibor Scitovsky (Eds.), American Economic Association, *Readings in Welfare Economics,* Homewood, Illinois, Irwin, 1969.

141. ____, "A Note on Welfare Propositions in Economics," *Review of Economic Studies,* Vol. 8, 1941.

142. Henry S. Shryock, *Population Mobility within the United States,* Chicago, Community and Family Study Center, 1964.

143. Herbert A. Simon, *Administrative Behavior,* New York, Macmillan, 1945.

144. Subcommittee on Economy in Government of Joint Economic Committee, *Economic Analysis of Public Investment Decisions: Interest Rate Policy and Discounting Analysis,* 90th Congress, Second Session, Washington, D.C., U.S. Government Printing Office, 1967.

145. Paul J. Taubman and Terence J. Wales, "Higher Education, Mental Ability, and Screening," *Journal of Political Economy,* Vol. 81, No. 1, January-February 1973.

146. Charles Tilly, "Race and Migration to the American City," in James

Q. Wilson (Ed.), *The Metropolitan Enigma,* New York, Doubleday, 1970.

147. James Tobin, "On Limiting the Domain of Inequality," *Journal of Law and Economics,* Vol. 13, October 1970.
148. Gordon Tullock, *Private Wants, Public Means: An Economic Analysis of the Desirable Scope of Government,* New York, Basic Books, 1970.
149. Ralph Turvey, "On Divergences between Social Cost and Private Cost," *Economica*, Vol. 43, August 1963.
150. ———, "On the Development of Cost-Benefit Analysis," in M.G. Kendall (Ed.), *Cost-Benefit Analysis,* New York, American Elsevier, pp. 5-14, 1971.
151. U.S. Bureau of the Census, *Local Government Employment in Selected Metropolitan Areas and Large Counties, 1970,* Washington, D.C., U.S. Government Printing Office, 1971.
152. ———, *Statistical Abstract of the United States,* Ninetieth Edition, Washington, D.C., U.S. Government Printing Office, 1969.
153. ———, *Statistical Abstract of the United States,* Ninety-first Edition, Washington, D.C., U.S. Government Printing Office, 1970.
154. Dan Usher, "On the Social Rate of Discount: Comment," *American Economic Review,* Vol. 59, December 1969.
155. William S. Vickery, "Decreasing Costs, Public Administered Prices and Economic Efficiencies," in Joint Economic Committee, 91st Congress, *The Analysis of Government Expenditures: The PPB System,* Washington, D.C., U.S. Government Printing Office, 1969, Vol. 1.
156. P.E. Vincent, "Reciprocal Externalities and Optimal Input and Output Levels," *American Economic Review,* Vol. 59, December 1969.
157. *Washington Post,* September 7, 1972, p. 1.
158. Burton A. Weisbrod, "Income Redistribution Effects and Benefit-Cost Analysis," in Chase (Ed.), *Problems in Public Expenditure Analysis,* Washington, D.C., Brookings Institution, 1968.
159. S. Wellisz, "On External Diseconomies and the Government-Assisted Invisible Hand," *Economica,* Vol. 44, November 1964.
160. Aaron Wildavsky, *The Politics of the Budgetary Process,* Boston, Little, Brown, 1964.
161. O.E. Williamson, "Administrative Decision Making and Pricing: Externality and Compensation Analysis Applied," in Julius Margolis (Ed.), *The Analysis of Public Output,* New York, National Bureau of Economic Research, 1971.

162. Dean A. Worcester, Jr., "Pecuniary and Technological Externality, Factor and Social Costs," *American Economic Review,* Vol. 59, December 1969.

163. Richard Zeckhauser, "Uncertainty and the Need for Collective Action," in Robert H. Haveman and Julius Margolis (Eds.), *Public Expenditures and Policy Analysis,* Chicago, Markham, 1970.

Index

Index

About the Author

Joseph A. Maciariello, assistant director and associate professor at the Institute of Administration and Management, Union College and University, Schenectady, New York, is an economist who has been a training consultant to departments of New York state government and private companies. He received the Ph.D. degree in economics from New York University in 1973. Dr. Maciariello is a contributor to professional and scholarly journals on the subject of benefit-cost analysis, project planning and control and management control in profit and nonprofit institutions.